DEAD MEN DON'T TELL TALES

GUY MARTIN

EBURY SPOTLIGHT

3

Ebury Press, an imprint of Ebury Publishing
20 Vauxhall Bridge Road
London SW1V 2SA

Ebury Press is part of the Penguin Random House group of companies
whose addresses can be found at global.penguinrandomhouse.com

Penguin
Random House
UK

Images in the picture section reproduced with kind permission from
North One Television, Gary Inman, Andy Spellman and Guy Martin.

First published by Ebury Press in 2021
This paperback edition published in 2022

www.penguin.co.uk

A CIP catalogue record for this book is available from the British Library

ISBN 9781529108941

Printed and bound in Great Britain by Clays Ltd, Elcograf S.p.A.

The authorised representative in the EEA is Penguin Random House Ireland,
Morrison Chambers, 32 Nassau Street, Dublin D02 YH68

Penguin Random House is committed to a sustainable future for
our business, our readers and our planet. This book is made from
Forest Stewardship Council® certified paper.

MIX
Paper from
responsible sources
FSC FSC® C018179

Contents

Introduction

THANKS FOR COMING BACK to catch up on what I've been up to. If you've read *When You Dead, You Dead, Worms to Catch* or *We Need to Weaken the Mixture*, you'll know the gist of the job. If not, then these books are written like diaries, with tales and details of some of the big, and not so big, stuff I've been up to since the end of the previous book. Like me, they're full of contradictions, because I'm writing what I feel at that time, and things can do a 180-degree shift a couple of months later. One example is me packing in the trucks part of the way through writing the book, then going back to working on them, for two days a week, before the end.

This book took about nine months to write. The first few chapters needed me to look back in my diary to remind myself of a few things, because the Nürburgring van, the world's fastest tractor, the D-Day job and the Arizona Trail Race (that was nearly the end of me) all happened close to the end of writing *We Need to Weaken the Mixture*, when my head wasn't in writing another book.

But, because I'm always making notes and taking photos, there's plenty to chew through, and if I couldn't remember something I had a word with those who were there with me.

Another thing that has changed a few times during the making of the book is its title. It was called 'Like a Bee in a Borage Field'. It was a way of describing how enthusiastic I was about stuff like the 300mph job. Borage is a crop that produces a certain type of oil used in the medical industry, and each field needs tens of thousands of bees to pollinate it. The bees go mad for borage, it's almost like a drug for them. They get off their faces on it and they're useless for days. So, if someone is like a bee in a borage field they're enthusiastic to the point of being addicted.

That was the title until I saw the words on a mock-up cover, when I thought, Maybe not. Then me and Sharon were watching a film and I said, 'It'd be far easier to kill him. Dead men don't tell tales.' Sharon said, 'You should call the book that.' I took it to mean, I'm still telling tales, writing these books, so I can't have killed myself yet. Simple as that.

I hope you like reading the tales.

Ta for buying the book.

Guy Martin

Lincolnshire, June 2021

1

She Was Trying to Educate Pork

YOU'LL HAVE GOT the gist of these books by now. They are written in chronological order, covering stuff I've been up to at any point from the end of one book to the end of the other. Some of it can be self-contained, like the TV programmes or the Arizona Trail Race, but this chapter began in *Worms to Catch*. It all started with me writing off my own Transit on my way to work in Grimsby early one morning. I turned a corner on the industrial estate, was blinded by the rising sun and ploughed into a parked artic low-loader trailer. While I was still working out how I'd done something so daft, another van came around the corner and did the same. I still don't know how.

Sometime later the TV lot were asking about races, and I mentioned the Silver State Classic road race, in Nevada. Then they came up with the idea of building a Transit and shipping it to America to compete in it. I told them the written-off van, that I'd bought back off the insurance company, was the thing for the job.

The story of how that all worked out is in *Worms to Catch*, and also, how we then took it to Bonneville to attempt to beat the outright top-speed record for a van, that was set at 176mph by Ford's own Supervan. I think Supervan had a Cosworth DFV Formula 1 engine in it, and it wasn't really a van, it was a space frame chassis, with a two-thirds-size lightweight plastic body over the top of it. A space frame is a lattice of tubes that makes the chassis, it's very light and rigid, and pure race car technology. So Supervan was the shape of a van, but it wasn't the dimensions, weight, design, or anything else to do with a van.

My van, which had been brought back from the dead, was still a Transit, but souped-up for the programme. Krazy Horse, the Suffolk-based car and bike company who'd been involved in the Wall of Death record, did a load of the work, and British racing car company Radical did a load more. The van was fitted with a Ford EcoBoost V6, 3.5 litre, direct injection, twin turbo engine; had a Safety Devices roll cage in it; a big front bumper and a wing on the back to try to improve the aerodynamics and roadholding. A roll cage is a frame welded and bolted to the interior, that follows the line of the roof and the front and rear pillars, so if the van lands on its roof it doesn't crumple. There was a load more to it, but those were the most obvious changes. It did the job at the Silver State Classic, people liked the programme, and the van touched 170mph. That's going some for a van.

After the race, the Transit was kept at Radical's USA headquarters, just outside Las Vegas, and a month or three later, I went out to Bonneville for the Triumph land speed record job, that I also wrote about in *Worms to Catch*. The TV lot said, 'While you're out there we'll do a land speed record with the Transit and be the world's fastest van, then we can make a separate programme on breaking the land speed record.' I always like the idea of killing two birds with one stone, but I was sceptical. The record stood at 185mph, and that is bloody motoring in a van.

When it came to drive the van for the first time on the famous Utah salt flats it was as nervous as owt, it felt like I wasn't properly in control of it, and the feeling of it was making me nervous. I'd driven it flat out on the road a few months before, but it felt totally different.

Before I did the second run I put the HANS device on, the Head And Neck Support shoulder harness that clips your helmet to your body to minimise head and neck injuries caused by high-speed balls-ups.

TV's mad when it comes to spending money. They'd flown the van out to America in a plane, in time for the Silver State race, and there was no expense spared for the Bonneville attempt either. They'd flown two of the Radical UK boys out there, and Dan from Krazy Horse too, but it turned out the van didn't have the horsepower to break the record. I was sat with my foot to the floor in top gear and the engine wasn't making enough power to pull top gear.

Later, I think the TV lot explained it away by saying the tyres were too wide, and that does make a difference. Bonneville is different. You'd think you'd want loads of rubber on the deck for the best tractions, but all the land speed boys use narrow tyres to get through the slippery crust of the salt to the grippier surface below. My tyres could have been narrower, but still, I had my foot

flat to the floor, and I wasn't gaining any revs or any speed, so that's when you know you've run out of horsepower. You have X amount of torque being made by the engine, and it goes for the path of least resistance. There's a balancing point where it's easier to spin the wheels on the surface than it is to push the van through the air: the friction of the wheels versus the aerodynamic drag of the brick-shaped van. We never got to the point where it was spinning the wheels due to the air resistance, so that shows we ran out of horsepower. You know you've reached the point where the tyres are slipping because the revs go up and the speed doesn't, the same as if the van has a slipping clutch. I'd be able to feel it as the driver, and the telemetry system would log it so we could see it on the computer screen. We were fighting physics, yes, when I was accelerating I was fighting the steering wheel while it found traction, but once it got up to speed, grip didn't make any difference.

We did two runs on the salt flats to get a certificate to be the world's fastest van, but it wasn't. I don't know who was telling them it was going to be, because I was never full of confidence it was going to do 185mph. I was told the van was making 700 horsepower, and it was hard to tell, because I'd never driven a 700 horsepower van before, but I was always doubtful it would break the record.

I did 163mph at Bonneville, which is fast for a van, but not the record, so the money felt like it had been wasted. There was no programme in being the world's second fastest van, and the footage they'd filmed sat on a shelf, or more likely on someone's computer, at North One Television.

The Transit was transported across country where it could be stuck on a container ship back to England. At that point I was thinking of converting it into something I could compete in for Time Attack events, and that's where the Transit saga got to in *Weaken the Mixture*.

What happened next in the life of my Transit Custom was, the TV lot were looking for ideas for programmes and thought about breaking the van record around the Nürburgring, the world famous, or infamous, 13-mile-long German track. A few people had set times round there in vans, and it was something we could aim for with a vehicle we already had.

I liked the sound of it, and, before I knew it, things were moving fast. Everyone who was involved in the initial van project, Paul and Dan from Krazy Horse, James from Radical, Rob the aerodynamics expert from Wirth Research, were asked to attend Cadwell Park racetrack, in Lincolnshire. The TV lot, again showing they're not afraid to spend money, had privately hired Cadwell for the day. The van was dropped off, and I was going to drive it, and then we'd be filmed discussing what should be done to turn the van into something more suited to setting the fastest possible time around the 12.94-mile track.

The Nürburgring has a cult following, for a few reasons, but the main one is that anyone can turn up on a 'tourist' day, pay for a ticket, which costs €25 at the time of writing, and do a lap with their own vehicle. You don't need a race licence or a fancy car, and there are no speed limits. So you can have a Lamborghini doing 190 down a straight, passing a camper van doing 45, and neither driver has had to prove they know what they're doing, beyond passing their regular driving test.

Dan from Krazy Horse and the lads from Radical had checked over the van, because it hadn't been used for a good while, and it had been sat in a museum. I did a few laps in it to get a lap time that was the zero point, that we could compare when we'd make the changes. Then there was a discussion, around a table outside the café, about what needed to happen to the van to break the record. It was all 'it needs these wheels and these brakes, and it needs to be lighter and more aerodynamic'.

All the while I was doing the TV thing, nodding and agreeing, but if you look at the programme, you can already get the gist that my heart's not in it, even though I'm not saying anything at the time. It reminded me of being sat in a casino in the town of Ely, Nevada, where the Silver State Classic ran from. The van was being mended and I was stood around like a spare part waiting for it to be delivered back to me. I wanted to be the man building the thing, but I felt like the TV presenter, because these experts had built the Carlos Fandango van, and there's me just rocking up to drive it. It was an amazing opportunity, and it was great to do the race, but it wasn't me.

We left Cadwell, the privately hired Cadwell, and the decision seemed to have been made that 'We'll do the same sort of thing with the Silver State job.' A plan had been drawn up: the van would be picked up on this date, be delivered to these boys for this, then this company for that; but it didn't sit well with me. The van had done the job, but I didn't like it. I like building stuff. I know I can be a disaster, but I want to do it. I thought about it for a day or two and spoke to Andy Spellman and told him what I thought. He is my point of contact, and the right thing is to go through him, not for me to get on to the TV lot and risk ending up shouting and swearing. They're nice people and that's not the proper way to deal with them. So I asked Spellman to tell the TV lot to leave the van with me, because I was going to prepare it for the Nürburgring.

My mate, Tim Dray, had said half-jokingly, 'Sling the engine in the back, boy', and I thought, Why not? The TV lot were on board. They probably knew it wasn't worth arguing with me. I'm not a prima donna, but they know if they want me properly involved I've got to be agreeing with the direction we're going in or I'll just go back to fixing trucks. They can't just wheel me in front of a camera, pull the cord in my back and I'll say whatever they want. This wouldn't be the easy way to do it, but it would be the best way to make a TV show I'd be happy with in the end.

So that was it. The first day, Tim Dray and Uncle Rodders (who's not my uncle) came over to my shed. We had a measure up, then I got a 9-inch angle grinder and cut a big hole in the floor of the van. There was no going back. We pulled the engine out, then the fancy dash came out, and we unbolted a load of other stuff that I either wanted to improve, was in the way, or we wouldn't need. Putting the engine in the back meant I had to rejig everything.

If you have a rear- or mid-mounted engine, you can't use the conventional gearbox in the back, you need a gearbox with a transaxle. The name comes from transmission and axle, because it has the gearbox and a diff, a differential, combined in one unit, with the driveshafts coming out of the transaxle casings. A transaxle is what you'd see on a Formula 1 car, or a Le Mans car, or anything with a mid-mounted engine. A normal front-engined, rear-wheel drive car or van has a flange on the back of the gearbox that a propshaft fastens to. The propshaft runs under the vehicle back to a diff that the driveshafts come out of. I hadn't done any research before cutting the Transit up, but I knew there was stuff out there and I'd find a solution.

I rang Quaife, the gearbox experts in Essex, to ask if they did anything, and they did. I didn't tell them that it was for a TV programme, I was just asking for advice, seeing if they could point me in the right direction. Adrian Naish rang me and told me they like what I do, mucking around in my shed, making stuff, so they'd sponsor me a gearbox. Mr Quaife, Michael, rang me to say, 'Tell me what ratios you want, and we'll sort it out for you.' And that was it, one massive headache avoided.

Quaife needed to know the wheel sizes and the maximum engine RPM, then they could work out the ratios. I told them we wanted the van to be geared for over 180mph, but Adrian explained that they'd have to specially make it, and it would take longer because they didn't have that ratio in stock. It would take another month, so I asked them to make a gearbox with what they had available. That meant the van would have a theoretical, maximum top speed of 165mph, not the 185mph it needed to beat the Supervan record, but sod it, I was going for the Nürburgring record, and if I didn't get a gearbox, we wouldn't have anything to film.

In the meantime, Quaife sent up some empty gearbox cases, while they were on with making the internals, so Tim Dray could make the back chassis subframe to mount the gearbox to.

I made the engine mounts, so the V6 was mounted in. Uncle Rodders was being a brilliant help. He's a big one for CAD – cardboard-aided design not computer-aided design – cutting bits of card out so we could suss the pieces of metal we needed to make to mount the engine. Once we had the design I had some of the engine mounts water-jetted and others laser cut, at Locate in Scunthorpe and Blackrow Engineering in Grimsby.

Another company that offered to help were Pro Alloy in Cambridgeshire. They'd worked on the van when Krazy Horse built it for the Silver State Classic. I contacted them asking for advice on what would be the best way to intercool it. I emailed them through the website explaining I had a Trannie van with an engine in the back, and because of the positioning, I didn't think I could air-to-air intercool it. Alex Oates got in touch and, like Quaife, said they liked what I do, and offered to make a bespoke charge cooling system. They were brilliant.

At that point I was still struggling with the rear suspension design and what I was going to do about that, and that's when Tim Dray came back in with another good idea. He told me to talk to his friend who runs Milner Engineering. They make 4x4 racing stuff, and were involved in the development of the Range Rover Evoque LRM1, a mad Group B rally-style Evoque.

The LRM1 looks like an Evoque, but it has a space frame with fibreglass and carbon fibre body panels, and, most importantly, it has a rear-mounted 6.2-litre, LS3 V8 engine. It is four-wheel-drive, where my Transit was rear-wheel drive, but it's a proper bit of kit, and we could use some parts of their dual-wishbone rear suspension. I still had to make a lot of the Transit's rear suspension, which was a bit of a fuckabout, especially as I had to do it a few times before I got it right.

That's just the engineering side of things, I had to drive the thing too, so I was having to learn the track. I've done a few laps around the Nürburgring on bikes, but not for years and I couldn't remember much of it. My way of learning it would be like I did when I was learning the Isle of Man TT: watch on-board videos and visit the track to do as many laps as I could fit in, and I did that, but the TV lot had another idea, and arranged for this state-of-the-art driving simulator to turn up at my house. It was a real fancy computer game thing, where you sit in a racing car seat with the pedals and proper steering wheel and a screen in front of you. It went in the spare room where I keep my pushbikes, and I'd have an hour a day on it when I could fit it in. I'm fairly good at learning long tracks, and this definitely helped.

North One also arranged for Dr Sherylle Calder to come from South Africa to Grimsby, to give me some brain training. How much must that have cost? A fortune! Dr Calder's thing is EyeGym, speeding up the time between the eye seeing, the brain registering and the limbs reacting. Her company had worked with all sorts of sportspeople. And she wasn't messing. She'd done a load of research into the track and was brilliant. We met in Grimsby, on the Nunny, the Nunsthorpe estate, one of the roughest areas of Grimsby. I was born in the maternity hospital on the Nunny – the hospital doesn't exist any more.

The TV lot rented a room in a community centre, where Dr Sherylle could set up her equipment and test me for the programme. She had worked with F1 drivers, and I, who was a decent go-er at the TT, was in a different league to some of the drivers she worked with when it came to reaction times. She wasn't impressed. She'd put loads of time and effort into the preparation and it was obvious she'd gone a fair way to learning the track herself, so I was going along with it for the right reasons, but I think it occurred to her she was trying to educate pork, because I'm far from a Formula 1 driver.

I was given a timetable of how many times I had to go on this eye and brain training computer programme, on a laptop at home. This was on top of the simulator, and everything that still needed making for the van. I was supposed to go on the brain training so many times a week, and I did, for a while, but with work and everything else, something had to give, and I have to say it was Dr Calder's eye training. I had a very mechanical view of it: I only have so much time left, so is that better spent finishing the van, or trying to improve my reactions, or learning the track better? I've been learning long tracks for a long time, and I haven't killed myself, so I'm obviously all right at it, but I realise there's a TV show to be made so we need things to talk about, and it's usually interesting stuff. The TV lot have to find as many of the little details for the viewers to get their heads around as they can or the show would be over in 15 minutes, and would just show me building shit in a van. People have this opinion of the Nürburgring, this mythical view of it, but it's just tarmac and bends, so I packed in the brain training and made sure the van would actually be finished on time, because we're not doing anything if that van isn't running.

I've mentioned this van record, but not given any details. The record I had to break was 9:57 set by Dale Lomas in a modified

Volkswagen Transporter T5, a boy-racered van, stripped out and chipped. I first met Dale in 2007 when I went to the Nürburgring with Dr John Hinds, straight after the Ulster Grand Prix. Dr John worked as a medic at the Irish road races. He was one of the flying doctors, who was sat on his bike, kitted up, ready to attend any crashes on his motorcycle. He was well-known to all the racers and fans, but, unfortunately, he died at Skerries in 2015, when he crashed himself.

I got to know Dale better through *Performance Bikes* magazine, where he worked for a few years. He left the magazine to move out to Nürburg, so his life could revolve around the circuit. People seem to get addicted to the Nürburgring, and I don't see the attraction. They get obsessed and move out lock, stock and barrel. At the time we filmed this programme, in 2018, Dale said he'd done 20,000 laps around the place. Twenty thousand laps of the same track! Jesus Christ, and it's only 13 miles. I got bored of the TT and that's 37 and three-quarters. Dale is a knowledgeable bloke, and a bloody fantastic driver. He likes using 50 words to describe a situation where one or two would probably do, though. He wasn't like that when he was a journalist for *Performance Bikes*, but I think he's reinvented himself to fit in with the car people. That's where the money is at the Nürburgring.

People want to be defined by how hardcore they are when they dedicate a big part of their life to the place, to become the Nürburgring man or woman. That's not me. I don't want to be defined by bikes or racing or a track or TV, I'm just someone who has a go. I'd rather be jack of all trades, master of fuck all.

When I was racing for TAS on the BMW superbike, in 2015, I was talking to one of the engine men who used to work for an LMP1, a Le Mans Prototype car racing team. I must have been struggling with a water pump on whatever project I was working on in my shed at the time. He said he used to be the water-pump man on the Le Mans team, so I was asking him about flow rates and he said, 'Ah, no, that's the main water pump, I just dealt with the secondary water pump, I didn't deal with the main water pump.' That's not a word of a lie, he knew everything about that secondary water pump, but absolutely bugger all about anything either side of it. Nothing! That confirms what I'm not. I have admiration for someone like Dale who has made his obsession into a career that he seems to love. Fair play to him, and he really is the man around there. No disrespect, but that's not for me.

Dale was involved in the programme. We went out to Germany to film him showing me around. He took me out for a lap in a Jaguar, and he was motoring, much faster than I would have to go in the van to beat his record. I ended up feeling carsick, because I wasn't in control and there's all the undulations. When you're holding the steering wheel, you're pre-empting it all, but not when you're a passenger.

We had a couple of Triumph Tiger 800s so Dale could take me on a tour on the outside of the track, stopping to spectate at different corners. We went to see Lauda Links, also called Lauda Left, where Niki Lauda crashed in the 1976 German Grand Prix. His car set on fire, with him in it. He was badly burnt, lucky to survive, and might not have done if some of his fellow drivers hadn't stopped and pulled him out. That was one of the problems with what most people know as the Nürburgring, but should really be called the Nürburgring Nordschleife, to differentiate it from the newer short circuit that the current F1 series races on. The Nordschleife is so long that it's hard to marshal, plus it's lined by Armco metal barriers, so if a car hits it, not only is there a violent stop, but the car is probably going to bounce and spin back into the track. That's exactly what happened with Lauda. His car was already on fire when it was hit by two more. The F1 drivers of the day already hated the place, but Lauda's infamous crash sealed its reputation.

Riding around with Dale, and being a passenger in that Jaguar, proved there isn't an inch of the track that he doesn't know, so even though my Transit would be more powerful than the VW he was driving, I'd be the weak link.

Another Nürburgring expert, Andy Carlile, was involved in the programme. He's another obsessive, the fastest bloke ever around there on a motorbike, who also moved his whole life out there. Like Dale, he earns a living instructing for track-day firms. Maybe the TV lot were worried about a conflict of interests if they had Dale instructing me how to break his record, so they asked Andy to do it. I doubt Dale was that bothered about me trying to beat his record, but I liked the way Andy described stuff when he was in the passenger seat. He was blunt, straight to the point. He seemed to have a good idea of what me, the vehicle we were in, and the tyres could take, encouraging me to get on the gas earlier, and harder, and keep accelerating.

Back in the shed it was getting to shit or bust time. I was still working five or six days on the trucks, and I was sorting the Transit every night. While I was loving it, Shazza wasn't. She moved back to Ireland for six weeks, because I was in the shed even more than normal. By this point I wasn't doing any of Dr Sherylle's eye-training exercises, and the fancy driving simulator was collecting dust.

Everything, every bit of the van, needed thinking about and there were countless problems to find solutions for. The turbos would hit the chassis rails so I had to make my own manifolds to reposition them. Luckily, Mark Hooker, who I worked at the truck yard with, helped out at the eleventh hour. He used to race grasstrack cars, so he knew what he was doing. I had planned for everything else, but I hadn't even thought about the exhaust. When Hooker came to visit we got talking and he said he could do it. He's a truck fitter, but a truck fitter who can make anything from anything. If your plane crash-landed in the desert, he's the boy you'd want with you.

He sussed the exhaust out, I got him the bits and the tube, and he made it. I didn't have to question him, he just got on with it. We can all overthink stuff, and I can imagine the TV lot would have subbed in a Formula 1 team to sort it, and we'd have been talking around it till the cows come home. The job would have been fantastic, but there would have been a whole lot of faff to get to the same point. Sometimes you need a person like Hooker who just comes in and does it, even if it's the first time he's done that thing. Proper handy man to have around.

He isn't the only useful mate I have by a long way. The Suzuki endurance lot, that I sometimes race with, were round here dynoing one of the GSX-Rs – putting it on the dyno, the rolling road machine that measures power – and saw the Transit on the ramp, in bits, and asked what I was doing with it. When I told them, they all shook their heads and said I'd never do it. Jez especially dismissed it, but as it got nearer the time, he realised I was going to manage it, and he asked if I needed a hand with any bits. I'd put a paddle-change gearbox in it, and I needed some wiring doing, and he's dead good, so I got him on board too. The paddle-change is levers mounted behind the steering wheel, making it possible to change gear without letting go of the wheel and reaching down for the stick.

With the help of the local yakkers I had the van finished in good time, and we took it to Cadwell for a track day, two or three weeks before the scheduled day of the record attempt. The van wasn't painted at that time, but it looked like a standard van again. I'd put a standard Transit bonnet and front bumper back on it, and unbolted the massive wing from the back doors.

Heading to Cadwell this time was different, and I was feeling under pressure. We'd built a mid-engined 500-plus horsepower Transit in my shed, me and a few mates, and the whole TV project was all on my head, because I'd told them 'I'm handling this'.

I gave the van a final once over while the camera crew were sticking little GoPro action cameras all over it, then it was time to roll out onto the track. I take a lap to make sure it all feels all right, check the gauges, then start speeding up. The van is bloody fast, and I was passing cars like they were standing still. I'd had it on my dyno by now and found out it wasn't making 700 horsepower, like I'd been told it was, but 500. Doesn't matter how you say it, 700 is not the same as 500, but still, it was fast.

Then it chucked a CV boot off. The drive shafts transfer power from the gearbox to the wheels. At the end of the drive shaft is a CV joint, a constant velocity joint, that connects the rotating drive shaft to the wheel, while allowing the wheel to move on its suspension. They've been widely in use since the launch of the original Mini, so they're nowt new, but they are clever. The CV joint is protected by a rubber cover called a boot. I thought it had come off because I'd packed too much grease into it, and as it had heated up, the grease expanded and blew the boot off. I'd learn later that wasn't the case, but we'll come to that.

I refitted the CV boot and got back on track. Then I flatted a front tyre. I was braking hard enough to lock the wheels, causing a skid that put a flat spot on the tyre. I knew then that I had to work on the brake bias, how much braking force is sent to the front and back brakes when the driver presses the pedal. I fitted a limiting needle valve to try to reduce the force the rear brakes were exerting.

But that was all, and really, I'd thought I was going to finish the track day and be faced with three weeks of no sleep, because I'd have to go back to the drawing board. I didn't have faith that something we'd built in the shed was going to work as well as it needed to, but other than the CV boot, I had ended up doing so many laps I ran out petrol. It left me thinking there was next to nowt wrong with it. That was the best feeling. This was a proper shed-built thing, and none of us had specific experience at what we were doing, but we worked it out.

Next, the van went to the paint shop for a full respray, and have the back doors repaired where the back wing had been bolted through it.

The week before the record attempt I travelled out to Germany to do some more laps, this time in a Suzuki Swift, a little hatchback, that a company in the area rents out. This being Germany, it was all properly track-prepared and spot on.

Andy Carlile came out in it with me, giving me advice and a bit of encouragement. The Suzuki is capable of lapping at about the same speed as I had to do in the Transit to beat Dale's current record, so it was good to get a feel of how fast I'd need to be going. There wasn't a single point on any of the laps where I was going too fast for Andy, and he'd calmly, and bluntly, tell me 'keep accelerating', and 'brake later'.

That was it, as far as preparation went. I had put the time in, learning the track on the computer, travelling to Germany to drive it and ride it, and also converted the Transit to mid-engine layout. Like everything, I could have dropped everything else and focused every waking minute on it, but that's never going to happen. I was feeling confident enough, though. I had just one week to wait to find out if I'd done enough.

2

Can You Smell Summat?

WE HAD A BUSY WEEK at the truck yard, before we got the Friday night freight boat out of nearby Killingholme. We went in two vans: my dad in his and me driving mine towing the Trannie, with Hooker, Jez and my nephew Louis split between the two vans.

We landed in the Netherlands, early Saturday morning, then drove to the Nürburgring. It was one of their tourist days, the ones where anyone can buy a ticket and do a lap. All that my van had done up to that point was that one track day at Cadwell, so it was still unproven, really. Anything could have gone wrong. Then it did.

The van shit the same CV boot off again, and got me scratching my head. I'd used drive shafts given to me by Ben Duckworth, who races one of those fancy Range Rover Evoque LRM1s. At first I just fitted them to get the driveshaft alignment right. They were second-hand, and even though Ben didn't tell me the history of them, there was no play in them, so I was happy to leave them on.

It turned out that the problem was the CV joint was picking up, by that I mean, something wasn't as smooth as it should be, causing extra friction, leading to it boiling the grease and that was what was popping the CV boot off. So it wasn't that I'd packed too much grease in there, like I'd thought at the Cadwell Park track day.

The driveshaft didn't fail completely, we were still moving, but it was obvious there was something wrong. I limped off the track and into the car park at the end of the lap. The CV joint was so hot you could hardly even look at it. I had only done one lap in the van at that point, and wanted to do some more. I had planned ahead, though, in case something like this happened, and bought two brand-new driveshafts from Land Rover as spares. So, me, my dad and Hooker set about it and changed the driveshaft there and then. We did it quickly enough that I got out for another five or six laps.

Again, I drove it till I nearly ran out of petrol, everything was working so well. We had a relaxed Saturday night, feeling quite smug that we could have a lie-in. I was looking forward to it, because I hadn't been having a lot of sleep over the last few months. We could have a beer on Saturday night, and then spend Sunday meticulously checking everything was tight, and topped up, before we went for the record on Monday. There would be pressure. We only had one hour on Monday morning, the day of the attempt. The TV lot had privately hired the whole track for one hour, at a cost of something mental like £20–25,000 for that one hour.

And that's what we did. Everything was going to plan on Sunday until I took one of the front wheels off, one of the last things I planned to do that afternoon. My mood changed when

I spotted a crack in one of the front brake discs. Holy-fucking-moly! The disc wasn't a regular Ford part, it was specially made by a firm in England. Now it was Sunday late afternoon, we were in Germany, and we had a very expensive Monday morning slot that needed paying for, whether we used it or not, plus the whole film crew, and a helicopter booked. We started making calls. Dale got on to someone in England, who could pick the disc up and drive it over for us to fit last thing on Monday morning. If that couldn't happen I was going to nick the standard brakes off my dad's Ford Tourneo people carrier and that would get me out.

Then Andy Carlile said he might know someone who had a good stock of brakes, so I gave him the cracked disc, and he headed off. He had to wait for the bloke because he was out, but a couple of hours later Andy came back with a smile on his face and a new disc in his hand. It turned out this special Transit front disc was the same as a Nissan GTR rear disc. He'd found one in the next village, delivering it to me at seven or eight at night, and none of that was TV bullshit. The chances of finding a replacement disc for an oddball Transit, on a Sunday afternoon, a few miles from where we were, were pretty slim. And we got it done. I still can't believe our luck. Sunday night could be summed up with the word relief rather than relaxation, but I was happy enough.

The record attempt took place on Monday, 15 October 2018. It was deep into autumn, in an area of Europe not known for great weather, but it felt like the middle of summer. It was T-shirt weather, dry as a bone. I couldn't have wished for better conditions.

We were up early, and met for breakfast, before I went off for a quick test drive and to fill the Transit up with petrol. Then the engine started missing, coughing, and not pulling right. Because we'd been in the back, and perhaps in the panic to sort the brake disc, maybe a boost pipe had got kinked, so I refitted that, but while it had been missing the engine had made a huge spike of torque and broken a ball joint in the tripod coupling, that goes in the gearbox end. The van was still running, but it was making a noise it shouldn't be making, and I wasn't happy, so I was going to have to pull the coupling out and change it. This was with an hour to go until our mega-money, private hire window started, and they didn't put all this in the programme. I just went quiet, got under the van and ripped it out. No one really knew what I was doing, except Hooker, who works with me and could see why I'd gone quiet, so he got stuck in. And it's a good job we did, because one of the couplings had broken, and I had a spare. I'd never built any race cars before, it had all been motorbikes, so I had no experience with driveshaft lengths and couplings. It was a steep learning curve, but I made sure we had enough spares in case stuff did go wrong.

I hardly had time to get in my fireproof race overalls and helmet, and the TV lot were tense. I'd already decided I was going to take Andy Carlile round with me on the record, and he was there waiting. Someone had pointed out that Colin McRae did all right with a co-driver and people didn't think he was less of a driver because someone was telling him what was coming up next. I thought, Oh, yeah ... And I asked if Andy was willing. It's not against the rules, so why not? He was more than happy to do it. I reckoned what I lost in the added weight of him in the passenger seat, I'd gain in his course knowledge. Or that was the plan.

Some people noticed I chose to drive in my work boots, not racing boots. The van had a standard Transit pedal box, my feet are used to feeling those pedals in those boots. I'd done 100,000 miles in that van, in those boots, I didn't need racing boots. The general reason for racing boots is to have better feel, and a narrower footprint, because a racing car's pedals are so close together. Racing boots make sure your feet are wide enough and no more. It wasn't because I was worried about looking like I'd gone full race-wanker spec, and that's why I wore work boots. I did it purely for mechanical reasons: my feet were used to the feel of pressing those pedals in those boots.

The van also had standard steering system: rack, ratio, and column, but no power steering. Once the engine had moved from the front to the back, there was a lot less stress on the front axle, so I didn't need the power steering. The benefit of no power steering is having more feedback to my hands on the wheel, and a better connection between me and what the front wheels were doing. I could have refitted the power steering if I felt I needed to, but it was dead easy to drive without it. A bit of a pain at standstill, but not when it was moving.

Because the track was exclusively ours a few things were different from if we were trying to set times on a track open to tourists. The most obvious difference being there that no one was going to get in the way. I didn't have to think about passing slower traffic, or have a section screwed up because there was a vehicle where I wanted to be. Also, I could enter the track at a turn called T13, named after the *tribüne*, that's German for grandstand. It's about 3 miles into the lap, meaning I could do nearly a full lap before

I started my timed lap, allowing me to accelerate towards the start line to use the first lap as a flying lap. T13 was renamed, in 2021, Sabine-Schmitz-Kurve, after the woman racing driver and Nürburgring expert, who died of cancer earlier that year. She held the van record before Dale. This was a decent advantage, because normally people would be driving out of the car park and accelerating from a low speed. Also, I was going to do a complete lap. Most people miss a length of the straight because they pull out of one end of the car park, onto the track, and pull into the other end of the car park at the end of their lap. It's like doing a lap of a racetrack, where you pull out of pit lane, do a lap and turn into pit lane, you've never actually crossed the start–finish line. The people who want to set, and compare, times have found a way around that, and they call it the bridge-to-gantry time, using two landmarks over the track that on-board GoPro camera footage can be timed to.

It was time to see if we could break Dale's record. Andy said it was the loudest vehicle he'd ever been in. It is loud, and there's a lot of shit going off, the whistles and the cracks of the turbo, and the noise of the gear change and the compressor, it's all action. And the noise caused a problem that I hadn't considered. We went out on the sighting lap, and straight away I realised it was a waste of time bringing Andy, because I couldn't hear him. The radio intercoms weren't loud enough to be heard over the noise of the van, the engine behind us was echoing around the tin box that the back of a panel van is. There was only a couple of points where I could pick up his hand gestures, telling me to 'Woah, woah, woah …' All the previous times he'd been in the passenger seat we'd been in a normal Transit, or the Suzuki Swift, so I didn't think about the possibility I wouldn't hear him. When I'd driven the rear-engined Trannie on Saturday I wasn't trying to hear anyone, I was just familiarising myself with the track and the van.

Before we set off, Andy had done a few pieces to camera, answering questions, and giving opinions that could be dropped into the programme to link one section to another. One thing he said was, if you take a vehicle around here at the speeds we're aiming for, 'You're playing with fire.' Good on him for still getting in with me, if he thought that.

The first lap was always going to be about getting my eye in, driving in a dead-controlled way, no last-second braking, then the next lap I was going to press on, but during that first lap the brakes had got up to their operating temperature, and the tyres had gone beyond theirs. The van weighed 1.95 ton. The tyres were designed for a Porsche GT3, that weighs something like 1.2 ton.

Also, as the brakes got warm they started locking up, so I was having to manually ABS it into corners. The back brakes were for a racing Range Rover Evoque, and they were so strong compared to the front brakes. I had six-pot calipers on the front, but they were just like souped-up Transit brakes, which is why I put a reducer valve in the system after the test day at Cadwell. I wanted to make sure the back brakes didn't overpower the fronts, so I fitted a needle valve, a car racing thing. The van had two feeds coming from the brake pedal, one feed to the front brakes, the other to the rear. The valve I installed had an adjuster mounted next to my seat, so I could dial down the pressure. The problem that I didn't realise until afterwards was the needle valve is just masking the problem, not solving it. As long as I didn't shut the valve completely, there's still a feed of fluid going to the rear brakes, so if I was braking into a corner, foot on the pedal for two or three seconds, the pressure would gradually leak past the needle valve and lock the back brakes anyway. So that's when I started manually ABSing it, quickly pressing and releasing my foot, trying to copy the way you can feel a car's ABS system pulsing when it's working. By braking like that I was making sure the pressure to the back brakes didn't build up. I was making this up as I went around on that fast-ish lap. All the while the tyres were telling me, loud and clear, that they'd had enough. They had overheated, lost their grip and were squealing. They felt like they were rolling off the rims, because everything was so hot and the brakes were so aggressive.

We finished the first lap, what I was treating as a sighting lap, with a time of 9:28, so I'd broken Dale's record, by 29 seconds, but the next lap was the one I planned to go for it. The first half of the lap was quicker than the sighting lap, so I was on target to improve on the time, but then I lost my pace. I was struggling to keep the van on the racing line because the brakes kept locking. It was becoming a handful, and I nearly put it in the gravel three times. Andy went quiet. I wouldn't have liked to be in his seat. I'm not an experienced driver and I was still learning as I went along, but at least my future was in my own hands. His wasn't.

Towards the end of the lap Andy shouted loud enough for me to hear him, 'Can you smell summat?' Smoke was coming into the cab. We didn't know, but there were massive orange flames licking off the engine. There was a GoPro camera or two mounted in the back of the van and it was catching what looked likely to become a bomb scene, while I was still flying around one of the most dangerous racetracks in the world. You don't want to smell burning, but all the temperature gauges were all right, so I kept driving as fast as I could. Then the van cut out, but it was unrelated. I went for another gear, because I didn't realise I was already in top, when I should have just looked at the gear position indicator on the dash. I think something in the software caused the power to cut after I'd tried to select seventh in a six-speed gearbox. The van came back to life and I carried on, but I was already hoping to get it over as quick as possible and get into our makeshift pits.

The fire in the back was caused by oil spraying onto the red-hot exhaust, and the oil was coming from a loose turbo hose. Nothing serious, other than the flames, and that's why the dash didn't show anything wrong. The fire looked dramatic, but all it damaged was the turbo hose and a brake hose. The fire was just the oil burning off.

Andy was already loosening his seat harness as we rolled into our pit area. He didn't want to be in the van a second longer than he had to. The comment he made earlier, about playing with fire, was on the money.

I can't have been thinking straight because I pulled to a stop right next to two petrol pumps. All we'd smelt was the smoke, and even though I know the 'no smoke without fire' saying, we didn't have a clue what it looked like back there. I just wanted to be as close as possible to where our vans were parked so we could open the doors and see what was up. Looking back, it wasn't the best decision I'd ever made.

With the fire out, the time was up. And the TV lot could say we had abandoned the top speed record, the one held by Ford's

Supervan, but you already know the gearbox I fitted wouldn't allow the van to go that fast, and it wasn't just the gearbox, the engine wasn't making enough power to pull the top gear we had anyway. So, if you watched the programme and heard the voiceover saying the speed attempt had been abandoned, that was a bit of TV bullshit. Yes, if the van had been still going well, and we had time left in our track slot, we might have attempted the record, but we'd have just been burning petrol for the sake of it, because my Transit was never going to beat the 180-odd top speed.

We broke the van lap record on that first out lap, so it was job done. The TV lot got the programme, and I learned plenty converting the Transit to mid-engine. I got to do a few laps of the Nürburgring, and also experienced the place as the only person on track, which not many people can say. I drove home with massive satisfaction. I wasn't having a lot of fun there, because there was a lot to deal with.

The programme that was called *Guy Martin: The World's Fastest Van?* – with a question mark – went out nearly straight away, in November 2018, and in the back of my mind was the thought, You watch, someone will smash it as soon as the Nürburgring opens again in April 2019. I thought my van had the potential to knock another 30 seconds off the record. I needed to sort the brakes, get some more weight off it, and sort all the little niggles. I'd found out the right way to stop the rear brakes from overpowering the front, with two master cylinders, working off one pedal, so you can reduce the force the pedal is exerting to get the bias right.

Going on for three years later, no one has tried breaking my time, and perhaps that's because it's a bit of a daft record. It's a fast van, but it's still a van. When I got back home, the van went straight up to my mates at the Grampian Transport Museum, up north of Aberdeen, and I kept having ideas. I was going to do all this and that, and when I got it back from the museum, I did another track day at Cadwell. I was smoking everything in a straight line, but I realised I'd done everything I wanted to do with the van and I'd had enough.

I'd sold a couple of cars I had but wasn't using, got rid of two Scanias that I'd ended up with, and told my mate Jim I wanted rid of the Transit. I don't know where he advertised it, but it sold within a day. A powerlifter champion called Marcus turned up, bought it, and has put it back on the road. And I felt miles better for selling it, and all the other cars and trucks. I've still got plenty of projects, but I felt so much better for getting rid of the stuff I have. I don't need it.

3

300 Miles per Hour

BEFORE I GOT INVOLVED with Triumph and their land speed streamliner, back in 2015, I had the mindset, Going fast in a straight line, what is there to that? Going to Bonneville Salt Flats sounded interesting, but how hard could it be? Once I got involved in their project, where they were hoping to break 400mph, and saw what was involved, I loved it. It wasn't just me sitting in the streamliner and pointing it in a straight line, I was giving a load of input, and it wasn't as easy as I initially thought.

Streamliner motorcycles are the fastest bikes in the world. They often have two engines, and look like a rocket or a fighter plane without wings. They're fully enclosed, so the bottom of two wheels is only just visible. The rider is in a cockpit, sat in a version of a racing car seat, looking through a windscreen. Streamliners need little jockey wheels that extend out like a plane's landing gear, because the rider can't put their foot down when they stop. In the early days of streamlining bikes they'd run on closed roads, but the top speeds the fastest streamliners are doing now means they can only get up to speed on dry lake beds, like Bonneville in Utah, or Salar de Uyuni, the world's largest dry salt lake, in Bolivia.

Trying to break land speed records is more of a science experiment than it is about finding someone with the bravery and experience to ride, or drive, the machine. Generally, I'd look at things and think, you have to have some balls to try that. That's why, in road racing, if you put the best rider on the worst bike they'll still do well, because it's about hanging it out. That's until you get right to the top and then you've got to have very good mechanical insight and be very naturally talented, and that's where I hit the brick wall – metaphorically and physically, sometimes. I was all right to a point, and did all right at certain sorts of racing because I had a decent mechanical insight and I was willing to hang it out there, but I never felt I was that naturally gifted. I wouldn't say Michael Dunlop was naturally talented either, but when he lined up on the grid he wanted it more than most. Ian Hutchinson, great rider, and perhaps he wanted it more than me too. John McGuinness had more natural talent than me, and good mechanical feel too. I could say that believing I lacked in natural talent was just an excuse for not winning. Perhaps I just didn't want it enough.

While I'm on the subject, I do still believe that TT racers are failed British Superbike racers, and British Superbike racers are failed World Superbike racers, and World Superbike racers are failed MotoGP racers. I'm generalising, but most riders who are in with a chance of winning are only doing the TT because they're not talented enough to earn a good living in another type of racing. A prime example is Peter Hickman. In the professional ranks, he's an average short circuit rider. Yes, he's won odd British Superbike races, but he's not at the sharp end all the time, yet when he transfers his skills to road racing he's a step above everyone else. Perhaps I'm being unfair. Maybe MotoGP riders wish they had the skills that make someone like Hickman or McGuinness as good as they are around the Isle of Man.

Still, when it suited me, I put my balls on the line. I did it plenty of times, but things had to be right. I learned when it was the time and the place to take the risks. I wasn't going to do it for fifth place.

Bonneville was a new challenge, and it wasn't the kind of riding where it felt right to use road-racing mentality, just chucking your brain out of gear and sticking your balls on the line, because you've got a much smaller window for error even compared to the TT. I think land speed racing is the most dangerous thing I've been involved with. From my experience, in land speed racing, it has to be perfect and you have to be 100 per cent in what you're doing, and if you're not, it's going to hurt, and because you're going so fast there's a good chance it's going to kill you.

I wasn't being paid by Triumph to ride their streamliner, they covered expenses and paid to fly a few of my friends out there, so I wasn't doing it for the money, I was doing it because I was into it. I don't make a fuss about stuff, but I sorted a will out after the first time I rode it, and that was before I had a young 'un. It felt bloody dangerous. I was prepared to do it, I wanted to do it, but that was the first time I thought seriously about a will. I think that was part of the attraction, that it really rammed home how dangerous it was.

I had a couple of stupid crashes in the streamliner, but at slow speeds when I was setting off. I had a massive moment at 190mph, the front wheel was going lock-to-lock, slamming the steering hard to the right, then hard to the left, as the power of the thing was pushing it in a shaky straight line. No amount of grip on the controls calmed it down, and we didn't know what caused it. I rolled off the throttle, it straightened out, I got back on the power and it didn't do it again. It wasn't a persistent problem, so it might have been an aero issue.

After three trips to Bonneville for Triumph's land speed record (LSR) project there was a big change of direction. The project had been run from Portland, Oregon, by Matt Markstaller but Triumph brought it to the UK. Matt was the truck aerodynamist and designer, who was the driving force and designer of the Triumph Streamliner. It had felt like a mishmash of energies from loads of different people, but Triumph's UK head office were footing the bill. I don't know how much they'd spent on the project, but $4 million rings a bell, and they didn't have a lot to show for it in terms of performance. I'd only been fast on it once, doing 274mph. That wasn't a fully committed run, and way off the 400mph they were aiming for, but what I learned was to go fast in LSR you have to learn to wait. You've got to have the right people doing the right thing and there's no room for half a job. People have spent a lot of money and a lot of time trying to do 400mph and the team that have come the closest is the American Rocky Robinson in the Ack Attack streamliner, with an official one-way run of 394mph.

Compared to Ack Attack and the Bub Streamliner, which is another two-wheeled land speed racer that had held the outright motorcycle record, the Triumph Rocket Streamliner was at the very start of its development, so the team were having to solve problems every time I got in it. The first time the problems were with the bike. The next time we flew out it was the weather. God knows how much it cost every time we went, because there was a helicopter sat on the salt for the four or five days we were there, and all these corporate guests and journalists were flown out, fed and watered.

Around this time Triumph were getting into Moto2. This is the class below MotoGP, with riders trying to step up from there into MotoGP. When Moto2 was first introduced, for the 2010 season, it replaced the old 250cc class, so the second-ranking grand prix class went from being a series for 250cc two-strokes to one for 600cc four-strokes. To try to keep budgets reasonable it was decided that all the teams had to use the same engine, and they couldn't tune what they'd been given. The teams could choose their chassis, but not their engines. From 2010 to 2017 all the engines were four-cylinder Hondas, then for the 2018 season, Triumph became the engine supplier, building a 765cc inline triple. It was the first time Triumph had been involved in the MotoGP series and they had a lot on their plate.

Compared to the land speed job, the Moto2 engine was a lot easier to deal with. They have no competition, they just have to make it reliable and make sure supply doesn't fail. When it comes to breaking the 400mph barrier there is no answer for 'how much is this going to cost us?' You can't write a cheque for 400mph. No one's ever done it and there are so many factors working against you.

It felt, to me, that Triumph had enough of the land speed attempt, even though they were making the right noises, asking me what I thought needed to happen to improve it. When we finished filming at the factory, for the *Great Escape* TV show, I sat down with some of Triumph's top bods to talk about the streamliner and I left thinking it was back on and it was happening, but, nearly two years later, nothing has moved. That might be more to do with the whole coronavirus thing, so I don't know. I still think there's a flickering flame for the Triumph job. I hope it's not completely extinguished, but I'm not the driving force, I just have to wait.

The experience with the Triumph at Bonneville Salt Flats left me realising that I'm into this, I'm into going fast, but I don't have the commitment or money needed to plough into a 400mph job. I don't want to spend all year building to have one go at Bonneville or Bolivia – just think of the expense of going. Even going to Bonneville you have to take everything, barring the kitchen sink, with you, and Bolivia is even worse, you're hours from the nearest hotel. Going fast is always going to cost money, but Bonneville can very easily be a massive waste of time and money.

I started thinking about other ways to go fast and decided I'd do my own thing. From the time I made that decision a bloke called Jarrod 'Jack' Frost became a big part of the story. Jack is 50-ish, and has been drag racing, motorcycle sprinting and top speed racing for 30 years. He grew up in Bradford, but for all the time I've known him he's been living in Northern Ireland. His company, Holeshot Racing, is the bedrock of British motorbike turbocharging. I got to know him through buying bits for my

Martek Pikes Peak bike, which is powered by a turbocharged Suzuki GSX-R motor. This is the bike I bought in 2009 and raced at the 2014 Pikes Peak International Hill Climb, that I wrote about in *When You Dead, You Dead*.

The first time I properly met Jack was when I went to the North West 200 in 2012. The North West is the biggest motorcycle race of the year in Northern Ireland, held a couple of weeks before the start of the Isle of Man TT. Like the TT it takes place on public roads, but it's a mass start race, not a time trial like the TT. At the North West, you used to practise Tuesday and Thursday and race on Thursday night and Saturday, so I had Wednesday off. I needed to get some bits from Jack, and drove the hour-and-a-half to his to pick them up.

At the time I was racing for TAS Suzuki, the official Suzuki road-racing team, and had spent the day before practising on the proper Carlos Fandango, trick as fuck, World Superbike spec Suzuki GSX-R1000, that I'd be racing that weekend on the Triangle, which is what they call the North West's circuit. It's not the fastest road race in the world, but bikes get radar trapped at 200mph, so you're not hanging around.

When I turned up at Jack's he showed me a Suzuki GSX-R1000K5, a road-legal Suzuki superbike, that he'd just finished turbocharging. 'Get a go on that,' he told me. I had my Martek at the time, but I'd hardly ridden it before I stripped it to sort it all out, so I had next to no experience riding turbo motorbikes. I was in my shorts, hoodie and I borrowed a helmet from Jack, then took the bike out on the shitty little lanes near Dromore. Jesus Christ, that Holeshot Suzuki was mental! It changed what I thought a fast bike was. The day before I'd ridden one of the best Suzukis in the world, on a fast circuit, with a team of experienced race mechanics doing anything and everything to try to make it the fastest thing that weekend, then this seven-year-old Suzuki, built in a shed, made it feel like a learner bike. That planted the seed. I carried on building the Martek, and I kept buying parts from Jack.

A couple of years later, in 2017, I had signed for Honda to race their Fireblade TT bike. After years of being the bike to be on, the new latest version of the Fireblade wasn't anywhere near as fast as it had to be to have a chance of competing at the TT. Jack gave me the idea of taking it to Elvington airfield, a former military airbase near York. It's the place in Britain to do land speed stuff, because it has a runway that is 2 miles long. Of all the runways in Britain people can rent for stuff like this, I think only Machrihanish in Scotland is longer, and people don't use that much because it's right on the west coast, over a three-hour drive from Glasgow, so it's a long way from anywhere.

Elvington's runway was extended during the Cold War to allow the heaviest US bombers to take off from there, but it was never used by the US. It has this massive apron, a huge parking area for storing machinery and supplies they might have wanted to fly onwards. It's the place the *Top Gear* lad, Richard Hammond, spannered himself, and where another presenter, Zef Eisenberg, an ultra-speed motorbike racer, was killed in 2020. Those things stick in people's minds, but a lot of great stuff has happened there, and people love racing their bikes and cars at Elvington.

As Jack said, if the Fireblade doesn't do 200mph there it's not going to do it at the Isle of Man, and if it can't do 200mph there wasn't a lot of point in doing the TT because it wouldn't be competitive. It was a good idea, and the team agreed to let me test it at a meeting run by Straightliners, a club that runs top-speed events around the country, but most often at Elvington. We turned up with the bike, a factory Honda superbike worth a fortune, a couple of Honda mechanics, and it took us all day to get this superbike to hit 180mph (and I still went to the TT, but, that's another story and it's in *We Need to Weaken the Mixture* if you want more details).

At Elvington that day there were road bikes, with £2,000 to £3,000 worth of parts, doing 200mph, and then there's Jack doing 250mph. Holy moly! When you see the speed with your own eyes it makes you laugh. They're the same kind of bike, but with a load more horsepower, and the sight of them blasting up the runway, so much faster than anything else, fried my brain. The seed had already been planted, but this made it grow. I wanted to go fast, at least as fast as the shed-built stuff I'd seen at Elvington.

After the TT of 2017 I packed in serious, contracted racing. I'd had enough. Since then I've done a bit of classic endurance racing on the Suzuki and some road races on my Rob North BSA, but I won't be signing for teams like TAS or Honda. I'd done all that, it was time for something new.

I had a word with Pete, who runs B&B Motorcycles in Lincoln and who I knew through the Classic Suzuki endurance team. I asked him to keep an eye out for a Suzuki GSX1300R Hayabusa, one of the fastest production bikes ever built, and the basis for a lot of fast turbo bikes. The Hayabusa isn't a sportsbike, like a Fireblade or a GSX-R1000, it's a sports tourer. It has a full fairing, but it's heavier, not as quick at changing direction, but it will do over 180mph straight out of the showroom. You could use a Kawasaki ZZR1400, another sports tourer, but the Kawasaki's engine is part of the whole chassis set-up – it's a type of monocoque construction, so the front of the bike bolts to the front of the engine, and the back of the bike bolts to the back of the engine. The engine is what they call a stressed member. With the Hayabusa the engine bolts into a beam frame that wraps around the engine. You could take the engine out and roll down a hill on what's left, and you couldn't do that with the Kawasaki. This becomes important when you start trying to bolt turbos and charge coolers to Kawasakis, because you don't have the same space as you do with the Suzuki. The package of the Hayabusa made the most sense for what I had planned.

Pete found me a 2012 Hayabusa that was a bit tatty, with 20,000 miles on it, for £5,000. It didn't matter that it had been ridden in shitty weather and wasn't as shiny as a brand-new one, because I was going to change so much of it.

By now I had looked into the whole straight-line thing a bit more, and I realised no one had done 300mph in a mile. By that, I mean going from a standing start to 300mph in one mile. The speed is just measured in the last 80 feet of that mile. Land speed streamliners, like Ack Attack, had been much faster at places like Bonneville, but they take longer than a mile to get up to speed. Once I learned about 'mile bikes' I felt like I had something I could really get my teeth into. The British don't have anything like Bonneville, but we have access to runways, so putting a mile cap on the record makes more sense for us.

Me and Shazza went to Elvington in the summer of 2019, where I rode my Hayabusa as a bog-standard road bike to get a datum, see what we were starting with. I did 183mph at Elvington, and put it on the dyno, and it made 182 horsepower. Not bad for a £5,000 bike.

I had started thinking how I was going to get to where I wanted to be. I'd built the Pikes Peak Martek, and worked through a load of problems with that, and for what I didn't know I rang Jack Frost. During all that I learned loads about turbocharging. I spoke to Jack about Hayabusas, asking what he'd do, and he told me all this and that. I asked him to price up converting the bike to the spec of one of his big-power Hayabusas. Exhaust, ignition, turbo, charge cooler, Inconel alloy valves in the head, spacer below the barrel to lower the compression, special bolts, special cams, this, this, this . . . He came back with a price of £27,000. For that, I give him my complete bike and it comes back ready to ride. I weighed up the pros and cons over a couple of weeks, going back and forth thinking I could do it all, but then decided to have him do it.

From the start I explained I wanted to run the bike on E85. This is an alcohol-based fuel, 85 per cent ethanol, 15 per cent petrol. Ethanol is called a biofuel and is produced from corn or sugarcane. It's sold out of pumps to use instead of regular unleaded petrol in Brazil and some US states, among other places. Running the Hayabusa on E85, instead of petrol, has pros and cons. You use a lot more E85, you get fewer miles per gallon, but the upside is the engine runs cooler, so it's knock resistant, because you're chucking a third more fuel through it. Knock, also known as pre-ignition or pinking, is the big problem to deal with when you're playing with big-power turbo engines. In an engine suffering from knock, the charge, that is the air and fuel in the cylinder, ignites before the spark lights it. It doesn't take long for knock to melt a piston, which is disaster for the engine. The turbo is compressing air until, in the case of my bike, it is two, three, even four times more dense than air in the atmosphere. You create a load of heat while you're doing that and that causes problems. Also, hot air is not as dense as cool air, and it can cause more knock and, in extreme cases, light the fuel before it even gets into the engine. It's on fire in the inlet tracts. Jack explained one of the most important ways he controls knock is with a British-made Syvecs ignition system.

Jack hadn't built a bike to run on E85, but said everything's doable. He was rebuilding his bike at the same time, so he converted his to run on E85. He's been brilliant and I like to think he's learned some stuff from me and how I've been developing things, too.

This type of land speed riding is far more realistic for me than aiming for Bonneville. I don't have to rely on that one week a year, when the weather's perfect, the bike's perfect. I'm better off running on a mile. I can go an hour-and-a-half north of home or an hour-and-a-half south and do it, but it's still a hell of a challenge.

4

It's the Toughest of the Tough

IN THE BOOK *Worms to Catch*, I wrote about the Tour Divide endurance mountain bike race. The 2,700-mile route follows the Rocky Mountains from Banff in Canada to America's Mexican border, so you're climbing and descending every day. It's self-supported, meaning you have to carry everything you need, for however long you're on it. There isn't a back-up truck or helpers. I wrote that the happiest I'd ever felt in my life was riding out of Sargents, Colorado, during that race. I had a full belly, I was doing this massive challenge and I'd just met similar people doing similar things.

Earlier that day I'd left a town called Salida, a real cool place in the middle of nowhere, knowing it was a big push to the next shop I'd be able to get food. I'd filled myself full of ice cream, and set off on the Marshall Pass, climbing to nearly 11,000 feet, thinking about the general store at the other side. I remember writing in my book, the one I made notes in every night: 'Fucking Brutal.'

I got there just as the small shop was closing, but they looked after me and the lass behind the counter made food for me. There were a group of American blokes cycling north, on the same route I'd been using in the opposite direction. One was an English teacher, whose rear hub had dropped to bits. Bicycle wheels get a proper hammering on that route, and the hubs, with the gear mechanisms, are relatively delicate parts. He had a plan, though, and got a taxi to the nearest bike shop to get some bits to fix it, while his mates waited for him.

I'm writing about this again now because, while we were there, a bloke arrived in a car and introduced himself as a cycling journalist. He was taking a few photos and talking to me. He knew I wasn't Terry Smith, the name I'd entered the race under. One of the group of riders I'd been talking to said to me, 'Do you know who that is?' I told him I didn't have a clue. 'That's Neil Beltchenko. He set the record on the Arizona Trail Race this year.' I told them I'd never heard of that either. This English teacher was surprised I was doing the Tour Divide, but I'd never heard of the AZTR – the Arizona Trail Race. 'It's the toughest of the tough, more of a crawling race than a cycling race, and he won it,' he said, meaning Beltchenko.

The way he said it was the toughest race stuck in my mind. He emphasised the race I was doing was sod-all compared to the AZTR. I was two-thirds of the way through a race I was convinced was the toughest mountain bike race in the world and I'd been told I was just playing at it. But it didn't ruin my mood, because I pedalled off into the dark Colorado wilderness feeling as happy as I'd ever been, and didn't stop pedalling till midnight.

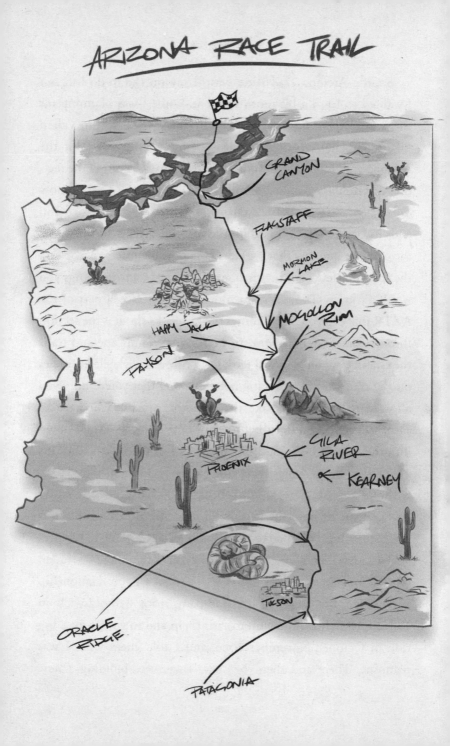

So, the Arizona Trail Ride was firmly on the to-do list, but I wanted to learn a bit more about it. While I was planning for the Tour Divide I found out about this online forum called Bikepacking.net. Visiting it again got me the start date for the Arizona Trail Race. There were two alternative versions of the race, the AZTR 300 (which is 300 miles long) and the AZTR 750 (now called the AZTR 800), that starts on the border with Mexico and ends in Utah. I was going to do the big one. I had a good look at the official route, saw that it gave all the possible places to stop and the special rules of getting through the Grand Canyon, things you wouldn't know. Though it's a mountain bike race, a part of the AZTR that everyone who knows the race talks about is the section through the Grand Canyon. To preserve the landscape and trails the Grand Canyon National Park has a rule of no wheeled vehicles on the trail, and Bikepacking.net explained that you're not even allowed to push your bike through the canyon, you have to carry it. The section starts before the South Rim, goes right down into the canyon bottom, then climbs out to the North Rim. It's 22.5 miles, and websites reckon it's a 12- to 15-hour hike. That's without a pushbike on your back. I didn't need any more encouragement from the forum. I'd made up my mind that this was happening, I just had to work out how was it going to happen.

I decided I was going to use a new bike, not the Salsa I'd ridden on the Tour Divide. Over the years I've had a good relationship with Hope, the bicycle parts company from Barnoldswick in Lancashire. I always drive up to visit them and to go out for a big ride in October, November time, and I told them what I was planning. There and then they said they were building a new pushbike, the HB130. They don't normally make full bikes or frames, they're most well-known for making CNC-machined alloy parts, like disc brake systems, stems, cranksets, hubs, chain wheels and lights, for riders and other manufacturers to fit to their bikes. In 2015 they'd started getting into making parts from carbon fibre, and combined with the materials they were experts in, they began making a frame they called the HB160 that has a frame set that is half carbon fibre and half alloy. It was really nicely done, like everything they do, but it was expensive, costing about £6,000. I got the feeling Hope didn't want to be one-trick ponies, so they ended up expanding their range of bikes with the HB130, the bike they said I could ride a pre-production prototype of in the race.

That was a big part of the planning sorted, and Hope said I'd get the bike in January 2019 but, it turned out, they gave me a prototype in February that I rode for six weeks. I only ended up getting the actual bike I was going to do the AZTR on two weeks before I left. I didn't really want to take a bike I hadn't ridden before because my body gets used to pedalling a bike in a different position and my joints seem to adjust to it, but the bike I took was very similar to the prototype I'd had since February, just with a few more refinements on it.

I wanted to ride the Hope because I liked being a small part of the testing process of this bike. I was going to put it through its paces. I love being part of that machine because their stuff's really trick and I like having trick stuff. It's quite simple.

While I was filming the D-Day programme in France, I took my bike and worked out how I was going to carry it. I'd never visited the Grand Canyon, but I learned it is a mile deep in places,

and where I was going to hike through, South Rim to North Rim, the North Rim is 300 feet, 90 metres, higher. It doesn't sound much but, I was going to find out, it is. I was trying to find photos from anywhere and everywhere of how people were rigging up their bicycles to carry them. I got hold of some lightweight straps that are used to secure the pipes on the haulage wagons I work on. Sharon was with me so I got her to take photos of me so I could copy what worked best. My Kriega motorcycle rucksack was man enough to carry the bike and it's designed to take a water bladder, that I'd need, so that was a big help.

I convinced myself I didn't need to do any special training to walk through the Grand Canyon. I'm not the best walker, so what's the point in knackering myself to train for it when I can just go and do it? I had the route map, and knew that when I climbed out to the top of the North Rim I only had 90 miles further to pedal till the finish.

My ankle is delicate and I'd been seriously thinking of getting a replacement one fitted before I decided to do the AZTR, but it didn't happen. The ankle problems all date back to the Southern 100 in 2003, detailed in my autobiography. After I broke it I was dead keen to get back racing, but I had to be signed off as fit to race by a doctor before the race organisers would let me race. I found an Irish doctor, well-known in the road-race world, who said he'd happily sign me off as fine to race, all I had to do was climb on his examination table and jump off, landing on just my bad leg. It's nothing anyone half-fit would be worried about but it was a proper leap into the unknown for me, especially as I'd only broken it six weeks before. I was sweating bullets as I stood on his table, looking at the lino landing spot, and gritted my teeth. The ankle held, and I was signed fit to race again, but Dr MacSorley told me it would be knackered in ten years because of the way it had been broken and how I was desperate to get back racing. I've had a good ten years out of it, but now, if I run on it, it's wrecked for the next week. It feels like everything starts moving in it.

When I set my mind on doing the AZTR I realised I hadn't left enough time to have the ankle operation, let it recover and do enough training for the race. I convinced myself that if I completely buggered it, I'd crawl the last 90 miles if I had to, so I wouldn't have to train on the walking job. Mind over matter, I reckoned, I'm strong enough.

I hadn't been pedalling enough either, because I was still working stupid hours on the truck job. I was setting off at four in the morning to get to work for six, just to try to get 30-odd miles in, but I didn't do one big ride. Before the Tour Divide I was riding to the north of Scotland, then doing the Strathpuffer 24-hour race up there. I was trying to have a structured three months of training before the AZTR, but I had it in my head that the race was going to be more of a mental than a physical challenge, more about being in the mindset to keep going than actually having the strength. I was confident I could pedal and carry the bike that far, because this race, at 750 miles, was so much shorter than the Tour Divide, which is 2,745 miles. I didn't think my back would be an issue because it never has been, even since I broke it at the Ulster GP in 2015 and had it plated. I'd grit my teeth. I reminded myself that it wouldn't be an issue.

I told the TV production lot that I work with, North One, I was going to do this race. It was never going to be part of a programme, but they needed to know I wouldn't be available for any work. North One told me the US MotoGP race was on at COTA, Circuit of the Americas, on the outskirts of Austin, Texas, in April, a few days before I was going to start riding. North One were making programmes for BT Sport and they wanted me to go along to the MotoGP race, to show my face there. That sounded like a plan.

The date of the race came around quickly and a couple of days after I'd finished parachute training in France, for the D-Day programme, I flew into Austin, Texas, with Andy Spellman, the agent I've worked with for years, the middleman between me and the TV lot. He runs the *Guy Martin Proper* website too, and helps with a load on the commercial side of things, from ordering the woolly hats, to making sure I'm where I'm supposed to be. It was good to see him for a couple of days, and especially in Austin. What a place. I knew about the city because I listen to radio DJ Zane Lowe, and his coverage of South by Southwest, SXSW, the massive annual music, TV and film festival they have there. It sounded like a right cool place, with a street full of different bars and bands playing all over the place day and night. I'd always thought to myself I'd go to the festival one day.

It was the wrong time of year for SXSW, but because it was MotoGP weekend it was still mint. I got to have a walk around a paddock and have a good look at a few bikes. Gary Hewitt was there too. He's a mate and his company, Elas, a business support company, was one of my sponsors from my motorbike racing days, so I spent a bit of time with him in Austin. There's also a big custom motorbike show, called the Handbuilt Show, in town the same weekend so I went there too.

There was a bloke at the custom show from Ireland, with an old Moto Guzzi that I'd seen at a bike show in Dublin years ago. The bike had been flown over and it was still owned by the same person. It was based on a 1971 Guzzi Falcone Nuovo and had been built by a couple of blokes from Cork, Don Cronin and Michael O'Shea, who call themselves Medaza Cycles. It won the Custom Bike World Championship a few years before. I'm not sure if it was Don or Michael there, but I had a good natter with him. There were loads of cool bikes.

In all I was in Austin for a couple of days and had time to mooch round a few bars and had a burger while watching the world go by. Me and Spellman rented one of those electric scooters each, where you have to put your card in the machine, which I don't like doing, and we had a cruise around on them. I really enjoyed the whole experience, but really I couldn't properly relax because I knew the pain was coming.

On MotoGP race day I had to get away from the track sharpish, because I was flying from Austin, Texas, to Phoenix, Arizona, and I had my bike with me, adding to the number of things that can go wrong.

The flight was delayed so I didn't land in Phoenix at 11 on Sunday night, then I thought I'd lost my pushbike in customs, but it eventually turned up. There's no train station, but I found a bus that would take me to Tucson. I was told I should've booked on the internet and it was too late to organise that, so I offered the driver $50 and he let me on. That took me to a petrol station on the outskirts of Tucson and from there I got hold of a taxi and told him to take me to a hotel. By the time I got in the room I couldn't sleep because I was as nervous as hell as the start of the race got closer.

Tucson is the nearest city to the start of the AZTR, but it's not that close. I could've biked from Tucson, but I had enough riding ahead of me, so I'd organised a lift through a pushbike shop in the city. A bloke from the shop took me in a massive 4x4, a Ford F350 pick-up, 65 miles out to the border, and only charged me summat like $100.

When the bloke dropped me off he looked around and said, 'I can't leave you here.' He told me he normally dropped groups of people off, not just one person. There was nothing there. I told him it was fine, this was the place, right on the fence that marks the border with Mexico.

I'd decided that the way I did the Tour Divide was the way I preferred to do things, setting off before the official start and doing it on my own, at my own pace. I like being by myself. I like riding my own race. I thought that if I set off with the group start of the AZTR, I might try to keep up with someone before I was ready for it. However much you know you should go at your own pace, if you see someone up ahead it's hard not to try to catch them and then blow up, by that I mean burn yourself out. I do the same when I'm riding with my brother, Stew. He's loads quicker than me, so I try to keep up and knacker myself. You can get away with it on a one-day sprint ride, but not on an ultra-distance race.

I watched the pick-up truck drive off and I can't remember exactly what time it was, but eight or nine at night and dark, not a light to be seen. It really is the middle of nowhere, so I had nothing better to do than pull out my bivvy bag and get me head down on the desert floor, for a six o'clock start. I had no tent, no proper sleeping bag. I don't think I could've travelled any lighter. It was nearly time to find out what all the fuss was about.

5

My Mind-over-Matter Spirit Was Shot to Shit

TUSCON IS THE NEAREST CITY, but the Arizona Trail Race starts near a little town called Hereford. It's 110 miles west of where I finished the Tour Divide. Though it's a race, most of the websites with information about it have a disclaimer that says, 'This is not an organized or sanctioned event in any way. It's simply a group of friends out to ride their bikes on the same route at the same time. We'll probably compare times afterwards, but more importantly, we'll compare experiences—the highs and lows the trail and mountains offered us.'

They say it isn't a race, for legal or insurance reasons I'd guess, but there is a winner, results and a course record. I went into the Tour Divide wanting to finish in a time of 20 days or less and did it in 18 days and 7 hours. For comparison, the record, at the time of writing this, is just short of 13 days and 23 hours, held by a British rider, the late Mike Hall.

The record for the AZTR was six days, so I thought I could possibly do it in seven days, eight at the worst. That would work out at only 80-odd miles a day. How hard could it be? If I was pedalling for 15 hours a day, something I didn't have a problem doing on the Tour Divide, I'd only need to do 5.3mph to cover 80 miles.

Those kind of numbers must have been in my mind because I set off with a smile. One of the few I'd have on my face for a while. The first 10 miles were easy enough. Then I got to the start point of the AZTR300. The AZTR300 and AZTR750 are both the same route, but the 300 starts 10 miles up the trail at a different time, ends at a town called Superior, east of Phoenix, and is roughly 300 miles long, with a record time of under 39 hours for the 300 course.

After that first 10 miles it was tough all the way to Patagonia, 44 miles in. The small town had a few houses and a burger bar, where I had a sarnie. I made a note in my diary saying I needed more mountain bike riding, because all I'd been doing was riding to work on the roads. I didn't feel like I was coping with the off-roading as well as I would've in the past. But I'd get used to it. Something I didn't expect was that this terrain was tough on my ankles already. The trails are so tough I had to keep getting off the bike and pushing, sometimes even dragging the bike by its wheel up the slope. Because I was getting off the bike that often, and I was using clipless, SPD-style pedals and shoes with cleats, that lock together to keep your feet on the pedals, and also so you can pull up as you're pedalling, not just push down, it meant I had to twist my ankle to unclip my shoe from the pedal. Just that slight twist, time and again, was giving my bad ankle a tough time. I had the pedal clips adjusted tight so my feet don't pull off when I don't want them to, but it made it that bit more difficult to twist them out when I needed to.

After Patagonia is Sonoita, 13 miles further, at 57 miles in according to the course notes. The notes are colour-coded, telling you where there's a spigot so you can get water, or showers if there's a campsite, where you can get food and how far you have to go off the trail to get supplies if the trail doesn't pass right through the town. I was trying to be half-sensible and not take detours for food, just getting it where the route passes a shop or petrol station. It turned out I might have been a bit too clever for my own good.

That night, when I was trying to sleep there was a massive thunderstorm, so I just had to go under a tree. Other than a light rain jacket I didn't have anything to put on to keep warm.

The next day was another hard one. Part-way through I realised I had to adjust my pedals. They have spring-mounted clips that grab a cleat that is screwed to the bottom of each shoe. I backed the pedals' spring pressure off. Doing that meant the pedals' clip wasn't gripping my shoes as tightly, so I risked my foot jumping out of the pedal when I didn't want it to, but I wanted to give my ankles a better time of it.

It was only day two, but my mind-over-matter spirit was shot to shit. I'd already started to think I was never going to finish. That night I found some campground toilets to sleep in. That's the dream on a ride like this, finding some public bogs that aren't too dirty to doss down in just when you need to stop. My sense of smell is bad so I can put up with quite a lot and if you're trying to set a decent time you don't want to be stopping too early in the day just because you see somewhere good to sleep. Keep pedalling.

I'd learned the hard way that a lot of the trail route was tough going up, but it was even tougher coming down. I had expected, like most people would assume, that however tough it was riding up, I could have a breather on the way down. No. There are parts, long sections, that are impossible to ride a bike on. Or impossible for me at least. There was so much debris on the trails, these goat tracks on mountainsides, that I was realising this really was going to be more of a hiking race than a biking race, just like the English teacher who'd first told me about the race, outside the shop in Sargents, had said.

The next day was more of the same. Pain, heat and the worst trail you could think of trying to cycle. I'd just crashed, coming out of Oracle. I caught my pedal on a rock or summat and went over the bars. Blood was pouring out of a cut on my face. I'm not one for taking selfies, but I took a photo of my face to see if I needed stitches, but I was all right. I met a Canadian truck driver who was on his holidays, pushbike touring around and heading south.

He was bedding down at eight in a hammock, but I was still riding till I ran out of light. I didn't have lights on my bike and I wasn't going to ride at night because the course was so lethal. I was asked if sleeping out in the desert on my own made me nervous, but it didn't. I never thought a hillbilly dressed as his mum was going to attack me with a chainsaw.

In the morning I got fed and watered at an old school American diner, next to a rundown Harley workshop. I filled my face. I'd not really had a proper feed since leaving Tucson. This diner was the first place I'd had proper food. I'd been living on petrol station shit, stodgy bread stuff, pastries covered in sugar, anything I could get my hands on to get calories in me. I walked into this diner thinking, 'Fill yer boots.' Sat at the counter, I was going over the ride so far and reminding myself, as if I needed it, that it's a lot tougher going than I expected. I'm not enjoying it, but my attitude had changed to be more positive, or at least more bloody-minded, and I've convinced myself that I'm getting to the end, no matter what.

The next obstacle, if that isn't too small a description of it, was Oracle Ridge. Getting to the top of any of the peaks on this ride was tough. The trails were sometimes like broken stone staircases. On the Tour Divide, by glancing up and looking at the Garmin GPS, I'd know I was nearly at the top and looking forward to rest, rolling down the backside of the climb, but not on this route, no, sir. Each time I kidded myself into thinking I could take it easy on the descent, the slope would be so rough it would be impossible to ride. I did the Tour Divide on a hardtail – the Salsa had front suspension forks, but no suspension at the rear. The Hope HB130 is full suspension, and I needed it, but there were boys doing the race on rigids, no suspension at all. They can't have had many teeth left in their heads.

By the end of day three I'd only covered 200 miles, which wasn't very good, but not as bad as it was going to get. I thought I'd be doing close to 100 miles a day, if not more. I was having to change plans all the time, consulting the route and being a bit more realistic about where I could reach before I ran out of food. Water was a problem, but less of one than food. I could find water and if I was worried about if I'd put chlorine tablets in it to decontaminate it.

Looking at the map there was a there was a town, Kearny, 7.5 miles off the route, that I could get supplies at, but I didn't want that

15-mile detour. So I thought I'd press on, but it was 90 miles to the next town, Superior. Thinking about it as I'm writing this I must have been off my head. I wasn't even averaging 70 miles a day and I was moving forward – pedalling, walking, crawling – for the best part of 17 hours a day. I don't know what made me think this was a well-thought-out plan. I look back and can't even imagine what I was thinking. Well, I can, I was thinking, I need to get to Superior.

There were other details on the route map that, if I'd done a bit more research or taken a bit more notice, might have helped. It was only after I got home I saw a phone number on the notes and realised that if I'd have rung it, the diner in Kearny would deliver food and water out to the trail, so I didn't need to detour at all, just make a phone call. I didn't have a phone that worked, so it wouldn't have made much difference, but maybe if I'd known I could've sorted out my phone before too. Anyway, it didn't even enter my head to do the detour. My thinking was I could knock off another 10 or 20 miles that night, meaning I had, at the most, 80 miles to get to Superior. I could see on the map that the route was next to a river, so I could get water and that was one less thing to worry about. I set an alarm on my phone (that wasn't working as a phone) and was packed up and on my bike at three in the morning. I got a mint start and had covered 50 miles by 11 in the morning. Thirty miles till Superior, what's the problem? Well ...

The route turned properly brutal. There was the odd bit of pedalling, but the majority was walking, me traipsing on the goat tracks with my bike at less than 4mph. It was horrible. And I was getting lost, losing the trail, looping back to find it and all the while knowing I'd made my bed. Kearny was way back, I had to push on. I was getting water from the river, but I'd run out of food. It was bloody hot, over 30 degrees.

Once I got home I looked at the path that my Garmin plotted, because it doesn't just tell me the route, it logs where I went, so I could see the route I actually covered on that day, and I could see that I'd lost my head. At times I was actually going in circles. I couldn't concentrate, I couldn't follow the path. At one point I was in a valley and thought I wasn't getting a signal for my Garmin, so I ploughed on, because I thought I was running alongside the route. When I realised I wasn't and I couldn't get out the end of this valley, because the sides were so steep that I couldn't climb up, I had to turn back and retrace my tracks. It's not what I needed to be doing. It's not improving my mood or mental state. I had buggered it up. Did I say I was out of food and it was fucking hot? I almost realise I'm making stupid mistakes even as I'm making them, but I can't do anything about it.

Things were getting serious, as serious as they ever have for me on a bike ride. I started thinking about my Spot Tracker. This is a little emergency device that events like this either make you take, or strongly recommend that you do. It's a way of people tracking you, so it times you and plots your route for timing purposes. That's how they can accurately time these kind of races. The Spot Tracker is also used as an emergency evacuation button. Back-country skiers and snowboarders, who go way out in the wilds, are some of the people who use them. You press the emergency evacuation button and the global rescue, whatever is needed, get alerted to try to find you. It's almost like *Thunderbirds'* International Rescue. You pay to register for the Spot Tracker service, then you pay the bill for whatever it takes to rescue you. It's only day four (day four!) and I'm asking myself, If it came down to it would I press the emergency evacuation button? I decided I would never press it. I'd rather curl up and die. You're paying for your life, but I'm not paying that.

I was walking again at this stage, struggling and thinking what my options were. It was late afternoon, the hottest part of the day, and I was baking. I'd got some brown water out of the Gila River and chucked a couple of chlorine tablets in to make sure it was OK to drink. Those tablets make it taste horrible, but then I put salt tablets in and that gives it another taste, still horrible, but not as horrible, and it wasn't going to kill me. I could see that pretty soon I was going to leave the river, so the only water I had was in my CamelBak bladder. I was nearly running out of options, and by this point I'm not enjoying one bit of it, even less than I was before. All I could do was keep plodding on, trying to drag my bike up another boulder. It hardly even matters that the brake pads have virtually worn away because the descents have been so hard on them. By now, I'm not going fast enough to need brakes.

Then I saw a woman, a bit younger than me, laying in the shadow of a rock. I asked, 'Now lass, what are you doing?' She told me she was hiking the Arizona Trail and said she was just keeping out of the sun. She'd been walking with some lads, but she was going to meet them 10 miles down the trail.

I told her I didn't mean to be cheeky, but could I buy some food off her. Hikers carry a load of food because they plan on being more days between refuelling stops, because they can't cover the ground a bike can, or not normally, anyway. She had a root around her rucksack and found some mashed potato I could have and it was the best thing, just the best thing. I ate it there while we had a natter. She told me she'd split up with her fella, who was a rancher on a cattle farm or summat, and that she'd been a heroin addict and got over that. She had a story. She was doing this walk to get her head together. She was nearly 300 miles in already.

By the time I'd finished the sun had gone down a bit and some of the heat had gone out of the day. The food had given me some energy so I thought I could crack on. I was still making mistakes and crashing, though. I carried on up the trail to near the point where I think she said she was going to meet the two lads she'd been walking with and I spotted them and introduced myself, telling them I met their mate. I'd only been stopped for 10 minutes, 20 at the most, when the lass comes plodding up. I'm on a state-of-the-art mountain bike, going as fast as I can, and had hardly gained anything.

I love the solitude of these races, but I was having such a miserable time on this trail that I was pleased to meet these people and to talk. I camped with them that night, but I didn't set my alarm. Mentally, I was finished. I thought I'd get to the end of the 300-mile route and call it a day. I felt the same when I woke up the next morning. They offered me some porridge, because I still didn't have any food of my own, obviously, and I set off, leaving the lass $20 because she'd got me out of the shit.

I really don't know what I'd have done if I hadn't come across those hikers. It was still 20 or 30 miles to Superior and before long I'd cut my hands from crashing. If I'd done that with no food in me I might have lost the plot. Instead, with some food and some sleep I had enough to keep going and eventually pedalled into Superior. I found the first diner and started drinking coffee and eating till it came out of my earholes, then I started crying. I'd had enough of the Arizona Trail Race. I thought I'd get on the road and start biking west to Phoenix, so I could get a flight home.

The diner was a breakfast place, so it closed at dinner time (that's northern dinner time, in the middle of the day). I got back on my bike and went straight to the local petrol station and carried on eating there, ice cream after ice cream after ice cream out of a self-serve machine. I wasn't going anywhere for a while.

During the day I kept going over the options. I realised that if I packed it in and went home now, I wouldn't be able to live with myself and I'd end up wasting another shitload of my life training to come back and do it. I had two choices, Go home and train to do it properly or put up with another five days of suffering? It's only five days of suffering, I can do that. Then I convinced myself the 300 course, that I'd been on so far, would be harder than the rest of it, course it would be, so it would be champagne and blowjobs for the rest of the race. Wouldn't it? I stayed in Superior all day, not setting off till six that evening.

After finally getting my head together, as best I could anyway, I started pedalling again and kept going till I ran out of light. By the time I had to call it a night I found this big, posh retirement community, that looked like an old Spanish villa, with its own golf course, right there in the desert. I thought at least I'd get a decent few hours' sleep on some lush, soft golf course grass, instead of the desert floor, but I got woken an hour later by something sticking in my arse. The golf course's fancy automatic sprinkler system came out of the ground to water the course overnight. So not only did I have a shit night's sleep, I was also wet through.

The next morning I do a deal with myself that I'll take the route's road section, from near Phoenix towards Flagstaff. For 2019, the year I did it, there were two options, with a new section called the Four Peaks. I was originally going to do that, but I was having such a miserable time I decided to do the alternative road section instead. It's a road, but it's a dirt road. Some American states get such bad winters that they leave the equivalent of smaller A and B roads graded dirt, instead of tarmacking them. Leaving them as dirt roads stops them getting ruined by frost and snow. Taking the dirt road route was a compromise, but I could live with it. I was going to force myself to finish the race, but I'd have to side-step the Four Peaks.

Again, it doesn't take long to realise that even the road section isn't easy in this bastard of a race. It's busy with traffic and there's 9,000 feet of climbing in 70 miles. That's 1.7 miles vertically.

Day six was Easter Sunday. I rode through another area full of mansions and found a shopping centre where I could fill my face again. I got talking to the local Italian-American old boys, proper well-to-do folk, while I was having a coffee.

I say these races are all about the solitude, but because there's so much of it, when you do meet someone they stick in your mind. Out on the road I met Dennis who was riding an air-cooled Suzuki DRZ400. He had a BSA Rocket 3, like my classic race bike, and he'd bought stuff from Richard Peckett of British firm Peckett and McNab, who my dad had raced for. He knew all about the kind of gearbox I had in my race bike.

I asked him where I'd get food and he told me a place called Pumpkin and when I got there I found it was proper hillbilly, with a feeling of Deep South. I was sat at the bar eating gammon and tayties, and the locals were shouting at the American football on the telly behind the counter. One of them looked at me so I said, 'All right?' and he looked down at my Lycra shorts and didn't say anything, but I thought, Oh, heck . . .

I slept in the corner of a car park that night and I didn't have to set my alarm as early, because I needed to call in at a bike shop in Payson to get some replacement brake pads. I hadn't brought any with me because I didn't think I'd need them. I underestimated how hard the course would be on them, and I've been riding with knackered brakes for a couple of days. Dennis with the Suzuki told me about this pushbike shop, but when I got there it has closed down. The note on the window said the owner had gone to work somewhere else.

The Easter Monday route was hard work. Again. And I was pissed off. Again. The trails were shit. More pushing than biking. I thought I'd rattle off this ride in seven or eight days, but I'd done seven full days, covered just 327 miles and had over 300 still to go, including the hike through the Grand Canyon that I had no idea how hard that was going to be. And I was having no fun. I decided I was going to take the road again the next day.

I was asleep when an Israeli lad passed me at two in the morning. He set off the day after me in the race. I was asleep, but I heard the loud noise of his bike's freewheel, ticking as he rolled, and it woke me up. He was the first person I'd seen who was competing in the Arizona Trail Race. I passed him later that morning, when he was kipping. He must have been doing the Mike Hall technique of riding till he could ride no more.

Day eight piled more misery because I was off the bike pushing most of the day. The Happy Jack Pass didn't live up to its name. On the Tour Divide's trails you'd get a 4x4 down the majority of the trails I rode, but on the Arizona Trail Route you would have to be some kind of enduro rider to even do it on an off-road 250. Then I got a puncture.

I was having a five-minute breather at the top of the Mogollon Rim and the Israeli lad caught me again. The section I'd just got up was that steep, I was on all fours, with the bike on its side, my hand on one wheel, dragging it up the slope six foot at a time. It couldn't have been a lot harder. I made it to Mormon Lake, a glorified campsite, just as the shops were closing. I got some hot food they stuck in the microwave and found they had AA batteries. The batteries were sold individually with a price tag on each of them. It all felt strange.

The next target was Flagstaff, a big city where I knew I could get fed and buy a new tyre. I'd done a fair few miles that day, a lot of them on dirt roads. I'd lost all the snot out of my rear tyre, making the pedalling that bit harder. If you've ever ridden a bike with flat tyres and compare it to when they're inflated properly, you know what I mean. The inner tubes I was using were ones designed to be more puncture resistant. The snot I described is a kind of jelly that can quickly seal small punctures, but if you get a big slash in tyre and tube, you're knackered, there's nothing it can do. And that's what had happened. I had patches to repair the tube, and a spare regular type of inner tube, but I'd broken my pump in a crash, so

I just had to carry on with what I had. And the tyre had had it too. I didn't want to wreck my rear rim, so I kipped for the night ten miles out of Flagstaff, then rode into the city and paid $160 for a bicycle tyre the next morning. One hundred and sixty dollars, for a bicycle tyre.

I carried on up the road heading to Tusayan, the town nearest the Grand Canyon. I was thinking, I'm a mountain bike rider, not a mountain bike pusher, so I didn't feel bad about being on the road and even stayed in a hotel that night. I used to think a toilet block was luxury, but I'd been having such a miserable time I treated myself to a hotel, a shower and more, a lot more, than my money's worth from the $20 buffet.

Tusayan is where the sightseeing helicopters take off from. Some come from Vegas, but the rest are from Tusayan. Everything that is tourism-based, connected to the Grand Canyon, is based at the South Rim, there's nothing at the North Rim.

I left the hotel at four in the morning and rode for two hours to get to the lip of the Grand Canyon, then strapped the bike to my back, with the straps and Kriega rucksack, and started hiking down into the canyon, hoping my ankle would be up to it.

Four hours hiking later I reached a place called Phantom Ranch, at ten in the morning. That's pretty much at the bottom of the canyon, but it's been all down and it's taken me four hours walking to descend 1,500 metres, or 4,800 feet, from the South Rim. I'd walk for about an hour and rest for five minutes. I know it was all downhill, but it wasn't easy, far from it.

Phantom Ranch was a bit of me. There was a lad working there who, if I remember right, said he did ten weeks at a time, then has a week off, then goes back for another ten weeks. Anyway, when you're down there, you have no contact with the outside world except the hikers walking past. No phone, no internet, nothing works down there. The donkeys, or mules maybe, bring the supplies down. If the tourists come this lad feeds and waters them, but there's nothing posh. There are a few cabins you can spend the night in too, that are said to be the hardest rooms to book in the whole of America, selling out 15 months in advance. If you want to book in you put your name on a list and people are chosen by lottery to be offered a room. It's not posh, but you just can't get a cabin because it's so in demand. And it's beautiful, looking down at the Colorado River that cuts through the canyon. You could go down there and forget about everything else.

It was so hot, perhaps the walls of the canyon trapped the heat. I read, once I got home, that the average temperature at Phantom Ranch in July is 41°C, that's 12°C hotter than the average temperature at the South Rim at the same time of year. I was there in late April, but it was still so hot I decided to stay at the Phantom Ranch until the sun went down a bit, then carried on trekking. I was hurting by then too, thinking perhaps I should've practised hiking after all. The theory I'd come up with, that I could grit my teeth and hike through the Grand Canyon, would have worked out fine, I reckon, if I hadn't spent so much of the last nine days pushing my bike up and down these unrideable trails. I'd been told how hard the Arizona Trail Race was, but I still thought I could ride the majority of it, and I'd get through the bit where it was illegal to ride, the canyon itself, by hook or crook, but I hadn't banked on my ankle being knackered before I'd even reached the canyon.

I spent a few hours at Phantom Ranch full of doubts again, thinking I might not be able to even make the finish line. While I was there, right near the bottom of the canyon, I was watching the coming and goings and finding out there's a breed of runners who do rim-to-rim runs, which is just how it sounds, down one side and up the other. It goes without saying that's hardcore. The distance is about the same as a marathon, with the added grief of how bloody steep it is.

Eventually I set off from Phantom Ranch, and straight away the climb was not easy. I was crossing rivers, or maybe they'd call them creeks, all the tributaries coming down to the main river, with water up to my knees and the bike on my back.

As I was slowly on my way up I met a British Army officer, leading a group on his way down. He recognised me and asked what I was up to, surprised when I told him it wasn't for TV, just something I wanted to do. He warned me there was a section that I had to be careful, especially with the weight of the bike on my back, telling me I'd be in trouble if I lost my footing. He was dead serious. He'd just been there and he was surprised I was going up, because no one really uses the route up to the North Rim, and hardly anyone compared with the well-trodden South Rim hiking trails, only the nutters who do the rim-to-rim stuff.

If going down was bad, climbing out was horrible. I started by walking for half-an-hour and stopping for five minutes, then walked for half-an-hour and stopping for ten minutes. I was in the middle of 28 miles of walking. It might not sound long, but it's more than a marathon and I'm not designed for it. Sweat was running off me.

I knew when I reached the section the army officer warned me about. The trail stopped and there was a slab of rock that I had to crawl across on all fours, still with my pushbike on my back. One wrong move and that'd be it, no one would know. They'd have to use the Spot Tracker to find me.

I got into the routine where I'd walk for an hour and stop for half-an-hour. I hadn't seen anyone for hours at this stage, so I got my sleeping bag out and kipped on the trail. It was only narrow and I was blocking the whole thing. It was the early hours of the morning and I'd had a couple of hours sleep and was getting my act together when this bloke came running past at five in the morning, heading in the same direction as me, up towards the North Rim. He'd set off from the South Rim, where I'd left from at ten the previous morning, and was doing the rim-to-rim. He slowed down long enough for me to ask him how far I had to walk until I got to the North Rim and then he was off.

Once I set off again it wasn't long before I was properly struggling. Parts of the bike were digging into me so I took the wheels off the pack and started carrying them, but it doesn't matter because I'm determined, again, to make it to the end.

Then matey, the rim-to-rim runner, starts running towards me. He's already reached the North Rim and he's on his way back towards me. 'You're nearly there!' he shouted as cheerful as you like as he went past. And he was right. It was only a half-hour until I made it out.

Just before I made the summit another AZTR rider, Josh Uhi, passed me. I climbed out onto the flat of the North Rim and sat down on the snow. I knew I only had 80–90 miles of trail left and it was not the hardest. Josh was still there as I was unpacking my bike and putting it back together. He'd done a similar race, the Colorado Trail Race, twice, so perhaps he had more of an idea of what to expect than me, but I wasn't putting on a brave face, I told him straight that I'd underestimated the challenge. He told me he'd done weeks of training with his bike on his back to get used to it.

Sticking to my rule of not riding with anyone else I set off alone, not waiting for Josh. About 20 miles from the Grand Canyon I reach a diner at a road junction. Up until then, from the North Rim to the diner, the roads are closed for the winter. I got some food and was just leaving when Josh comes in and we say we'll see each other at the finish, and I get back on the bike for the final stretch.

I stop to talk to a photographer who has travelled to the area to shoot wild mustang horses, then carry on some more.

When I reach the finish line there aren't any emotions except, Thank fuck for that. No tears, no joy, no whooping, just relief. When I say finish line, it's a point on the Garmin screen, where the Arizona–Utah state line is. There's nothing there and just one person in a car, a woman waiting for her husband who is finishing not far behind me, so we get talking.

My mate from home, Dobby, was going to fly out and meet me at the finish line, as a bit of a holiday, but I texted him around the time I was close to packing it all in, and told him not to bother because I was coming home. So I didn't have a plan for how I was going to get away from the finish. I was just going to pedal east to a town, some civilisation, somewhere I could travel onwards from.

I didn't have a flight or anything booked. The nearest town was 50 miles away and it was four in the afternoon, but luckily, this woman says she'll give me and Josh a lift to Kanab, Utah, 50 miles west, where there's a Holiday Inn. She was happy enough to have the pair of us stinking her car out. She had an old Labrador in the car, and it was nice to see a dog. It felt strange going west because I want to be going east, I want to be heading home.

Josh and I booked into the hotel, but we were both so tired we didn't bother having a celebratory beer. I just slept.

The next morning the woman on reception says I should head to St George, further west, a couple of hours from Las Vegas. From Vegas I can easily get a flight home. But I was stood there, with my bike, no trousers and no buses to get out of the place, when fate dealt me some more luck. A lass overheard me asking how to get to St George and said she'd give me and Josh a lift. Her and her mate, a lad, were going that way. She worked with juveniles, taking them on camping trips, and she was just back from one and heading that way. She was mint and did us both a massive favour.

I was dropped off in St George, a place I'd never heard of, still with no plan of the next part of the journey home, but I knew I had to find a box I could put my pushbike in so it could be loaded onto the plane. I rode about town till I found a pushbike shop and they let me have one of the boxes that new bikes are delivered to them in. Next I had to find some duct tape to make sure it wasn't going to split the box, but now my bike's in a box and I've nowt to ride on. I booked into a cheap motel, got on the internet, sorted a flight out, then booked a shuttle from St George to Vegas for the next day before spending all night watching NASCAR and dirt oval car racing because I couldn't sleep.

At the airport I paid $60 to sit in the lounge and filled my face. I was still in the same clothes I'd had on for two weeks, sweating through the Arizona desert and sleeping in bogs and on golf courses. My sweat has taken all the dye out of the T-shirt and sent it from black to a toxic baby-shit brown. I wouldn't be mistaken for your average business traveller.

If you've read my other books, you'll know I've wanted experiences that break me and this nearly did, but I finished it. No one was cutting bits off me, but I had suffered. Travelling home I wasn't in the best state of mind. I have honesty Tourette's as it is, and coming back from a race like this makes me ten times worse, so I'm not the best to be around after it. I don't regret doing it, because now I've done the world's longest and what a lot of mountain bikers reckon is the world's toughest. It ended up taking me ten days. I'd made a mistake. I hated it, from day one. There were some nice views, but I got sick of them too. I couldn't look at them anyway, because the trail was trying to kill me. It's over a year since I finished the Arizona Trail Race and I thought time would heal, and I'd forget the pain and remember some of the good parts, but no. Not this fucker. Still, move on to the next thing . . .

6

Night Fright

THE TV LOT STARTED TALKING to me about doing a programme about Operation Overlord, better known as the D-Day landings, sometime in 2018, with an idea that filming would get going in early 2019, before I did the Arizona Trail Race. The way they present a new idea differs from time to time, but it usually starts with an outline being described to me in dead simple terms, sometimes by either of the two directors I work with, James Woodroffe or Ewan Keil, though sometimes it comes through Andy Spellman.

In the case of the D-Day job, James Woodroffe was in charge of this one, so first he got a feel for the job, how likely a programme is going to happen, how long it would take to film, if they were able to get the permissions and, sometimes, the help from companies or organisations they'd need. Then he'd take the idea to his bosses at North One Television, to make sure they're thinking along the same lines. They'd usually describe it to Spellman, who has a good idea if I'm going to be interested or not, then they'd come to me.

It's not like I'm some kind of diva who needs isolating or that I'm making people jump through hoops, but there's a lot of work to be done and boxes to be ticked before it's even worth mentioning it to me. I'm nowt special, it's just the way most telly programmes are made.

If James thinks he can get it made for the right kind of money, and I'm up for it, then North One's bosses speak to Channel 4 to make sure they're interested. There's a deal been done that I only work with North One, like I have since I started, and that the programmes will be shown on Channel 4 first. North One are a production company, they make all different kinds of programmes, from my kind of stuff to live sports coverage, for different channels. They used to make the Isle of Man TT coverage, and they first came across me there when they were filming some stuff. Andy Spellman was one of the producers, and thought I could do more than talk about bikes and how to make a cuppa tea, and one thing led to another.

Sometimes it can be over a year from an idea being discussed with me and filming eventually starting. Other times it can, or has to, happen a lot quicker, but it's never less than four months' worth of planning.

James said summat like, 'Are you up for doing something on D-Day? We'll train you up to parachute into Normandy,' and I think, Why wouldn't I do something like that? But I don't go for everything they put in front of me, far from it.

A few years ago, they asked if I wanted to learn to fly a Spitfire for a programme and I turned it down. It would be great to fly a Spitfire, but the amount of time it would take to become qualified, and how many days I'd have to take off work, didn't seem worth it. How is it going to improve my life? I'm never going to buy a plane, even though, for the 300mph job, that I'll get back on to in a bit, it sounds like it would be ideal. When I'm trying to do 300mph on my Hayabusa I'm riding on runways, so I could fly in, take all my shit out and ride my bike, but to carry all the stuff I need, which isn't even a vast amount of gear, I'd need a bloody Hercules.

Even if you get the pilot's licence you have to keep getting it renewed. It's just a hassle. I couldn't work on my own plane. I'd have to pay an approved specialist to do it, so there's no sense to it, as great as it would've been to fly a Spitfire. The only reason I can imagine for me to get a pilot's licence is to be a flash bugger, unless I can get something big enough to make it worthwhile. I'd always need my van, because wherever I'd land 'my' Hercules I'd still need a van to haul my shit from where I landed to where I'm going. If I paid someone to drive my stuff and meet me when I flew in it would make me the ultimate flash bugger and I'm not doing that.

The journey to these airfields is part of the adventure. When me and my mates, Francie and Benny, went to Spain for a track day in March 2020, the main point was the road trip with a bit of riding on the end of it. It was a pain at times, three of us in a Transit van for over 20 hours to the south of Spain, but there was a point, when we were outside a Spanish filling station in the middle of nowhere, that looked like the Gobi Desert. We'd stopped to fill up and were having a coffee, not that I'm much of a coffee drinker, and I thought, Ah, that was worth it. Five minutes, having a brew with a couple of mates, then go to ride my bike and come home, job's a peach. So that's a long way of saying if the programme doesn't light a spark in me, I can't get the enthusiasm to go through with it, but the D-Day programme had loads of different elements and sounded like it was right up my street.

Filming started with the restoration and rebuild of a Douglas C-47 Skytrain, what is better known as a Dakota. The plane is owned by Charlie Walker, and he was in charge of the rebuild. Charlie is part of the family haulage and storage business, Walkers Transport, but he's also a commercial pilot, flying private jets for people. He's not a messer. This actual aircraft, called *Night Fright*, was heavily involved in World War II, as part of the USAAF – the United States Army Air Force – flying from RAF Membury in Berkshire. Charlie explained it was used to drop paratroopers, tow gliders, evacuate wounded troops and fly supplies to the front line.

The TV lot had found out about this rebuild and jumped on the back of it. Doing this meant they just have to go with it. They couldn't dictate anything, but the benefit is they're not paying for anything either, so it's the only way to make it realistic.

When we turned up to the hangar where the plane was being restored, I saw it was a repainted but otherwise bare fuselage. It was being restored at Membury too, the place it was based in the war. I drove down with my dad, who also got involved and was filmed and shown in the finished programme. He's mad about the history of World War II, so it was good to be able to get him involved now he's retired. We visited the project for over a year. The place they were working was a bit of a shit-tip, if I'm being honest, not what you might expect from a place restoring aircraft, but the level of detail they were going into was every bit as good as anything that's being done at the Imperial War Museum, Duxford or Biggin Hill.

They were putting five coats of paint on every component and there was talk of 10,000 parts that needed painting. They weren't cutting any corners and it was a long job.

That is the opposite of how it was built in the first place. At the height of preparation for the D-Day invasion in 1944, the Douglas factory was finishing one Dakota an hour. It wasn't just Dakotas either, it was everything that was being used in the war and the factories were under such pressure to supply. I've been to a place that restores Spitfires and was shown around by the boss. They had original Spitfires that had been maintained but hardly touched since the war, and none of the panels lined up, things were overhanging, the rivets didn't line up. They looked tatty, not because of their age, but because of how they were built. Then I was shown one being rebuilt with panels they'd remade and it was perfect. That was the same with the original Dakotas and the one Charlie was restoring. During the war they just chucked them together, because chances were they would last two weeks before being shot down, but Charlie wanted to make sure *Night Fright* could fly for another 70 years.

When I was visiting the Membury workshop I'd get involved, but I wasn't doing anything too detailed. Bit of drilling, bit of paint stripping, bit of spannering. I went at least half-a-dozen times, and right from the start I was pessimistic it was going to be finished in time for the D-Day flight, but those boys knew what they were doing. They are all proper lads, enthusiasts who are massively into it. When we first turned up, the engines were ready, it was just (just?) a case of bolting it all together, but they weren't rushing anything. The detail was absolutely perfect.

Night Fright had an interesting life after the war. It was used by small American airlines into the 1960s before being sold to the French Air Force as a trainer. In the mid-eighties it went back to America, where it was converted again, this time into a civilian cargo plane. It was still working into the 2000s and was nearly scrapped ten years ago, but was saved by enthusiasts. During all this time it's been chopped and changed a ton of times, so it was a job to find the parts to get it back to the proper wartime spec. The bulkhead, the wall between where the pilots sit and the back where the paratroopers would fly, was specific and different to the one that had been fitted at some time during its post-war working life. Charlie found the right kind of bulkhead in Colombia and had that sent over. Those were the lengths they were going to during the rebuild to make it the best flying Dakota, the most original, in the world. And I'm sure it will be.

7

I'm Not Much of a Fighter, but I'll Have a Go

WITH THE DAKOTA on the go, it was time to start turning me into someone who could jump out of it. The British and American paratroopers were dropped into Normandy six hours before the invasion by sea, and their mission was to put as many of the big guns out of action as possible, before the troops started landing on the beaches. To get me prepared there was a week of civilian parachute training after a taste of the Parachute Regiment's beasting. When James the director was telling me about the training, the more brutal he made it sound the more interested I was.

The army training day started at Catterick Garrison, just at the side of the A1 in North Yorkshire. It was early in 2019, a cold, damp day at the back end of winter. First, I watched the new recruits go through some of their six-week basic training. They were on a massive, scaffolding climbing frame, assault course thing they called the trainasium. I was there to see a real make- 'em-or-break- 'em part of the introduction to the regiment.

I was stood with one of the current Parachute sergeants watching the recruits getting a beasting. The sergeant I'm with isn't leading the training, so he's smirking a bit, and he's earned the right, he's been through it, all the officers have, and he's smiling at my reaction because they're not mucking about. I was watching for the best part of an hour, laughing and shaking my head, but I'm not laughing at the recruits. If it came across like that in the programme then that's wrong, because it was more of a nervous laugh. I'm sympathetic to them. No one really wants to be in their shoes, but everyone can imagine what it's like and everyone knows it isn't going to last forever. I think all the shouting and screaming is part of breaking the spirit of the individuals, so the army can build on top of it and turn them into what they want. It's like breaking a horse. I have respect for what they're doing.

I was watching the process of their spirit being broken and enjoying it, because, in a way, I think it's what I do to myself with some of the bicycle races I do. I break my own spirit and build myself back up stronger. They'd love to tell the staff sergeant to eff-off, but this is what they've signed up for and it's all part of the greater good. Everyone understands this, even if it's bloody uncomfortable. There was a little bit of me that thought I might join the forces when I left school. If I knew what the Paras was going to be like I might have thought more seriously about joining. I think it's a great life.

Before long it came to my turn to climb to the top of the trainasium and get shouted out. We weren't allowed to do it on

Ministry of Defence equipment, probably due to insurance and liability. They can't risk having some bloke from a TV programme falling to his death off a bit of their equipment. It would take up too much time explaining to be worth it, so the TV lot had their own replica of the assault course made just for me, on some land ten minutes' drive away. It was at an adventure assault course-type place that companies send their employees to for team-building exercises, so some of the stuff that was shown in the programme was already there. The rollers made out of car tyres, where I went through like wet washing going through an old mangle, that was already there, but the massive scaffolding structure was built just for the TV. Talk about commitment.

Right from the start I was nervous of my bad ankle. I told James, the director, that I'd prefer to do the parachute training after I'd come back from the Arizona Trail Race, but, because the D-Day commemoration was set in stone, it turned out the only window everyone could get was before I flew out to Arizona. So I'd do the jumps, but I was nervous it was going to break my weak ankle and knacker my chance of doing the race.

Once we'd left Catterick Garrison, an ex-Para sergeant major, Keith Sharkey, took over and was going to treat me the way the famous regiment treat their recruits. Once I got togged up in the camo gear, and it was my turn to start the training, the camera crew stepped back and let the former sergeant run the job however he wanted to. They weren't talking to me or asking me questions, they were just filming what was going on.

Sharkey had a crew with him, all ex-military and playing the parts of the soldiers doing the training. And they meant it. The rough treatment was all right with me because I wanted to sample a small part of what the Paras are put through. If that was a case of someone getting right in my face shouting at me or dragging me around by my collar through the mud, I was happy to take it, and I did everything to the best of my ability. I don't know how it came across on telly, but it wasn't fun. I wanted it to be as authentic as possible and I wanted to do it right, but there was one bit when they took it easy on me, and that was the running. I didn't do as much of it as a recruit would on the same day, because while I could have run around that day, I would've struggled to walk the next day, my ankle is that bad.

I climbed to the top of the 18-metre-high trainasium to tackle the bit that took the most mind over matter for me, the same section some of the recruits had also struggled with, the balance bars. Mine looked exactly the same as the one at the army base. There were two lengths of scaffold pole, about shoulder-width apart, that link two towers of the trainasium. The idea is to shuffle across, stood up straight, feet on these smooth metal poles. The worst bit is halfway across. There's a short length of scaffold pole, linking the two balance bars, but it's above the bars so you have to lift one foot at a time to step over it. The crossbar, with the scaffold joint, is a good six inches proud of the balance bar, so you've got to lift your foot quite high. I got to it and the bloke playing the staff sergeant was shouting at me not to stop, to get straight over it. I didn't hesitate for long before I stepped over, but then lost a bit of confidence, even though I'd done the hard bit, and bent over to put my hands on the balance bars for a bit of safety. 'Staff' didn't like that and encouraged me, in the strongest terms, to get my hands off the bars and stand up straight. I did as I was told, got my act together and carried on with it. It's all of 40 foot off the ground, easily chimney height of a regular two-storey house, so there's a fairly sudden stop if you hit the ground and it's going to hurt.

There was another bit, I think called the illusion jump, that was an easily cleared gap of five or six feet, from one platform to a lower one, but it was high off the ground. If it was jumping from one kitchen table to another you wouldn't think twice, but that high up, with all that scaffolding ready to knock your teeth out, it was a different matter. I did that all right, though. My reasoning was, I'd seen it done, so it can be done, so I'll have it.

After the trainasium it was onto the assault course, under these bars, over these bars, commando crawling through the fields, then after all that it was time for the milling.

Before we were talking about the programme I had no idea what milling was, but James knows what presses my buttons. He told me it was a bit of a boxing match, but it turns out it's a lot simpler than that. You can't back away, you're just throwing punches while the other person is punching you around the head.

Our staff sergeant told me the rules, but there weren't any rules that I remember. I was wearing boxing gloves and the kind of headguard boxers train in. I shaved my head a couple of days before, I needed a haircut anyway, so I thought I'd play the part. I had no nerves going into it. It's only a minute of pain, how hard can it be? There's no point in worrying about it.

Just like when the Paras are milling, there was a circle of blokes, all these ex-military fellas brought in by the TV lot, to give a feeling of what it's like when the recruits do it. They stood in a circle, shouting encouragement at whoever is their fighter, and were ready to give you a push back into the middle if you strayed too close to the edge. All the Paras have a story about milling. It's not something they forget.

I'm not much of a fighter, but I'll have a go. There's no sizing each other up in this fight, it's straight into it. The bloke I was up against was a lump, two tours of Afghanistan behind him, and I landed a good one on him early in the fight. He admitted that once I did, he wasn't about to take it easy on me. The punches were coming hard and I knew I'd been hit. He was dealing with torque, I was dealing with horsepower. Everything I had to do, I had to do it fast, because I didn't have the same weight behind the punches as he did. He put me down, but everyone was shouting at me and pulling me up to get back at it. There wasn't a referee looking in my eyes to check if I was OK. Once you're vertical it's straight back into it. I think they respected me for having a go, and I did get some blood out of his nose.

They were hard fuckers right up to the end and once we were done we were shaking hands and everything was back to normal. It reminded me of when I stayed at the worst hotel in the world in Latvia. The bloke who ran it, who was playing the part of a Soviet-era prison guard, was twice as brutal as the Parachute sergeants, but as soon as we finished this hard-looking head of the Gulag said, 'All right lads, see you later.' He told me he was going wakeboarding, climbed on his pushbike and off he pedalled. It's not an act, it's part of the process. The Para training is serious, because it has to be.

Harvest time. It's about as full-on as farming gets. If it's dry, you're working.

The business end of the world's fastest tractor.

Last-minute changes at the Nürburgring. That's Hooker with his head poking through the rear wheel arch.

My dad and my nephew Louis. Both are always up for a road trip and some spannering.

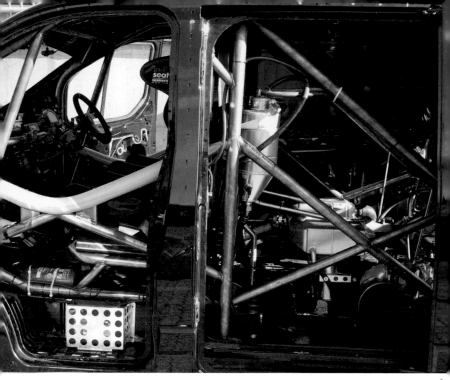

How trick is this Transit?

Having a natter with Andy Carlile, my co-driver for the van record.
Brave man and calm even when the Transit was on fire.

At the Handbuilt Motorcycle Show in Austin, Texas the weekend of the US MotoGP.

On the MotoGP grid with Neil Hodgson.

In France, working out how best to carry my pushbike through the Grand Canyon.

Tucson hotel room, deciding what I can bin before I set off on the Arizona Trail Race.

'I can't leave you here.' Sunset drop-off in the middle of the desert. Time for a kip before an early start on the ride that nearly killed me.

Evidence of one of the many crashes on the AZTR.

Took what I think is my first ever selfie to inspect more damage.

The hikers that saved my life with rice pudding.

Boiling half to death and riding on snow in the same day.

One of the great places you find when you need food in the middle of nowhere.

My Hope HB130, made in Lancashire and carrying everything I took for two weeks' rough camping.

Plenty of reading material on the shelves at home.

Is everyone's fridge covered in stickers?

A mate from the truck yard I was working at back then came with me, because he was an ex-Para. I remember he brought a roll of the little coffee bean stickers you put on the cards to get a free coffee from McDonald's, so we could get one for the drive home. If that's what's sticking in my mind, it proves I wasn't overcome by the experience of being punched in the head by an ex-Para. Now it was time to start jumping out of planes.

8

Hubert the Jumpmaster

THE NEXT PART OF THE JOB was the jump training and there were different parts to that too. The first was a visit to Langar airfield, Nottinghamshire, to do a tandem jump with the Red Devils, the Parachute Regiment's display team. I mean, what an honour, they are the men. I was with a Red Devil called Dean, and the experience was very different to the beasting at Catterick, all very calm and polite. Really, there wasn't a lot of training, just the basics of do this with your arms and this with your legs, and I'll tap you on the head when you need to put your arms in. Those boys are so on top of what they're doing there's nothing to be nervous of.

The airfield is right near the UK headquarters of tractor maker John Deere and I was excited to see their 9RX quad-track things from the plane. Next we're at 13,000 feet, it's time to be chucked out of a plane and it was bloody brilliant. It was another of those days when I thought, I can't believe I'm here, getting paid to experience this.

There are a few obvious differences from this kind of tandem jump and the one I was leading up to. For the Red Devils tandem jump, I'm strapped to an expert, and we are free falling from an altitude of 13,000 feet, about 4,000 metres. For the free fall, you leave the plane and you're falling like a stone, for about 30 seconds, until the person in charge, in this case, Dean the Red Devil, chooses to pull the parachute release cord, when you're about 3,000 feet from the ground.

The jump out of the Dakota, what the paratroopers did on D-Day, is called a static-line jump, and is usually from 3,000 feet, about 1,000 metres, or less. The person jumping out of the plane is wearing a parachute that is clipped to a rail inside the plane, by a 15- or 20-foot strap. This is the static line. As they fall the strap is pulled tight and it yanks the parachute canopy out of the bag. As part of training they tell you to count to three then 'Check parachute' – look up to make sure it's the shape it needs to be and not tangled. If it is tangled, you have to get it off and get your emergency chute out in a hurry.

We were into spring 2019 by now and it was time for me to go to France for the static-line parachute training. It took place in Normandy. Me, Shazza and our daughter Dot drove down in my van with our pushbikes in the back. Like the road trip to Spain for the track day, this was part of the adventure. We met the TV lot in Kent and drove down together to Omaha Beach, near the villages of Sainte-Honorine-des-Pertes and Vierville-sur-Mer. On the way to the airfield where the training was going to take place, we visited the war graves at the Normandy American Cemetery. The site must be 100 acres of graves and memorials and visitor centres, what an amazing place.

Everything to do with TV is insured up to the eyeballs. The researchers and producers have to write page after page of risk assessments, then put it all in front of specialist insurance companies. Every now and then the insurers ask for a change. Some are so small I don't even get to know about them, but this time the insurance company said I had to jump with a modern rectangular parachute, not a round one like they used in the war. When I found out I dug my heels in. The goal was to make a realistic programme worth watching and I thought this was a detail worth sticking to. The rectangular canopies are supposed to be safer, but round ones were used for D-Day. I told them I wouldn't do the programme if I couldn't use the round parachute and eventually it was agreed that I could, so we ended up at the Round Canopy Parachuting Team training centre, in Normandy, with Hubert Achten, our Belgian jumpmaster.

For the static-line jump training I was in a group of World War II enthusiasts, men and women, who all had their own historically accurate gear. They had to jump however many times a year to keep their licence current so they could jump during the D-Day commemoration. The majority were British, but there were some French too. A lot of them had got interested in all this after watching *Band of Brothers*, this dead-good TV series about what happened after D-Day, when it all came to a head in Bastogne, the Battle of the Bulge. *Band of Brothers* is based on the experiences of American 506th Parachute Infantry Regiment, part of the 101st Airborne

Division, who pushed on from the Normandy beaches into Belgium and the Netherlands.

On a previous trip to Europe, when I was endurance racing the Classic Suzuki at Spa in Belgium, me, Shazza, Dad and my mate Tim Coles went from Spa to Bastogne to visit the museum. It's the best museum I've ever been to and stopped me in my tracks. They have German tanks, King Tigers, with the sides blown out. There's no attempt at softening of the brutality of the war. So I could see why the folks on the jump school had got so into it.

The training was a week long and pretty basic – you're learning how to roll when you land, how to steer the parachute. There was a bit of steering, but the round parachutes are nowhere near as responsive as the modern rectangular ones.

When it comes to civilian parachute jumps you have to wait for the weather to be right, so you're not blown onto power lines or a motorway or summat, so there was a fair bit of hanging around, but then the time came.

We walked in line out to the school's Cessna 208 Caravan, a utility plane used for cargo, passengers, training, all sorts. It's a model that dates back to 1981 and is still being made now. Caravan is its real name, not a nickname. The film crew wanted me to be first out of the plane every time I jumped, so they knew which one I was and they could get a camera on me. None of the other folk who were jumping were bothered that I was always first, because nearly as soon as the first person is out of the plane, the last person is out. You have to be that quick. Ten people are out the door in summat like eight seconds.

The plane would do a fly over the landing point and Hubert would drop a bog-roll streamer so he could gauge where we'd have to jump out to have the best chance of hitting the landing zone. When Hubert says jump, you jump, and, being first, if I stuttered and didn't jump straight away we'd miss the spot.

At this point I had put a fair bit of effort into preparing for the Arizona Trail Race. Not as much as I should have done, but a fair bit. Everything was in place and I didn't want to knacker the job the week before I was going, so my dodgy ankle was on my mind all the time.

When I was coming in to land I was favouring my left ankle, the better one, which might have been asking for more trouble because I wasn't dispersing the energy through both ankles, I was putting more stress on one of them. The first jump I did I landed on the runway, but it felt all right and I walked away without a problem. On another jump I was blown off course, couldn't steer back and landed in a neighbouring farmer's field. The design of parachutes changed from the round type to make them easier to steer, so I was getting a bit of authentic World War II inaccuracy. When I hit the deck, the parachute canopy was still open and there was enough wind to keep it inflated and I was being dragged along this ploughed field until a bloke jumped out of his tractor to help me. I wasn't hurt, but I was on the wrong side of the airfield's perimeter fence and had a bloody long walk with my bundled-up parachute back to the main gate and into the airfield.

We had been sat around for ages, waiting to see if the weather would let us go up for another jump, to keep practising. When it turned out that wasn't going to happen James came up with the idea of doing some more filming. He'd thought of a way to explain why the D-Day landings were at Normandy, not at the shortest point over the Channel, which is what the Germans were expecting. We drove around, found a beach he could get above to film from, found a rake and I marked out the different beaches and the flanks on the sand. I marked a rough curve to depict the Normandy coastline, then five arrows pointing at the landing beaches, codenamed: Utah, Omaha, Gold, Juno and Sword. At each end I raked a couple of crosses to show the paratrooper landing sites. I like doing stuff like that, on the hoof.

The real downside of the week at the parachute centre involved an experienced parachutist who was part of our training group, a young bloke, younger than me, who had a heart attack while we were on the ground and died there in the training centre. It was a reminder, if anyone needed it, that you never know what might happen next.

We couldn't jump on 6 June, the anniversary of D-Day itself, because President Trump and other leaders were going to be there and the whole airspace was locked down for the actual anniversary. The latest that civilian jumps that could be done was two days before, and we were going to fly a few days before that. There was going to be summat like 20 Dakotas going up on the 'official' jump day and that wouldn't give the TV lot the flexibility they needed. They wanted to film air-to-air from a helicopter, James loves a helicopter, and they couldn't do that if there were 20 other World War II planes in the sky, so we did it on our own day that bit earlier.

Charlie Walker had contacted Pete, a Dutch pilot, and arranged to use another survivor of D-Day, a Dakota called *Drag 'Em Oot*, because there had been hold-ups with *Night Fright* and that plane wouldn't be ready in time. *Drag 'Em Oot* earned its name because it was used for, among other missions, picking up landed gliders as it flew very low over the ground, dragging them off the floor and pulling them back into the air. You wouldn't believe it was possible if you hadn't seen film of it happening. The owners say *Drag 'Em Oot* has 30 bullet holes in it from D-Day.

Charlie and Pete flew up here, landing at East Kirkby airfield, south of Louth, on the Saturday before the jump. We all went to my sister's pub in Kirmo, The Marrowbone and Cleaver, for some grub, then Shazza drove me and my dad to East Kirkby. Charlie was in his element in the cockpit, straight into character, doing all the pre-flight checks, getting everything running, it was magical to watch. From there we flew the Dakota to Membury, the airfield that is both where Charlie was restoring *Night Fright* and one of the airbases the Paratroopers flew from in 1944.

They weren't going to rent the whole plane just for me to jump out of, so the TV crew invited a load of people who were on the training week I did in France to join our flight too. Not only did it look more authentic, they all got another opportunity to jump.

Me, my dad and the TV lot stayed at a hotel down the road from Membury. Also there were a load of the lads who were jumping with us the next day. The next morning we set off leisurely, taking off for Normandy late morning, all of us in the back, parachutes on, Hubert, our jumpmaster, in control of the job.

Our flight roughly followed the route of the Pathfinders, the much smaller advanced force who secured strategic bridges and set up communications that allowed targeted bombing and, later, larger missions. The programme included interviews with survivors of D-Day, including one of the Pathfinders, Bob Stoodley, who is the grandad of British Superbike racer Christian Iddon.

Obviously there was no chance of anyone shooting at us or being caught by the SS, like Bob Stoodley was, but I was still getting a feel of what it must have been like on D-Day. When we got to the jump point Hubert dropped a paper streamer again, but he wasn't confident so he told the pilots to loop round and do another pass so he could drop a second one. Hubert is very precise, and because we were the only plane that day, he had that option. If it had been later in the week, with another 19 planes in the air, it probably wouldn't have been possible. We'd have just jumped and had to deal with it. I'd been stood up all the time, me in the door, while Hubert's sussing the job, wind blasting me in the face, the noise of the massive engine and propeller on the wing, just in front of me. I'm staring Hubert in the eye. He's not looking at me, he's totally focused on the streamer and the landing, but I can see his face, 'No, no, no . . .', then it's, 'Go!' And all of us are out of the door as quick as that.

There were 25 of us ready to jump in the back of the Dakota. Half jump on the first pass, then the plane loops for another pass so the other half jump, otherwise they'd be spread all over the landscape.

As I push out of the door, a warning Dean the Red Devil gave comes back to me. He said watch your head because people are known to have jumped out Dakotas and hit their head on the tail. You'd feel that at a combined impact speed of what? Over 180mph.

From leaving the plane to landing on French soil takes about three minutes. It feels like one second you're checking the canopy's up, the next you're looking for the landing point and preparing for the landing. They'd even lined up French customs officers to check our passports when we landed. No one was doing that in June 1944.

My grandad, on my dad's side, was part of the D-Day landings. He was a Royal Marine and was on the beaches a day or two after. Twenty-five years previously, when I was a kid, my grandad, me and my dad went to Normandy for the 50th anniversary. We were over there for ten days taking in all the history and commemorations. Even with that bit of knowledge, and visits to the Bastogne War Museum, I still learned a load making this programme. I knew the importance of D-Day, but didn't really know what stage of the war it was at, so one of the main reasons I had for doing this programme was to help me fill in the holes I've got about the history of World War II. Now I know where D-Day was in relation to the Battle of Britain and the Dambusters and all of that. I'm still learning, but I'm fascinated by this period of history. There's a BBC podcast, *The Bomb*, about Oppenheimer and the development of the nuclear bombs that were dropped on Japan, and all that. It's eight hours long and I've listened to it three times. But jumping out of a plane and learning while you're doing it is better than listening to a podcast.

9

Blokes in Vans
Giving It a Go

JACK FROST, at Holeshot Racing in Northern Ireland, had my Suzuki Hayabusa for eight or nine months, turning it from a 180mph road bike into one of the fastest things on two wheels. I rode it at Elvington in the middle of 2019, Jack took it away with him, and I didn't get it until the first meeting of 2020, when he brought it back for a Straightliners meeting at Elvington. The Suzuki looked very much like it had when I bought it: all the standard bodywork, standard exhaust end cans, but now with a turbo and massively powerful engine hiding under the standard bodywork.

I couldn't wait to feel the difference. I pulled my leathers and helmet on, and got the feel for the bike running down the runway, from where we park up to the start line. Everything felt OK, and I did the first run a bit gingerly, with no boost, just learning and feeling out the bike. Without boost the bike doesn't feel that much different to normal. Then I added more boost, meaning the bike would make more power, and rode a bit harder. I did 10 or 15 runs, getting the feel for it. By the end of the first day of riding it I had clocked a 257mph terminal speed. The fairing, the shell that covers the bike's frame to make it more streamlined, was trying to fly off, so we were taping bits closed, but this was a bog-standard road bike with the turbo engine on its first ever run, and there were no problems except for a couple of loose fairings fasteners. No drama, no special techniques or an army of mechanics: just get on, point it at the horizon and let's have it. I loved it.

The bike went back to Northern Ireland with Jack because he wanted to finish a few bits and check a few things, like you would with any project like this. I drove home thinking it was great and that I'd never felt anything like it, but also realising I had a long way to go to be able to go 300mph in a mile. I also had another reason for knowing this kind of racing was for me, it's very leftfield and that is part of the attraction. Land speed racing is niche. It's blokes in vans giving it a go. It's not cool. It's not sponsored by Monster.

Over the next couple of months I rode the Hayabusa at Elvington every time they held an event, and the bike would go back with Jack. I'd turn up, Jack would bring his and my bike, and it was fast, and it never missed a beat, but I was itching to get my hands on it because there were things I wanted to change. You can't argue with what Jack does, because he builds the fastest bikes in the country, but there's always details I think I can improve. I usually have my own views on things and there were bits and pieces I wanted to do my way, and then start to really develop the bike with my own ideas and experiments.

Soon, the Hayabusa looked less like a road bike. I fitted a bigger fairing and big seat unit, making it far more enclosed and aerodynamic, but that brings its own problems. Because the surface area of the bike is now increased it's more easily affected by wind. I'm looking for conditions with wind speed of no more than 2m/s, that's metres per second. If you really have to know, and it hurts me to write this, but that's the equivalent of 4.5mph wind speed. I've got it into my head that pressures must be referred to in bar, not psi, and wind speed is m/s not mph. I do realise I say all this, but I'm trying to do 300mph in a mile, so I'm the ultimate contradiction, but if there's anything I'm consistent with it is the contradictions. Anyway, because the wind speed is so crucial, I'm glued to a weather phone app, that all the local farmers I know use, called yr.no.

As I've done more runs and my speeds have risen, if I don't think I can go over 270mph I don't normally bother starting the bike. I might not go faster on a run than 250, but if I don't think there is potential for 270, I'm just wasting fuel. I'd got to the point, with the big fairing on the bike, that I have convinced myself the window of opportunity, where the conditions are ideal, is something like four hours a year. It's become a fight against the wind and unpredictable thermals created when the sun comes up. What I learned from the Bonneville Salt Flats in Utah is, if it's possible, you get there before the sun comes up and you're ready to go at first light, because once the sun warms the surface and starts reflecting back it creates these thermals. If you haven't done your record run by 9 or 10am you're not going to do it. It's not to do with headwinds affecting top speeds, it's the sidewinds that

make it dangerous. Weather apps can predict general wind speed and direction, but the thermals are so local you just have to suck it and see. Lower speed and unfaired bikes aren't affected by wind the same way, so they can run later in the day.

These outside forces make everything more of a challenge, but it all adds to the achievement when things do all line up for a fast run.

10

Tokyo: Micropigs

BEFORE ALL THAT, we flew to Tokyo to do a travel programme in July 2019. I'd been to Japan three times before. The previous times I'd been, like nearly all my travelling before I started the TV job, were motorcycle related. The first two trips were for motorcycle launches for *Performance Bikes* magazine. One launch was the 2009 Kawasaki ZX-6R, the other was the Yamaha R6. When big bike companies, the size of Kawasaki or Yamaha, launch a new bike they would fly journalists from magazines around the world. Back then there might have been as many as seven or eight journalists from the UK alone flown to Japan. You'd get there on day one, usually have the next day to acclimatise and be shown either something touristy or something to do with the company, have a presentation of the details of the bike that night, then ride it the next day or two, before flying home. They were always four- or five-day trips including the travelling, shorter if the launch was in Europe. I'd been doing stuff for *Performance Bikes* for quite a while when they sent me on a few launches and the experiences were mega.

The third time I went was to test the Mugen Shinden, the electric racing bike I was asked to race at the Isle of Man TT in 2017, my last TT. Mugen is a car and motorcycle performance parts and tuning company, founded in 1973 by Hirotoshi Honda, son of the Honda founder, Soichiro. They're linked to the Honda Motor Company, but not owned by them. I travelled to the test with 23-time TT winner, John McGuinness, who'd raced the Mugen a few times before, and I crashed it during the test. The first person to ever crash it. Not my finest moment.

Sometimes I get in the mood when I'm chuntering to myself, 'Fuck motorbikes. I don't want to be defined by motorbikes', but I have to remind myself that they've been very good to me. I bet there have been times in interviews where I've sounded dead disrespectful to the motorcycle world, but I don't mean to be because I owe it a lot.

I've always loved visiting Japan, so once the dust had settled after the Russia and Ukraine programme in 2018 and they asked where I wanted to go next, I said Japan. It wasn't the only place in the running. I'd like to go to Tel Aviv, the Gaza Strip and Bethlehem to see it with my own eyes and suss it out, but I don't think a dickhead like me could do it justice. I'd like to find out more about the Arab world and their views and beliefs. I've spent a lot of time in tractors lately listening to podcasts from around the world, stuff like the investigative journalism podcast, *The Bellingcat Podcast*, learning all sorts of stuff and I want to learn more, but it's a difficult subject and region to cover in the kind of programme I do, so we'll have to have a good think about it.

Those previous three times I'd been to Japan it felt like another planet to me, like nowhere I'd ever been before, and I loved the place. So that was it, we were going to Japan. The TV lot never ask specifically where I want to go in a country, or what I want to see or do, and I don't bother giving them any requests. They sort the whole trip out, and just tell me when I've got to be at the airport, and if I have to bring my motorbike gear or whatever.

The one thing we do now, that other TV shows probably don't have to, is sort out a pushbike for me to borrow. I don't come back from any of the trips complaining, I've loved them all, but I admit my head went at the end of the Russia and Ukraine trip and I turned into a bit of an arsehole. We'd been away for the best part of a month and it was too much. I still enjoyed everything we did, but being away for that long, travelling nearly every day, loads of internal flights, next to no chance for me to do anything physical, put me in an awkward mood and I didn't make it easy for the people I was working with. I'd had enough, I wanted to be home, working on trucks, getting a sweat on. It was a mental thing, and we learned that burning off energy on a bike helps my mood, so I do that now. Everybody is wired up differently, aren't they? And that's what's needed to keep me happy and running smoothly. The Japan trip was 16 days including the flights, which is spot on. And I had the use of a mountain bike for some of the time.

I went out pushbiking for a couple of hours every morning I could, to give Brian a bit of a workout. I talk about this little madman, Brian the Chimp, but really it's just a way of talking about my mental health. The idea of the chimp came from the

Professor Steve Peters book I've mentioned in previous books of mine, *The Chimp Paradox*. I've learned what I need to do to keep things on an even keel, and for me, especially when I'm on a trip away filming for a long time, out of my normal routine, I know that going for a good bicycle ride is what needs to happen. I'm happy to get up before everyone else and go for a ride around, early in the morning.

When I was out on the bike I was fitting in with the Japanese anyway, because I was told there are 8 million bikes in daily use in Japan. I was given a GoPro camera and did a bit of filming that was used in the final programme too, so it all worked out.

The crew on the Japan job were James Woodroffe, the director; Amy, the producer; Nat and Max, the cameramen; Andy, the sound-man; Jess, the production assistant; and Stew, the medic, security, extra pair of hands. Every programme I make is directed by either James or Ewan Keil. The director is in charge of the job, telling the camera people where they need to be, what they need to point at, and for how long. The director is also the person I talk to when I'm doing a piece to camera, they're at the side of the camera asking me questions to get me going. The producer is the director's right-hand, making sure everything happens when it's supposed to and everyone is where they're supposed to be, overseeing the nuts and bolts of the job so the director can concentrate on what's being filmed. Nat the cameraman, or director of photography if we're being technical, and Andy the soundman work with both direct-ors so they've been on just about every job I've done. Max is brought in for bigger jobs, or ones where we're tight for time, to film different angles and different set-ups, to allow more to be filmed every day. The production assistant, sometimes called the runner, makes sure we don't run out of anything, keeps the wheels greased, and generally helps the producer make sure everything happens when it's supposed to, or to get us back on track if owt goes wrong. We worked with a Japanese translator/fixer, Yu, who had helped with the research and recce'd pretty much everything and everywhere we were going to film.

I'd usually be up early and go for a ride for a couple of hours and be back for breakfast. I got in bother a couple of times in the past, because I'd got lost in China and got back to the hotel late. Now I've picked up a tip from Stew, who happens to be an ex-Royal Marine and comes on these longer jobs. Whenever he gets to a place we're staying he looks up to get the position of the landmarks, so he has a rough idea of how to get back if he got really stuck. It's a lot more important skill to have in the military than it is when you're doing a bit of filming, but I've got into the habit of doing it too. I do back it up with my Garmin or my phone, though, too. One morning my phone battery died when I was out so I had to sit in a hotel for half-an-hour having a cuppa, waiting for it to charge so I could find my way back. You live and learn. I like getting lost and working out how to get back.

The bike was also used in one of the segments to show the workings of a very Japanese, high-tech bike park. There's a little kiosk above ground, with a slot, or holder, to push your wheel into. When you press a button, a door opens, the pushbike disappears through it and into underground storage. You're allowed inside and the bicycles are delivered to racks until the owner returns and gives the ticket, or code, for their bike back. The robot arm goes off to fetch the bike and delivers it back to street level. Everything is so precise and well-oiled. The robot arm is like something out of a modern car factory. It's just amazing and the kind of thing that sums up Japan for me.

I bet there have been loads of programmes on Japan, but I wouldn't have thought many will have covered as many different subjects as we did over two programmes. One day I'm in the guts of the world's most advanced bike shed, the next I'm underground in the MAOUDC, Metropolitan Area Outer Underground Discharge Channel, a flood defence system. Flood defences; you wouldn't think it was a subject to get the average Channel 4 viewer's heart racing, but I didn't worry that we'd travelled halfway around the world to see some flood defences, because I'm not like that and I knew they'd be very Japanese – whatever we were going to see would be. The TV lot don't line up any dud visits and this flood defence system was an eye-opener.

Japan is 50 per cent bigger, in area, than the UK, but it has nearly twice the population: 126 million to the UK's 66 million. They have the problem that the majority of Japan's landmass is uninhabitable. It's a string of islands and the middle of most of the islands is forest-covered mountains, so the majority of the population live on or near the coast. Tokyo is one of the original megacities, and, for a time, they poured more concrete there, annually, than anywhere in the world. Because of that, when it rains, and they get properly heavy rain in typhoon season, there's no land for it to soak into, because everything's tarmac and concrete. Not only that, Tokyo is built on land that five rivers cross, so that makes it prone to flooding too.

To solve the problem they constructed this massive flood defence system.

First, we went in the control room and it was very 1990s. All the keyboards and phones had gone the piss-yellow colour old office equipment used to go, but because it's so specialised and cost so much it's not going to be replaced, like a phone or a PC in a normal office would. It ends up being a time capsule of when it was installed and a lot of Japan is like that. It's a very rich country, but it had this massive boom time in the 1980s and 1990s and a lot of what I'd call the infrastructure dates back to then. When I think of something as being 'very Japanese' I think of places like the flood defence control room, stuck in the nineties (even though it was all finished in 2006). There's no USBs, everyone's on serial ports.

The most memorable part of the system are massive underground tanks, propped up with huge concrete columns that both support the roof and baffle the water running into the tanks. When there's risk of flooding, 3.9 miles of channels are opened, allowing water to run into the tanks. Rain fills the underground caverns and is then pumped out into the largest of Tokyo's rivers and into the sea. The tanks fill up three or four times a year. The time and money invested into building them blew my mind, but I couldn't help thinking it was their own fault because they didn't foresee the problem.

We filmed in the turbine room where four converted jumbo jet engines have been installed, that, instead of spinning to create thrust, drive a pump. They can shift enough water to empty a 25-metre swimming pool in less than three seconds. While we were in the turbine room I was asked to do what the TV world calls a 'piece to camera'. If you watch my programmes I never present like a normal presenter, I am either talking to someone on-screen or I'm answering questions from the director off-screen. You don't usually hear the director's voice, because the filming starts after he finishes talking. So they'll say summat simple like, 'Tell us what that felt like?' and that's enough to set me off. David Attenborough doesn't need to do that, of course, he knows what he's doing and he does what a regular presenter does. In the turbine room underneath Tokyo I did a rare bit of normal presenting, and I realised I can do it when I have to. I have to know what I'm talking about and have a bit of conviction, I can't just spiel off. I have massive appreciation for what presenters do, but I can't do it unless I'm into it. I can't be excited about a vegetable lasagne. I make a point of saying I'm not a TV presenter. I just have a natter with the people who I work with.

Floods aren't the only natural disaster Tokyo has to deal with and they have a centre designed to prepare people for earthquakes, typhoons, tsunamis, and getting out of a building when there's been a power cut. It's free to attend because they want people to be prepared.

I went in the typhoon simulator to feel what it's like to be in 70mph, hurricane-force winds. I had a post to hang onto and I needed it. They let Nat the cameraman in with us and he was getting rattled about. I wasn't worried about his camera kit because he's equipped for every eventuality, including simulated typhoons.

They put six-year-olds in there too, so when the next typhoon or earthquake hits it's not a shock to the kids. The earthquake simulator wasn't messing around either. The guide told me what

I had to do: hide under the bed until I felt it was over, then grab a cushion, put it on my head, and escape the room. I wish I had the cushion when I was in the blackout corridor because I smacked my head on the wall trying to find my way out.

We don't get typhoons or hurricanes in Britain. We get the odd flood, but they're rarely bad enough to cause a loss of life. We don't get earthquakes worth talking about, but we still talk about the tremors we do get. Over there they have a lot to deal with, but they just get on with it. Over here we dither and worry about everyone and everything and set up an enquiry or a cross-party steering committee to look into everything and never get on with it. We're ditherers. In a way I'm patriotic, but in another way I'm embarrassed to be British. We're given the impression, from those in government, that we're taken seriously by other countries, but no one gives a fuck about us. We're a tiny island who did a bit a few years ago. Travelling to places like Japan and Russia made me realise this.

The scale of the flood defence was impressive and the civil engineering was right up my street, but I don't think you can do a programme about Japan without covering the technology they use before the rest of the world catches on. To make sure we ticked that box, we visited an old folks' home, another one of those filming days that, if you saw it on paper, you might scratch your head, but was another good one. We learned how automation and technology are used to look after the pensioners, and there's plenty that they do that nowhere else seems to.

The population of Japan is getting older because the younger generations aren't bothered about shagging or meeting anyone.

They'd rather sit at home reading manga comic books and searching the internet for freaky porn. For lots of the population, life is all about work; maybe that commitment to work grew out of the post-war rebuild, the success led to success and that's the way the country had become brainwashed after the war. By the time they've finished work they're too tired for a relationship and they just want to knock one out to extreme porn. That means the average age in Japan is increasing and there aren't younger generations in the same numbers, so the population is aging, and decreasing. I've read that Japan's population is predicted to drop by 20 million in the next 30 years, simply because more folk are dying than being born. They're already the oldest large nation in the world, so old folks are a big issue for them, as they should be for most countries.

While I was there I was sat with one of the old women who was stroking one of the animatronic pets they have to keep the old people company. This one was a seal pup, but they have other animals. Part of me thinks it's not a bad way to see out your days, stroking a robot mammal, but it did make me realise we go full circle if we live long enough. When you're a kid someone's wiping your arse and you play with toys, doing simple memory games, and that's what the old folks were doing in the Japanese retirement home. They had a robot teacher leading a roomful of residents to join in with memory games. Perhaps British retirement homes will have robot bingo callers. Maybe they already do, but I haven't heard about them.

Another bit of advanced technology, this one more for the benefit of the people who worked there, was a kind of exoskeleton that the carers wear when they need to pick someone up out of bed. There are electrically controlled pushrods that extend to help you straighten your knees and back when you normally wouldn't be able to. It works a treat.

While the old folks' home used robot and toy animals to keep their residents happy, we also visited a place that used real animals to do the same job: the piglet café. Because people spend so long at work they don't have pets in the same kind of numbers that we have them, so they went mad for the idea of cat cafés, that spread around the world, and the next thing was the piglet café. You go in for a brew and sit on low cushions while micropigs walk around, being stroked, sitting on people's laps.

There were some 20-something computer programmer blokes when we were there, and they were having a great time. I'm not sure if these place help folk deal with stress or what, but they were all dead happy, and Yu, our translator, was mad for it. I can appreciate it, but I'm not the kind of boy who would normally hang around in a piglet café. There's nothing better than coming home and stroking your dog, but if you haven't got a dog and there's an opportunity to have a cuppa while you're stroking a cute piglet, then fill yer boots.

One thing though, there's no such thing as a micropig. There's no miniature pig breed, those are just very young piglets and they're going to grow up into someone's dinner. If anyone tries to sell you a micropig check the size of their windows, because they saw you coming. A micropig is going to turn into 25 stone of porker.

Another day of filming in Tokyo was with an old bloke, well past his retirement age, but it couldn't have been more different from the old folks' home. Seisakujo Iwai is a master lathe operator, a craftsman who has earned the right to be called a *takumi*. To become a *takumi* you must put 60,000 hours into your chosen specialist profession. Work that out over a normal person's working year of 37-and-a-half-hour weeks, and 20 days off a year, and it's over 33 years. Iwai-san, the '-san' is like Mr and a sign of respect, had stood at his lathe for well over 30 years. He was in his 80s, and had made stuff for nuclear reactors and components for satellites that are still in space. His workshop was in Minamikamata Street, I haven't forgotten that.

Meeting Iwai-san was one of the days where I thought, What a lucky bugger I am. Getting the chance to work with someone like him, at the coal face. They say that he's more accurate than a CNC (computer numerical control) machine, but that's not true, because a CNC machine is just as accurate as the person writing the programme. Everything he was doing could be done by CNC, but to watch him work his manual machine, where you wind the handles yourself, was just brilliant. He let me do some passes with the cutting tool, on a part he'd been working on for days. I felt the pressure, proper pressure. Wind that handle one degree more than you should and the week's work is ruined. There is nothing, not one thing, you can do to recover it. Stick it in the scrap bin and start again. I'm not sure the TV lot realise that and how much it meant to me, and why should they? It's not their world, but to be able to do that in a Japanese *takumi*'s workshop is my favourite memory of the trip.

We measured the part and it was slightly too big, and I mean slightly, 10 microns. I asked if we should have another pass, but he said leave it. He went and had a fag and by the time he'd finished his Silk Cut the piece had cooled enough that it was the perfect size. I love stuff like that. If you're wondering how much 10 microns is, a human hair is 70 microns.

Iwai-san is a proper old school toolmaker, a highly skilled machine operator who can make anything a lathe can physically make to the tightest tolerances you can imagine. His workshop wasn't tidy, but he knew how to wind those handles. Now, in most what you'd call advanced countries, a place that is expected to make advanced components has to look the bollocks and have all the bells and whistles to be taken seriously, but Japan seems to respect the person doing the job, more than the manager or the salesman who's out the front in their suit. I like that Japan realises a workshop doesn't need to be spotless to be able to produce good work.

I didn't need to speak the language to know what Iwai-san was thinking and I did enough to impress the Japanese *takumi*. I've been working on machines, like, since I was 15, but I am self-taught. I suppose I'm a failed toolmaker and a failed farmer. Those are the things I'd like to be really good at. I look at those boys with such respect because they've got the feel for it. People comment, and I'm told the programme did, that there isn't a younger generation coming up who are willing to put in the hours to become a *takumi*, and that skills like this are being lost, but that's only partly true, because things have changed and there are factories all over the world that can machine stuff as accurately as him, using CNC machines. The end result is as good, but I do think it is a shame that there won't be people like him around forever, and there are benefits to doing the odd one-off job the way he was doing it. The exact level of skills might be lost, but the ability to do the job is not. That's the price of progress. It's a dying trade, but as long as there are machines like his around, people will still use them, and teach themselves to use them.

We were rattling through the filming and next up was going for a drive out with a club of custom truck owners. We might have been given a bit of a false impression that they were more outlaw than they were. They were just lads into their trucks, but it was good to see. I don't care what you're into, but you've got to be into something and those boys were passionate about their trucks. I've worked with drivers at Moody's who want the horsepower, they want the flashing lights, and you can think, You sad bastard, get a life. But I'm the same about other stuff. That's their hobby, let them get on with it.

The trucks were old-fashioned compared to British stuff. There were a few tippers and vans with huge whale-tail bodykits. That style of customised van is called *dekotora*, decoration truck. Some are covered in a thousand lights, others have 1970s plush upholstered interiors that look like something out of a sultan's palace. They're painted, plated and polished to within an inch of their lives. When we were parked up on a very quiet side street not bothering anyone, the police arrived and started taking names. While they were doing that a Japanese saying was told to me: 'The nail that sticks up gets hammered.' If you don't conform they'll come for you. I can appreciate the reasons for Japanese wanting conformity, it makes for a very pleasant country, but I'm with the *dekotora* drivers. I don't want to conform.

We were out with the trucks at night, so we could see them all lit up, but we'd usually be back to the hotel from a day's filming at six or seven. They're full days, but they're not hard for me. Everyone else is sorting things out, thinking what needs doing, from which angle, and I'm the performing monkey.

I hardly ever feel any pressure when I'm on a filming job, at least not from being in front of the camera. If I have to jump out of a plane, or take the controls of a *takumi*'s lathe, then I feel the pressure of that, but that's nothing to do with filming. So while the crew are working to set everything up I'm reading or having a look around or just listening. It's the best job in the world.

11

Being *Bushido*

A MASSIVE HIGHLIGHT of the Japan trip was finding out about the motorcycle sport of autorace. It only takes place in Japan and its sole purpose is for people to bet on it. The betting industry is very restricted in Japan. You can only bet on four sports: horse racing, speedboats, track cycling and autorace. I didn't know how secret the autorace world was until we started filming, but the film crew lined up the best guide, former 125cc Grand Prix World Champion, Haruchika Aoki, who is now an autorace rider.

The track is in a place called Kawaguchi, a city of 600,000 folk in the huge Greater Tokyo Area, and the people who turn up to watch aren't into bikes, they're just gamblers, like some people who turn up to a midweek horse race or watch it in a bookies. It's a motorbike race, but they could be watching a speedboat or a greyhound go in circles, because it's just about the betting.

The autorace track is a tarmac oval within a stadium. When they have series of races, the riders race over the space of a few days, then have time off. While they're racing they live at the track, isolated from the outside world. They're not allowed to meet outsiders, and they have to hand over their phones, so there's no access to the outside world, in an effort to stop the races being fixed or the public getting information to help them place bets.

Haruchika Aoki explained no outsiders normally get let behind the scenes. So, first I was having this access, unprecedented as they say all the time nowadays, and not only that, they partner me up with Aoki. Haruchika is the youngest of three brothers who all raced in grands prix, and he's five years older than me. The other autoracers riding when we were there ranged from a 19-year-old lass to the oldest, a 70-year-old bloke.

Autorace bikes are the strangest-looking machines. They look a bit like 1960s speedway bikes, with rigid back ends (no suspension), skinny front forks, a little petrol tank tucked in between the frame tubes, narrow wheels, no brakes and handlebars that look like they've been run over by a Scania. The right grip is down by your knee, the other is nearly at chest height, but when the bike is leaned right over in the corner, and the rider has their left foot on the floor, the bars make more sense. The bikes are powered by a specific Suzuki 600cc parallel twin engine, made just for autorace, and the whole bike is designed to go left on a very smooth track.

The riders look after their own bikes and can tune them within a certain degree to get an edge. They'd go as far as changing the valve springs for certain weather conditions. These are the springs, about 4cm long, that close the valves in the engine's cylinder head. I change them in engines I'm tuning, uprating the standard ones for ones of different material or more heavy-duty, but once they're in, it wouldn't occur to me to try to change them to make an advantage for certain weather conditions. All the autoracers' valve springs were nearly identical, they'd share the same part numbers, but within the manufacturing tolerances you'd have some very slightly stronger than others and they'd go to the bother of changing them. That level of marginal gain is mad.

Haruchika liked talking to us, I think, because he's travelled the world for years, he speaks decent English, he probably liked the change of scene for the day. He took me to the works canteen and gave me a lesson in slurping ramen, Japanese noodle soup.

It sounds like racing there is a good job. I doubt you'd retire from grands prix and become an autorace rider if it wasn't pretty good. I heard wage figures of £80,000 a year, so that's not shabby. There aren't many British Superbike racers earning that. And the life isn't as restricted as we'd been led to believe before we arrived. I was told the riders were only allowed home for short periods of the year, but that wasn't true. They're just in the track digs for a few days at a time. Haruchika had kids, but he didn't seem that upset about having to stay in the autorace barracks. Maybe he likes the peace and quiet.

He took me to the autorace practice track where they all train, to have a ride around. I realised I'd been right next to it when I tested the Mugen. I'd seen autorace bikes go round and John McGuinness was getting really excited about them, he knew all about it and I hadn't heard of it then. That was two years before.

The idea was for me and Haruchika to have a bit of a race for the cameras. He gave me a two-minute lesson. You set off in the gear you race in, so there's no gearshifting. They don't wear steel shoes, like dirt trackers or speedway riders, but something like a nylon sole, something sacrificial, to scrape along a bit like a kneeslider.

It's completely different to dirt tracking, but there's something there, because you're just turning left, that made it feel a bit similar to what I'd done before. The difference is there is so much grip that I never got to the point where I was feeling something move, or sensing the tyres beginning to let go. It meant I didn't know how much faster I could go. I have a lot of motorbike experience, but it was such an alien thing. I was riding the thing so hard, I felt anyway, and I still wasn't getting any movement. And autoracers are the fastest things imaginable on their smooth, tarmac oval tracks. There's a film of a race between a Suzuki GSX-R road bike, a Suzuki World Superbike and a Suzuki MotoGP bike, and the autoracer beats them all.

Like most of these situations, I just get ten minutes on the bike for the TV, and that's great, another fantastic experience, but I'm not going out there to push any limits. Haruchika made it look more of a race than it actually was. He could have smoked me, but instead he was riding in a way he looked like he was pushing and then just got past me before the line. He was completely on another level, and wasn't about to let me win, but he was too polite and too much of a pro to blow me into the weeds. Not that there were any weeds. This is Japan, everything was spotless and in order, of course.

From Tokyo we travelled 320 miles to Kobe, a city on the coast near Osaka, to film another couple of sections, including me trying fugu, the poisonous pufferfish. On average a handful die of fugu

poisoning every year, but it's mainly people who are trying to prepare it themselves. I was 100 per cent confident I was going to be all right. We're making a TV programme, no one's going to die, are they? We're not pushing the boundaries.

The restaurant were fugu experts and their speciality was a £50, five-course meal all made from this one fish. The final course, saving the best till last, was described as either the egg or sperm sack of the fish. It's a delicacy. We know all about food described as a local 'delicacy', but there's not much I won't eat, and I haven't got a great sense of taste anyway, a result of getting my head kicked in, as a teenager, on a night out in Lincoln, so I was tucking in and it was nice enough. I was asked to describe the taste, and came up with Spam. I wasn't looking, but I'm told the chef's face dropped. I'm not sure how much English he knew, but he knew enough to get the gist. He shouldn't have been upset, there's nowt wrong with Spam.

Another impact that the shrinking, aging population is having on Japan is the lack of workers willing to do manual work. We visited a fishing town, near Kobe, where workers from Vietnam have been allowed visas to enter the country and work in the fishing and seafood industry. Japan has very strict immigration rules, but there are so many more jobs than people to fill them in Japan that they've had to open their immigration to fill the essential jobs. I spoke to a woman from Vietnam, who had five kids back home. She'd been a lawyer, but she got more money in Japan working on a fish farm getting a normal Japanese wage. It's like Eastern Europeans in England who earn a few quid, send some home and maybe move back eventually. A couple of lads I work with on the potato job are from Romania, and I always used to work on trucks driven by Polish drivers.

By the time we filmed at the fishing place we'd been away from Tokyo and the borrowed bicycle for a few days and I was feeling it. I think I must be the opposite of most people, because I stiffen up and feel like I can't do anything if I've been taking it easy. On the way to the fishing place my knees, hands, ankles and back were killing me, because I hadn't done anything physical. I was seized up and sore, quietly thinking to myself, I hope I'm not going to let anyone down today. I was only 37 then, but I've got a fair bit of metal in me, and I think that's probably it. If I bike every day I feel brand new, but if I have a day off I feel second-hand; two days and I feel terrible.

One day we can be filming in the calm of a fishing dock, people sat cross-legged preparing equipment for growing shellfish, the next we're in the middle of the madness at a Shinto firework festival in Toyohashi, where I was included in this annual, religious festival. The day started with me helping to carry a bloody heavy wooden frame, with a bloke stood on the top of it, up and down every street in the town. To miss a house was bad luck, or disrespectful. I was leaking by the end of it. It was definitely exercise, so I wasn't complaining, but I felt it.

The team of people I was with are all educated blokes, and their year seems to revolve around this, and I love that dedication to one thing. The group that I was part of explained they train throughout the year for this one weekend, the whole day was very choreographed, but I got let straight in.

Fireworks are a huge part of the day and we went to a Shinto temple to have the fireworks blessed. Groups of blokes from neighbouring villages congregate to set off homemade explosives. They start setting them off before it's even dark and it goes on all night. It's madness. I'm not sure if the idea is to try to outdo each other, but that seems to be what it turned into. They reckon these homemade fireworks are so volatile that when they're being assembled they have to pack them full of gunpowder at night, when it's cooler, to lessen the risk of them going off during packing.

Huge fireworks, bigger than anything I've ever seen, bucket-sized, homemade explosives are held by the people as they're going off. Some of the blokes take their shirts off and lie down while being showered by huge sparks, and they're being very *bushido*, showing no emotion, and having the calm attitude and respectful behaviour of a samurai. I think I was the only one wearing earplugs. I was given a firework to hold, and even though it wasn't the biggest there, it was still massive. I was waiting and waiting for it to go off, holding my breath, then Bang! I'm trying my hardest not to flinch and let the side down, and doing my best to be *bushido*, but also making sure I didn't blow my arm off.

Yokohama is the neighbouring city to Tokyo, and the second largest Japanese city, in terms of population. I was shown around Kotobukicho, one of Yokohama's slums, by a British bloke, Tim Gill, a university professor. He'd lived in the slum at one point when he'd been on the bones of his arse, that's how you end up with a place to live there. This being Japan, the slum wasn't like something out of India or South America or even the rough parts of Grimsby. It was mint, everything was in its place, everything tidy, even round the back of places it was still tidy. There were little gardens that people had made themselves, just on the street, growing plants in window-box type containers, but fastened to the street furniture and the fences round the communal bin dumps.

The area was kept in check by the yakuza, who are the Japanese mafia. The Japanese don't like crime, but they like organisation and conformity, so organised crime, that's OK.

Tim said it wasn't a good idea to film in this area, so I was filming everything with a GoPro. He was explaining all about the yakuza and illegal gambling. Gambling isn't illegal, but is restricted to the sports I've mentioned, the pools, lottery and pachinko, a sort of pinball slot machine the Japanese are mad about. We went to an illegal betting shop and put the equivalent of £10 on a speedboat race, one of the four sports you are allowed to bet on. I don't know what made this betting shop illegal, but it was.

While we were exploring the seedier bits of Japan, Tim also showed me a 'love hotel', in the same yakuza-run Kotobukicho area, the kind of place where you book a room by the hour, and it hardly cost any more to stay for the whole night, so you knew what kind of clientele they were appealing to. These kind of hotels are where blokes go with prostitutes, and are also used by people having affairs. He explained you could choose off the menu what outfit you want the hooker to dress up in.

I'm fascinated by the yakuza and I'd stepped into their world in Tokyo when I got a tattoo. On the plane to Japan, James had said we were going to meet a traditional tattooist, and I could have one if I wanted. No pressure, it was up to me. I've got tattoos, but I'm not *into them*, into them, and this was a bit yakuza-ish, because the Japanese still associate tattoos with criminals.

It was our first day in Japan when we turned up at a flat in a very quiet block, where Horihachi the tattooist worked, and, I think, lived. We got talking and I decided on the spot I'd have one done. Me and my mate Gunster gave each other our first tattoos. Mine was on the bottom of my foot and I did the 'This Little Piggie . . .' nursery rhyme lines on his toes. We didn't start with the neck or whatever folks do now. The following year I had one on my leg. So being in Japan, in what felt like an underground tattoo spot, was a good reason to have one done, especially when the others were done when I was pissed-up in Grimsby.

I chose traditional cherry blossoms, very Japanese, very yakuza, and lay on the floor for over two hours while Horihachi did the job. He didn't use an electric gun for the main part of the tattoo, he stabbed the ink in by hand, using metal needles on the end of a wooden handle. The ink is special, different, I'm told, to the kind of ink used outside Japan and retains its colour and brightness for longer. It's still vibrant 18 months later.

Hiroshima made a big impression on me. When I was in the city I was wrapped up in all the emotion of it and the few facts I knew at the time, and it made me think, Why did this have to happen? What was the need for it? I didn't have the facts at hand, but I know a lot more now, because I'm fascinated. I didn't concentrate at school, not in history or maths, but now I love them. I have a pretty good grasp of maths, because I've learned it in relation to something I'm into. I can work out volumes, CNC tool paths, cutting rates, and all sorts of stuff. I've learned as I've gone along because it's been practical and I can see the purpose of it, which I, and lots of kids, struggled to when I was in the classroom. Perhaps the interest in history comes with age, but I can't get enough of it.

The war with Japan and the war with Germany is all thought of as World War II, but they were pretty much two different wars. They're tied together because Germany, Italy and Japan signed an agreement in September 1940, stating an enemy of one was an enemy of the other two. Japan were really at war with China, whose territory they were trying to expand into. They were empire building under the Emperor Hirohito. America weren't involved in World War II for the first two years, but they were concerned about what Japan were doing and worried they might try to invade islands under American or European rule in South-east Asia. America pushed a load of battleships, destroyers, submarines and aircraft out to Hawaii, in the middle of the Pacific, pretty much halfway between America and Japan. Japan noticed this, and, without warning, bombed the US naval base at Pearl Harbor, Hawaii, on 7 December 1941. The 'without warning' bit is important because Japan hadn't declared war on America, so the attack was a shock to America. The president at the time, F.D.R. Roosevelt, declared war on Japan, and, because of the agreement they signed, a few days later Germany declared war on America, and that changed everything. The Americans were supporting Britain and its allies, but hadn't sent troops. After Pearl Harbor they did, and if it wasn't for the Americans we wouldn't have won. The Germans traipsed through mainland Europe without much resistance, and we were doing all right, but we are kidding ourselves if we think we'd have won without the Americans.

The decision to drop the bomb on Hiroshima was made because America believed the Japanese would never surrender, they'd fight till the last man standing. Dropping the bomb to end all bombs was to force them to realise they couldn't win. Still, there wasn't a peep out of Japan for three days after the atomic bomb went off. There was no sign of weakness, not a hint that they were considering surrender. So the second H-bomb was dropped on Nagasaki. Again, nothing for three days. America were ready to drop another when the Emperor of Japan finally made an announcement that they must accept the shame of surrender with the words, 'We must endure the unendurable.' It was forbidden for soldiers to surrender and there had been years of talk of the Japanese civilians having to fight to the death too.

My grandad was shipped from wherever he'd ended up in France at the end of the war in Europe to South Africa to prepare for a land invasion of Japan, because the war was still going on there. VE Day, Victory in Europe, the end of the war with Germany, was 8 May 1945, but the bomb wasn't dropped on Nagasaki until 9 August the same year, leading to the Japanese to finally surrender on 14 August.

You'd have to wonder about my grandad's chances of surviving the D-Day invasion and all that followed that, and then having to survive fighting the Japanese defending their home soil at a time they believed it was a massive honour to die for their country. Not good odds, I'd have to say.

We visited Hiroshima's famous memorial, the domed building, one of the only structures that remained standing, and only because it had a steel frame. It's been left as it was in 1945, damaged by the blast. I also took a ride on one of the trams that dates from before the bomb. The Japanese had that very tram running just three days after the bomb was dropped. What commitment. The first ever nuclear bomb is dropped on the city, completely flattening it, vaporising people so there wasn't a single trace of them, poisoning the land and water for miles around and they got the trams back up and running in three days.

There aren't many other sites that commemorate what happened to Hiroshima, but it was a memorable experience to be there, one of only two places in the world nuclear bombs have been used against a population, and to see what the resilience of the Japanese people built out of it.

The trip to Hiroshima couldn't have been more different to another day spent sampling some *onsen*, the natural springs in the city of Noboribetsu, on the northern island of Hokkaido. The whole place was geared up for tourists to come for a soak. The water is geothermally heated by the Earth's core; the hot springs are full of minerals, making the town smell of boiling batteries, sulphur, strong enough for even my rubbish sense of smell to pick up on. I had to wait for the pool to empty before we were able to film, so I was sat in an automatic massage chair for half-an-hour thinking, I'm getting paid for this.

You're supposed to go in naked, but I had my shorts on. I wasn't going to get my little fella out. I know I have before, when we made the boat programme, but I was young and stupid then. The pool was mega, 50°C, much hotter than I'd have a bath, I was almost worried about it boiling my internals, but it was great.

The whole town was beautiful, with half-tame little deer walking through it.

In those two weeks we filmed in and around Tokyo, Kobe, Yokohama, back to Tokyo, on to Hiroshima before going to the northern island of Hokkaido, for the last thing we filmed: making a katana, the samurai blade, with the master.

The katana-maker, Korehira Watan, was another *takumi*. His job was to make the shape of the sword, before it went to another specialist to be sharpened for a week, then it would go to someone else to be polished for a week.

The different steel he beat together to get the right amount of strength for flexibility is a science. He'd get it up to temperature and beat it all together. At first he had me and his apprentice beating the red-hot blade with lump hammers to help shape it. I've been hitting things with hammers since I was a kid, and he seemed happy to trust me. He tried me with a bit of a sharpening and said I did all right at that, so he got me involved with tempering the cutting edge. It was a long old process, but I loved it.

Yu was brought in to translate. They don't normally allow women into their workplace, because they say the flames are female and the fire will get jealous if a woman appears. Anyway, that all went out of the window because Yu was there and she was getting a bit anxious about us doing a good job. Watan-san, the master, was watching the colour of the flames with eagle eyes while I held the blade in the fire and the apprentice stoked the fire. Watan-san would give the word and I'd pull the blade out for him to inspect. There were no temperature gauges, it was all experience, eye and feel for the job. I pulled the blade out, but it wasn't ready

My Rob North BSA. I still get a buzz from road racing this bike.

BSA and Martek at the Almeria track, in Spain, with *PB* magazine.

We had some good days working on *Night Fright*, even if it wasn't ready in time for the D-Day commemoration.

The kit World War II paratroopers wore to be dropped into Europe.

That's a face that says, 'These lads say it's going to be ready in time, but I'm not sure it will be'.

In front of the *Drag Em Oot*, the Dakota we used in the end, with Charlie, Pete and my dad.

Shit or bust time.

The TV lot, and our Japanese fixers, at Honda's museum.

Dekotoro vans. I loved how much these boys loved their vans.

I didn't want to ask what the tissues were for. Some things are better left unspoken.

The Atomic Bomb Dome, Hiroshima.

One of Hiroshima's trams that was running within days of the bomb being dropped.

With Haruchika Aoki at the Autorace headquarters. Very few outsiders have ever been let in here.

Under the watchful eye of Iwai-san, the takumi. What an honour.

Ah ... I'm not good at relaxing, but these Japanese 'onsen' spas were spot on.

Helping make a katana blade with another takumi, Wantan-san.

Japan summed up for me in one photo.

so it went back in. Eventually it was out and I had to quickly plunge it in the water. It was tense, and, like with Iwai-san and his lathe, if I'd had buggered this up there was a lot of time and work wasted. These specialists don't have to let me get involved. They've nothing to gain, they're not being paid, but they do it because, I'm guessing, they can see we're enthusiastic and not complete idiots.

Watan-san was very happy, saying the tempering was close to perfect. They test the strength and quality of the katana by chopping into a sheet of steel stood on its end. We got Stew, the ex-Marine, on the job. He's a big lad, and took a big swing cutting further into the metal than anyone before according to Watan-san. It was a great experience.

The sword maker and his apprentice were both fully committed to work six-and-a-half days a week for however many years to master their trade, and I love all that, the dedication, the commitment, but would I want it? I have a massive amount of respect, because I couldn't have that commitment. I'm a jack of all trades. I'm all right at a few things, but I've never excelled at one thing. It's almost like being a monk, giving your life over for one purpose. It's not normal. It's a bit more common in Japan, but it's definitely still not common. You could say I had the same attitude about motorbike racing, I didn't master it, but I don't regret one thing. I'd love to be a better welder, but I'm good enough to get by. That's me. Good enough to get by. Maybe I should watch the finished programmes to see if I can improve or do things a bit differently, but perhaps that would take the shine off things if I tried too hard. I'm only doing TV for the great experiences. I'm not doing it to be famous. I don't want to be on *I'm a Celebrity Get Me Out of Here*.

Now I've done travel programmes in China, Latvia, India, Russia and Ukraine. I've enjoyed them all for different reasons. I told the TV lot before I went that Japan was like nothing else on the planet, but after two weeks I came away thinking I'd sold them a dud, because it is more normal than I thought, just a nicer version. Why can't we be more Japanese?

12

Hang on, Dickheads, Why Am I Ordering Another 200 Spoons?

LOTS OF PEOPLE THINK of *The Great Escape* as a motorcycle film because of the famous Steve McQueen section at the end, but that was never in the original script. How I understand it is, McQueen had the idea at the eleventh hour, and you've got to say he was probably right to put his foot down, because it's what everyone thinks of when the film is mentioned and it's one of the most famous and favourite war films, and the jump is up there with the most famous film stunts of all time.

North One came up with the idea of me doing the famous jump for a programme. It never entered my head that I might be comparing myself to Steve McQueen. Now, everyone knows Steve McQueen was mad about motorbikes, and his name and image are used to sell all sorts of stuff, with loads of people wanting to look like him, and why not? If that's what floats your boat. I did tell the TV lot right from the start that anything to do with me and off-road riding smells like hospital. That didn't put them off and planning started in 2019, with filming ending in October of that year.

The gist of the programme was me learning to jump so I could attempt clearing the fence that McQueen's character, Captain Hilts, crashes into, leading to his capture by the Germans who were chasing him. I would also learn about the actual escape much of the film is based on, and life in Stalag Luft III as a PoW, prisoner of war.

The film was released in 1963, 56 years before we started filming. I don't think anyone else had had a good go at copying the jump, and if they had, I doubt they went to the lengths this programme did. Even though McQueen was the star, it was his mate, Bud Ekins, who did the famous jump. Ekins and McQueen raced off-road together, even representing America in the 1964 International Six Days Trial, in East Germany, so neither of them were messers. Ekins was also the most successful Triumph dealer on the west coast of America in the 1960s, so when it came to doing the stunt riding for the film, the pair of them only wanted to ride Triumphs, not BMWs, which would have been more historically accurate. It made sense for North One to get Triumph involved, and they lined up a stunt rider called Andy Godbold to be the bloke to teach me to jump. Ewan Keil was the director in charge of this programme, and when he explained it to me, his idea wasn't that we were just going to film me doing a similar jump, we were going to the actual hillside in Germany where the filming took place in the early sixties.

I've done a lot of stuff on motorbikes, but the thought of jumping dirt bikes made me nervous. The first day of filming was with Andy Godbold at his home near Swaffham in Norfolk. As soon as I met him I felt more relaxed. He's a professional stuntman, on bikes, in trucks and fight scenes, with dozens of credits in all sorts of films including some massive blockbusters. He was an amateur boxer, raced top-level British championship motocross and launched his own stunt team, Bolddog Lings FMX, that go around motorcycle events and country shows doing all the backflips and everything. He's a proper do-er.

Andy has a track and jumps set up on his land. He had a small oval track and he wanted to see how I was on a bike. He didn't assume I was going to be this or that, he just wanted to see for himself. I got on his Husqvarna 450 motocrosser and did a few laps, going dead slow, because the track was so small and tight. I've done a bit of flat track and what have you, but I've never been a proper off-roader, and he wanted to assess what my level was.

After doing a few laps, Andy asked me to start attempting some small jumps. They were on what they call a tabletop, so I rode up a short ramp and just landed on the flat. The idea of starting on a tabletop is if you come up short you're landing on flat, not trying to jump what they call a double, which is like two humps of a camel. If you come up short on that you land on the incline of the second hump, and that can hurt because you're almost stopping dead, like jumping into a wall.

I didn't feel confident, even on the tabletop, but Andy was telling the TV lot he thought I was too confident, saying I was going too fast. He saw that I was using speed to mask the issues, those being a lack of experience on this kind of bike. Using speed to mask the issues is all I've ever done, even though I didn't think

I was doing it that day, and before long I crashed. Those 450 motocross bikes are animals. I've got one set up as a dirt tracker and with the less grippy dirt-track tyres they're a usable thing. You have to be gentler with the throttle or the thing just spins up, but when the same bike is fitted with knobbly tyres, that gives that much more traction. I got crossed up after hitting a stone on the take-off ramp, but because I didn't really know what I was doing, I panicked, put my foot out in mid-air, and landed without being in control. The next thing I know, I'm in a heap. With experience I wouldn't worry about being slightly out of shape, I'd be thinking about how to ride it out. It's all experience and I didn't have it, but I was going to get it.

People who've seen the kind of races I competed in could be confused that I'm nervous about jumping a dirt bike at 30mph. Oliver's Mount, Scarborough, was my first road race and there are a few jumps there so it just got me into it, but Scarborough is nothing like the Irish races or the Isle of Man TT. Tandragee, Skerries, the TT . . . there are bloody big jumps on all of those road races.

At Cookstown, in Northern Ireland, you have to commit as you take off. Once you're in the air you're between two telegraph poles and if you've got it wrong on the approach you're in trouble, because, obviously, there's no steering the thing when both wheels are off the floor. At the Isle of Man TT, you're hitting the jump at Ballacrye in fifth gear on a superbike, at the thick end of 170mph. That's faster than most people will ever travel on wheels in their life, and we're taking off on a motorbike between stone walls and trees, jumping 40–50 feet. Not high, but bloody fast. There's nothing like Kells though. That was my first Irish road race, that would be the most extreme because of the speed and how vicious it all feels. Kells jumps in a straight line and then there are other, what I'd call, technical jumps, at Armoy, Cookstown and Skerries, where the approach is crucial – it's not just balls out, pin the throttle in a straight line stuff. The other thing about these road races is there's no possibility of thinking, I'll back off here and see what this is like. If you're turning up to those races wanting to finish near the front you've got to be on it from the first lap of practice. That means you're hitting the jumps as fast as you possibly can, otherwise someone's up your arse. They are wild. And all this on a bike not really designed to jump.

Even explaining it all, I don't really know why, but I can't relate the jumps on the roads to what I was learning on the dirt bike. I don't know what the issue is, and why I struggle so much. All I know is I have to keep plugging away; the more I do it, the better I'll get. I crashed on that first day because I thought, Shit! while I was in mid-air, but it should, and would, become second nature to not panic, just deal with it.

At the end of the first day with Andy, I was told to jump off an 8-foot ramp into a foam pit, a massive metal skip full of chunks of upholstery foam. All the freestyle motocross stunt riders use foam pits to perfect new tricks. They usually ride a little bike until they get confident, then move to the big bike. Andy explained a rider might do 200 backflips into the foam pit before they feel confident to try it in the real world. You don't want to come up short on a backflip, so you practise the rotation, landing on your wheels in the soft foam, until there's no doubt left in your mind. I rode the same minibike the stunt riders learn on, a little 100cc bike, tiny thing. The idea was to get the feel of what it was like to ride up a ramp that tall and launch off the end of it. And it felt good. What a great thing foam pits are, I was thinking, while the digger arm swivelled over to hook the bike out of the pit.

The next part of the training involved building a track at my house. Luckily, I've got enough room behind the house. JCB are always up for helping out and dropped off a bulldozer, roller and a 360 digger. Andy brought his mate Dan Whitby, who runs the stunt-show parts of the business, and we built a dirt jump.

I already had a thousand tons of muck that I wasn't doing anything with. A mate of a mate was building a house and had nowhere to put the muck that they'd dug out for the footings, so I said I'd have it. That was about five years ago. They were dumping it here before I moved in, while the house was being rebuilt, but I thought it would come in handy for summat, and it did.

Andy and Dan were telling the JCB's driver how the jump should be, and when it was done I had a few goes at it, on my own Honda 450, while the film crew were filming. The JCBs were left here for a week, so I made a bit of a track, with a berm at the top, so I could keep looping round and hitting the jump. Just doing that might have been enough to set me up for the big jump, but it wouldn't make much of a programme, so the next day of filming involved taking me to a motocross track to get me used to tackling bigger jumps. Andy said I should come and meet his mate Carl, who used to race. I didn't know it was bloody Carl Nunn. He was a British champion, won a World Motocross (MX) race and was ranked sixth in the world in 2006. He was just introduced as his mate, Carl.

We mucked about for the day, a full day with Carl Nunn! Watching him was great, seeing what he could do, whipping the bike sideways off jumps. He wasn't trying to show off, it's just what he does. The big thing he was telling me was about my foot position. I had to get my feet on the pegs right. I was on my toes, because that's how you do it on a road race bike, where I should have had the arch of my foot on the footpeg.

Up until now I was riding 450cc motocrossers, the Husqvarna I rode at Andy's and my own Honda, both pure dirt bikes, but I'd be doing the jump on a big Triumph road bike, and it was decided with Triumph that I would use their Scrambler 1200 XE. It was a good bit of advertising from their point of view because the 1200 XE is one of the most expensive bikes they sell. The bike that McQueen and Ekins rode was a Triumph TR6 Trophy, pretending to be a German Army BMW, and a modern Bonneville T100 is a lot closer to one of them, in size, design and suspension travel – that's the amount of movement the forks and shocks have before they bottom out. The Scrambler 1200 XE is a big old beast, so it still felt like it would be a bit of a challenge.

We went to the factory in Hinckley, Leicestershire, and spent part of the day in the prototype department, mucking about with the bike I was going to jump. We took some bits off the brand-new Triumph, trying to make it a bit lighter. Triumph say the dry weight, that's it complete, but with no oil in the engine or petrol in the tank, is 207kg. Does it help if I write that in stone, so you can compare it to your own weight? That's 32½ stone. The Honda CRF450 and the Husqvarna 450 weigh 105kg with oil and a splash of petrol, so almost spot-on half as much as the Triumph. Like I said, a big bike.

The Scrambler was painted a metallic green as a bit of a nod to the olive drab bike in the film, and Triumph had their expert give me a lesson on how to paint pinstripes on the petrol tank. Old school pinstriping is not something you pick up in an afternoon, but I had a go at it and even my best attempt was a dog's dinner. Fair play to Triumph, though, they left my mess on it.

While I was at the factory I got to ride the actual bike that Steve McQueen rode in the film and that the stuntman, Bud Ekins, jumped. A bloke called Dick Shepherd owns it, and has loaned it to Triumph's museum. He was at the factory and they got the bike out in the car park for me to have a little ride around. It's been restored so it looks brand new, with a few extra dents expertly put into the exhaust silencers. They reckon it's valued at £1.5 million.

Triumph delivered another Scrambler 1200 to my place for me to practise on the little track we built behind my house, and once it arrived I didn't ride the Honda CRF450 again during the rest of the training. First time I rode the Triumph Andy told me to just take it easy, but I must have jumped 30 feet. Straight away I felt the Triumph was a nicer thing to ride than the motocross bike, and it was better for jumping, as far as I was concerned. Even though it weighed twice as much, it was so much nicer to ride because it was a dead torquey thing. It's a retro, big metal tank, twin shocks on the back, but modern, upside-down forks and radial Brembo brakes. I was glad to get on it, because I still had the opinion that 450 motocrossers are madness. They're not that different to what the best in the world race, so it's like selling MotoGP bikes down the shops. The motocrosser is like a light switch, and it feels so racy. A dickhead like me should not be riding a bike like that.

Because the Triumph has so much mass, once you drove it at the jump that's the way you're going. It's not easily knocked off course by a stone on your launch ramp. Now I had the bike and the jump, so when I got home from work I'd ride the Triumph for half-an-hour and was getting more and more comfortable. I must have done well over 500 jumps on it.

The shows North One make with me often have a scientific, historic or educational part to them, because it helps the programmes fit a category of being educational. This is important because Channel 4 set itself up to be a public service broadcaster and it has to follow guidelines, one of them being to produce programmes of 'an educational nature'. It ticks a box for the channel and makes it that little bit easier for North One's programme ideas to get the thumbs up if they can prove we're doing that. That's part of the reason we spent a day filming with Hugh Hunt, the professor who we've done a few things with over the years, including the Wall of Death record. It was him who calculated the ideal diameter of the wall for the speed we needed and the g-force, that's the force you feel pushing you into your seat as a jet accelerates for take-off, a human could be expected to withstand.

We visited him in Cambridge, a place I've only ever driven past on my way somewhere else, but it's beautiful, and we were there on a scorching summer's day. Hugh explained how the gyroscopic forces affected the bike in mid-air. I took my Rourke pushbike and they wanted me to do some jumps, but the seat post had seized in the frame and I had the seat right up my arse, which isn't ideal when you want to jump. I'm going to take Shazza and Dot to Cambridge for an ice cream and a cup of tea, then go see Ken Fox, the Wall of Death expert, who's not too far from there.

I had already got used to the gyroscopic effects and how the rotating masses of the bike affect it in the air, but having Hugh explain it was good for the programme. Revving the engine raises the front wheel, jabbing the back brake makes it dip. You don't want to land front wheel first, but neither do you want to land with the front wheel too high, so you can learn to do those simple things to balance it out and make life a bit easier for yourself.

Andy set up another couple of bits of training with people he knew. One was a day's trial riding with Katy Bullock, another stunt rider, that was another full day of filming down at Swaffham, but I'm told it only made a minute of the finished programme, making it a bloody expensive minute. That's nothing to do with Katy, she was great, but there's just so much to fit in, and I suppose it's better to have more than you need, come the editing process, than be panicking about not having enough.

Andy also set up some boxing training, and it was one bit of the filming that I might have struggled to explain how relevant it was, but I went along with it. It was summat to do with core strength, but really, I was jumping one fence once, not doing the Dakar Rally. I think it came from the TV lot crossing the 't's, asking Andy what kind of training they could put me through, so it didn't look like I just rode a bike in my backyard a bit and then did the re-creation of this famous jump. It was maybe a little bit of TV bullshit, but only a little bit. I was sparring with someone Andy Godbold knew, and at the end of it, and writing this now, it makes me think I'd like to get into a bit of amateur boxing. I love the discipline of it. The other thing it makes me think is how much the TV lot like filming me getting punched in the head. First it was the beasting with the Paras when I was preparing for the D-Day landing programme, and now this.

An easier day was spent at Louth cinema with John Leyton, one of the stars of *The Great Escape*. John played Willie Dickes, the tunnel king, though I'm not sure if someone was having a laugh with that character name. He was in a load of big films in the 1960s and also sang the number-one hit, 'Johnny Remember Me'. It was one of the highlights of the whole programme to watch the film with him, as he told me stories he remembered.

The motorbike part of filming was good fun, but the historical part really fascinated me and made for more unforgettable days of filming. North One brought the historian Guy Walters on board. He'd written the well-respected book, *The Real Great Escape*, published in 2013. He knew the escape inside out, and had strong views on it. For his bit of the programme, we flew into Berlin and drove to the site of Stalag Luft III, near Żagań (Sagan), in Poland, the prisoner-of-war camp where the actual 'great escape' took place.

Luft in the camp's name is German for air, so this camp was just for captured airmen and run by the Luftwaffe, the German air force. Perhaps because all airmen thought of themselves as superior to the regular army, the Germans treated their prisoners with more respect than you might think. While no one wants to be in a PoW camp, there were far worse camps to be in Germany, and that's before you think of the Jewish concentration camps or the horrors of the Japanese PoW camps.

Guy explained that the officer who was the driving force behind the mass escape was an upper-class squadron leader called Roger Bushell, and the character closest to him was played by Richard Attenborough in the film. Bushell had been shot down over France, been captured, and already escaped once. He was in hiding in Prague, Czechoslovakia, when the Germans went on a mass hunt after one of Hitler's right-hand men was assassinated in the city. Bushell's hiding place was given up and he was recaptured and ended up in Stalag Luft III. Guy explains that the Czech resistance who were hiding him were executed, but Bushell was sent to another PoW camp. The SS killed whole villages of people they thought were connected to the assassination of Hitler's SS chief, so, Guy argued, Bushell should have known what was waiting for anyone who was caught.

How it was explained to me was that Bushell believed, and convinced his fellow prisoners, that it was their duty to try to escape, but actually, it was the duty of the airmen to avoid capture, not to try to escape once captured. Guy explained that a lot of prisoners thought that these mass escapes weren't the best idea because they caused too much heat, and forced the Germans to act. If it was just one or two at a time, it's just a little leak that they could live with, but if the pipe bursts they have to sort it. He also gave me the impression that a lot of the prisoners in camp had the opinion that they'd done their duty, they'd already ridden their luck because, as airmen, they'd all survived being shot down, and that they would prefer to see the war out in the PoW camp. I can't make a comment about any of that because I've never been in their shoes, but it was 1943 when they were on with the digging, for the escape that went ahead on 24 March 1944. That means they'd been at war for four years already.

Bushell's plan was to dig three tunnels in case one or two of them were found or collapsed. The three were called Tom, Dick and Harry, Harry becoming the longest and the final escape tunnel. It was 104 metres in length, but stopped just short of the treeline they were aiming for. There's a memorial, a gravel trail, showing the length of the Harry tunnel. That's all there is at the site of the camp.

Another thing I learned was how much aid the Germans were allowing into the camp from the Red Cross and the families of the prisoners. For a lot of the time the food wasn't great, but at times the prisoners had better supplies than the guards. Germany was on the bones of its arse, too, the population were poor because so much was being spent on the war effort. The soldiers, many of them not fans of Hitler or the Nazis, could be bribed with Red Cross supplies that were being sent in.

The prisoners had sports days, with loads of equipment, built their own theatre and would put big productions on. The Germans didn't mind because they thought content, distracted prisoners were easier to deal with. The photos of the costumes they made were something else. Because there were obviously no women in the camp, some of the parts required the PoWs to dress in drag. One of the prisoners caught the eye of one of the German soldiers, and made the most of that to his advantage. He talked the German into getting him a camera, saying that the amateur dramatics department, who put all the theatre shows on, wanted to take photos of their costumes and props, and they got one! What they really needed it for was to forge false documents and passports. The lengths they went to were incredible.

While we were in Poland, Guy took me on the actual route through the forest the 76 escapees took to get to the nearby town and railway station. It's hard to imagine how they felt walking in an occupied country. I wondered if they were lulled into a false sense of safety that this was a game. They catch us, we try to escape, and if they catch us again it's a slap on the wrist and back in Stalag Luft with its theatre and aid packages from Britain. But that's not how this escape went, which I'll get to soon.

In Żagań there's a statue of a Triumph motorcycle that as we know had nothing to do with the actual escape and was a piece of fiction, and wasn't filmed anywhere near Poland anyway. There's also a statue of a bear with an interesting wartime connection. The statue shows the bear holding a cannon shell and is a memorial for a real brown bear, called Wojtek. He was bought as a cub by Polish soldiers in Iran, in 1942. Wojtek travelled with the soldiers through the Middle East towards Italy, where they continued to fight. Wojtek saw the soldiers carrying boxes of ammo and, the story goes, started copying them, but, being a bear, he could easily carry more. He also copied them smoking and drinking beer and was taught to salute. The army liked the bear so much they gave him the rank of private and even slept next to him to keep warm. Some people have doubted the story that the bear helped, but there are British eyewitness reports of a bear helping carry ammo. Can you imagine being in the middle of the madness of a battle, turning up at a new camp and they have a bear loading trucks?

Wojtek's military career wasn't over, he was promoted to corporal and the Polish 22nd Artillery Supply Company put him on their badge. After the war, the Polish army division he was part of were stationed in the Scottish Borders until they were demobbed in 1947, and that's how Wojtek ended up seeing out his days in Edinburgh Zoo, with regular appearances on the kids' TV show, *Blue Peter*, dying at the age of 21 in 1963. The bear stuck in my mind, even though I didn't know his story, because someone told me there was a connection to Grimsby. It turns out there's a wooden sculpture of Corporal Wojtek in Weelsby Woods, Grimsby.

Another military historian we filmed with was Phil Froom, an expert on the secret devices that British military intelligence designed and kitted out soldiers and aircrews with. There were fantastic things like uniform buttons that would come to bits and have a compass inside. Another was a plain white hankie that turned into a map when you peed on it.

We filmed that part in the Drakelow Tunnels, near Kidderminster. This was a secret, underground 'shadow' factory built to supply the aero industry. All aboveground factories were at risk from bombing raids, and the British government had been planning these kind of factories since the mid-1930s, already fearing another war with Germany. This one was run by Rover, the car company, and made parts for Bristol and then Rolls-Royce aero engines. It was a massive site, dead impressive.

North One had commissioned a mock-up tunnel, the same dimensions as Stalag Luft III's Harry, so I could recreate digging the tunnel and show how tight it was. I was sliding up and down the tunnel on a little buggy, like a mechanic's roller board that they lie on and roll under a car or truck on. I'd learned, when I was with Guy Walters, that 600 men worked on the three tunnels and they'd nicked 4,000 bed boards to strengthen them. There was always the fear of tunnels collapsing, because they were deep, 9 metres, 30 feet, underground, and fed with air from pumps the prisoners made themselves. They dug naked because, one, it was bloody hot and hard work and, two, so they didn't ruin their uniforms. They were down there digging, shitting and pissing where they worked. I also read that 2,000 pieces of cutlery went missing during the time they were working on the tunnels. If you were a German soldier, wouldn't you think, Hang on, dickheads, why am I ordering another 200 spoons this month? Perhaps they were coming in with the supplies. I know they made the wheels for the trolleys from tins that the powdered milk was sent in in the aid packages. It was tight in the tunnel, but I'd have got stuck in, I think. It'd be summat to do to pass the days.

Guy also explained that they redistributed 4 tons of soil in two hours, without the guards seeing. There was the added difficulty of the dirt being dug out being a lot lighter in colour than the regular top soil so it had to be mixed in or camouflaged somehow, and they managed to 'lose' a load of it under the seating in the theatre. There was so much clever planning and ingenuity involved, but the whole escape was soon to be proven to be a bad idea, like some of the prisoners feared.

Only 3 of the 76 who escaped through tunnel Harry would reach safety, and none of them were Brits, they were two Norwegians and a Dutchman, all pilots. Like some had argued, the size of the escape put too much heat on those trying to escape and most were rounded up soon after the breakout was discovered. The film, *The Great Escape*, is described as a Christmas family favourite, perhaps because of the famous theme tune and memories of Steve McQueen on the motorcycle, but you'd leave the cinema in the mood to slash your wrists. The film ends with recaptured soldiers being executed, machine-gunned in the woods. This isn't how it actually happened, but the order from Hitler was to kill 50 as an example to other PoWs. The SS did it one or two at a time. This was a war crime, and treated as one as soon as the Allies found out about it. These were the Nazis. Who thought it was going to be any different? It wasn't 'The Great Escape', it was 'The Great Mass Murder'.

While the film is American, with American stars, there weren't many Americans left in Stalag Luft III on the night of the escape, and only one took part. The 50 escapees executed were a mixture of British, Australian, Kiwi, Polish, South African, Canadians, Lithuanian, French, Norwegian, Argentinian, Belgian, Greek and Czech.

The camp commandant disagreed with the order, but there was nothing he could do. He was Luftwaffe not SS, and he paid for a memorial to the murdered escapees out of his own pocket. There's a lot more to it than I'm describing here, of course. Bushell, the squadron leader who pushed the plans ahead, felt that any attempt to escape would pull German resources away from the fight and into searching for the PoWs on the run, but Guy Walters didn't agree with that, and there's evidence to show it made bugger all difference, so the 50 who were executed died needlessly. Perhaps that's all with the help of hindsight, but it was a grim end, and definitely not my idea of a feelgood, family favourite.

The date set for the big jump was coming up and we had one more filming day planned in the UK. Just a week before the jump day in Germany, we went to Andy Godbold's place again to test the ramp that his mate, Paul Vickers, had constructed for the job.

The weather was terrible, everything was soaked. Andy rode the Triumph and looked like he was struggling to keep it on two wheels, but everyone was dead keen for me to try this ramp before we went to Germany, so Andy found a length of carpet somewhere. He said we could use it as a run-up, but I was thinking, What are we getting into here? Things were beginning to reek of hospital, but he tried it and it worked, so I didn't have any excuse. I launched about six feet in the air and we were back on track. The carpet worked a treat and I got to the point I was comfortable, so we could start altering the ramp, edging it further from the landing, and putting half a degree into it to make it steeper. If you put me in that position now I think I'd panic, because I haven't ridden a bike that big for well over a year and it looks so much more intimidating than it was. Still, I managed to hurt my ankle that day. The energy of the landing has to be dispersed somewhere, it's a heavy bike, not going very quickly and landing on the flat. If I was going a lot faster the landing would be more gentle because you're dispersing the energy. It's the difference between a plane landing and a plane crashing. I was almost belly flopping. That ankle is becoming the subplot for the whole book.

Andy told me not to take the Honda 450 to Germany because I was used to the Triumph, but I disagreed. I thought it was a new jump, new surroundings, and even though I hadn't been using it to practise on since the Triumph turned up, I wanted to take my Honda 450. I'd been jumping more comfortably on the Triumph than the motocrossers, but I thought I'd be better off attempting the jump for the first time on a bike that's designed to jump, to build my confidence.

I drove out to Bavaria with the 450 in the van, and Triumph took their bike. I went out on the Killingholme freight boat to the Hook of Holland, like I'd done for the Nürburgring, and started on the fair trek out to the Austrian border. The plot of the film is that Hilts, Steve McQueen's character, is jumping into neutral Switzerland, but the location it was filmed in is much closer to Austria. I was listening to Guy Walters's book on audiobook as I drove out.

The TV lot plan every detail of everything we do, pages of notes, plans, insurance up to the eyeballs, experts and fixers at every stage, but things can still go off the rails, and this was one of those times. North One had been dealing with one farmer, let's call him Klaus, who owned the land that *The Great Escape* had been filmed on. The scenery looked exactly the same as it had done in 1962, when McQueen filmed there. Between the TV lot doing the recce and us going to do the jump, it seems that Klaus had sold some land to another farmer who didn't want us jumping into his land. Klaus didn't want to fall out with his neighbour and wasn't willing to budge. The TV lot might have been asking for a few changes, because that's the TV way: want, want, want, want . . . and that was it, the farmer had had enough and he really took the hump. Ewan the director must have been pulling his hair out.

Then the back-pedalling started. We had a fixer, a Geordie called Kevin, and he helped sort the job. As far as I was concerned there was never a risk that the job was off, they'd always get it worked out. I've done enough of these and seen the TV lot deal with problems chucked at them, and they've always ended up solving it one way or another – sometimes there's a bit of palm-greasing. It's what they do, they're professionals, so I never doubted it.

While all that was happening, Channel 4 and Triumph wanted some publicity photos taking so we did that next to a barn that was in the film that's still standing and not looking much different from 57 years ago, except there was a massive pile of manure next to it.

The building of the ramp started a day later than expected, because of Klaus, but the weather was beautiful. It was October, but you wouldn't believe it. Once we'd done all the photos and press stuff, it was time to start practising on the actual jump. I could tell Andy worked in the film world because he wanted nothing left to chance and had a schedule of practice jumps: this height at this time, then we progress to this, we do this, this, and this, and do the final jump ten. I went along with it. At first, anyway.

I got the Honda out because, like I said, it's the bike made to do jumps, and I don't think it was the wrong decision, but every time I jumped I landed like a sack of shit. I was nearly battering my head off the handlebars. I did four or five jumps and stopped for a think. If it's this bad on the 450, what's it going to be like doing a jump this big on the Triumph? I didn't crash, but I was hurting. I don't know what I could've done differently. Andy said I was going too fast, but I thought it would be worse if I was going slower.

I found myself remembering doing the land speed record on the pushbike on Pendine Sands in Wales, the time I was in the slipstream of the racing truck, pedalling at 79mph.

We'd spent a while doing these jumps in the afternoon, and that evening I had a word with Ewan and Andy telling them that this felt like it could end in tears, and I wanted to do the jump once on the Triumph and that was it. I didn't want to do any more building up, starting small and working towards the final big jump. I wasn't being awkward for the sake of it, but I stuck to my guns. Both Andy and Ewan were trying to talk me into doing a five-foot jump, then eight-foot, but I wasn't having it.

When we got the Triumph out I wanted it to be shit or bust and if I crashed, so be it. It was a little bit like the Wall of Death experience. Ken Fox was the Wall of Death expert, but it got to a point where I was the only person who had experience of that bike on that size of wall and I'd become the person to listen to. Andy was by far the most experienced jumper, but I'd done over 500 jumps on that Triumph, I know my body and my limits, and it was time to trust my judgement. All those motorcycle races I've done, making hard moves on roads that don't give you a second chance, and I'm still here. I have to remind myself that I do know what I'm doing. The reason I'm here is because I listen to myself. When it's not right, have a rethink. I wasn't being bull-headed. I'll do it, but I'm only doing it once, because this feels like it's going to shit.

They couldn't really argue. Ewan had made it clear he wanted to wait until the sun was in the right place, for artistic purposes. He wanted to shoot at the same time Bud Ekins had been filmed, so it looked as much like the original as possible. That meant I had to wait until about four in the afternoon. I don't think I've ever felt under more pressure. Neil Duncanson, the boss of North One, was there, John Leyton from *The Great Escape*, and everyone who we'd filmed with was there, all in the one hotel. We had a medic so I had my ankle strapped up. I'm not sure if it helped, but it was a bit of a placebo. I reminded myself that when I'm in certain situations my brain goes into a mode where I can deal with it.

The time came around and I was sat on the Triumph, all ready to go, blue jumper with the sleeves cut off and some chinos to make me look like Captain Hilts. Everything was ready, the weather was perfect, and they had 101 different camera angles covered, because they knew they only had one chance to get it. I rode off, not even looking at the jump, turned around and aimed for it, tootled into it, and cleared the big jump, the one McQueen's character failed to clear in the film. It was a heavy landing, but if they'd have asked me to do it again I would have because it turned out the Triumph was far nicer to land than the motocross bike.

Then it was time for a few celebration photos and thanks to everyone involved. John Leyton looked like he was getting a bit emotional. It must have brought back a lot of memories. He'd been there when the real jump was filmed and so had Klaus the farmer.

Andy had managed to teach me how to jump a motorbike, and I put the effort in and got the job done. I'd have been embarrassed if I hadn't managed, though, because Bud Ekins did it on a 1960s road bike with no helmet.

13

Saturated in Horsepower

EVEN WITH EVERYTHING else going on, the 300mph job was always in my mind. What can I do to go faster? How do I make it more stable? Who can give me some advice? Because there are so few days when the conditions are ideal, I started looking for places other than Elvington that I might be able to use. Through John McAvoy, a mate who writes for *Performance Bikes*, I heard about Cottesmore, in Rutland. Cottesmore was an RAF base, but now it's an army base, so the runway only gets used half-a-dozen times a year for Hercules touch-and-go training. Through John's dad, who was the chaplain for the base in the 1980s, we made contact with Richard Chesterfield, Cottesmore's commanding officer. I'm sure I have heard him called the commandant, but that sounds French and I won't use French words if I don't need to. I won't use the word garage, because there's a British word that does exactly the same as that: shed. Anyway, Richard's the man. He's into bikes, and owns an old BMW GS. He's a big tank man, high up in the

7th Armoured Division, the famous Desert Rats. I love talking to him. With the help of John McAvoy I managed to set up an arrangement where I could use their runway as long as I gave them enough notice, and Richard was on site. I started going there in 2020, with my dad helping me.

In the run-up to a day at Cottesmore, I'd contact John and let him know there looks to be a good window of weather coming up. I'm not usually telling him anything he doesn't know because he looks at the forecasts as much as I do. We look as far as ten days in the future and get a feel for the weather. If it looks good he contacts the army base to see if it's possible for us to run on that day. Nine times out of ten the answer is yes, so we keep an eye on the weather to see if it's improving or the forecast is getting worse. Obviously, I'm not running in the rain, so it has to be a fine day with next to no wind.

I load up the night before and get there for about seven or half-past. I have to sign on at the front gate, then meet Richard in his office. The office looks fairly normal, except there's a shell, an armour-piercing tank shell, on his desk with a depleted uranium core. It's not very big, but it's so heavy because depleted uranium is 59 per cent heavier than lead. We drive out to the runway, unload the bike and get the kettle plugged in. At Cottesmore we have access to a disused pilot's mess that dates back to the Cold War, with badges and plaques of squadrons from all over NATO on the walls. We put a tyre warmer on the back wheel, I don't need one for the front, and fill up the charge cooler tank with antifreeze that I've chilled in a freezer to -20°C.

With John and my dad we have dead-set routine. John meets me at the start, my dad goes to the halfway point, and I just get cracking. Even with the turbo Hayabusa's massively powerful engine, it starts on the button like a regular road bike, though I plug in a starting battery, so I don't drain charge from the two small batteries I have on the bike.

The nerves start once I know I'm going to go fast. Nothing compares to this, not sitting on the start line of the TT, not lining up for the start of the Le Mans 24-hour, nothing.

I just set off like I'm leaving traffic lights in town. It's not a racing start, it's just a smooth getaway. First gear on my bike is like top gear on a normal Hayabusa. This bike is geared for 311mph. It sets off slowly, then finds the turbo, and the engine RPM starts feeling the benefit of the forced induction, then it just goes, and it's accelerating like nothing you've ever experienced.

On a dyno I've seen, realistically, 550 horsepower, with 3 bar absolute boost pressure, but we're struggling to control the boost with the wastegate I currently have and it lifts the head off the barrel, it's making that much power. From data that the on-board system has logged, I've seen, for short spaces of time, 4 bar absolute, so that might be 650–700 horsepower. That's coming from a 1.3-litre engine. When I say 3 bar absolute, that's another of my recently adopted ways of talking about things. An absolute boost pressure takes the atmospheric pressure into account, so at sea level, that is pretty much 1 bar (actually 1013 millibars or 1.013 bar). It doesn't matter if you're pulling 3 bar absolute at sea level or the top of Pikes Peak, the only difference is everything is working that much harder to make 3 bar when the barometric pressure is only 800 millibars, at the top of a Colorado mountain, for instance. It's harder to get the air in the engine because the air density is lower at altitude. Boys talking in psi? I don't want to deal with it. It's old-fashioned, it's gibberish. Imperial? Pounds per square inch? Absolute shite. Things like that annoy me, because there's no sense in those numbers.

So, the Hayabusa has the ability to make over 700 horsepower at the rear wheel, but I don't have the ability to use much more than 550.

I don't want wheelspin, so I'm fighting that with the back brake. I want to be proactively controlling the power with the back brake, so when I'm ready for the power I release the brake and go. If the back wheel spins up suddenly, and I have to close the throttle, it causes a seesaw effect of the transitioning chassis, and affects the traction. If that happens, I've lost shitloads of momentum, and I have to wait for the turbo to spin up again and that's all dead time, the run is gone. Once I'm in the boost, I need to stay in the boost. If I have wheelspin I've buggered it up. I end up in a cycle of closing the throttle and ending in a big trough of torque, which means when I open the throttle I get this big spike of boost. I'm trying to use the back brake as throttle control, which is something I've brought from road racing and I'm not sure if any of the other mile riders do it. This bike makes 400Nm of torque, a standard 186mph Hayabusa makes about 150Nm. You can tame a superbike with the back brake, no problem. I'd ride the back brake all the time at the TT, but you can't with this bike. No chance. I'm just doing what I can to calm it down.

I'd been fast at Cottesmore once, other than that it'd been runs of 250mph. One day I was there with John McAvoy and his mate Michael Rutter, the British Superbike racer, North West 200 legend and multi-time TT winner. They were doing stuff for *Performance Bikes* magazine and let me come along with my bike. I was running a north-easterly direction up the runway, like I normally do, but Rutter, who was riding a Honda RC213V-S, the £137,000 road-legal MotoGP bike, said it felt a lot smoother, less wind turbulence, running the opposite way. I tried that and did 272mph, the fastest I'd been. It wasn't what I thought was the ideal part of the day, because the sun had been up for a while, but we'd fallen lucky with a lull and the conditions were close to perfect. I did another run of 273mph, then 276. I was happy. Richard came and said it was going to stay like this for another hour, so I got the bike back out of the van and tried again, but didn't go as fast again.

On that 276mph run I was only on full throttle for 0.8 of a second. It's not about getting clean gearshifts or wringing the throttle, it's all about getting that bike settled so you can try to use the power. The duty cycle of that wastegate was working to 40 per cent. The wastegate allows unused turbo pressure to escape. So, in effect I was only using about half the potential of that bike, because half of the potential energy is being dispersed through the wastegate rather than going through the turbo. I'm saturated in horsepower, I just need to be able to use it.

On a good run I could be in top gear, that's sixth gear, for 0.2 of a mile. I've never been in a position where I have the throttle on the stop in fifth and on the stop in sixth. When I rode the Honda RC213V-S that Rutter was testing, this ultimate road bike, it was good to ride a bike with the throttle on the stop. It felt like I could be smoking a cigar at the same time. I was thinking, How nice is this?

On the Hayabusa, I'm looking for the cones with the big markers on them to signal the end of the mile, because I have to get it stopped. The one thing I learned early on was you don't sit up. I did once and it nearly got nasty, because sitting up, out of the protection of the screen, at 270mph is a bad idea. How I didn't get blown off the back is a mystery because the wind nearly ripped me off the bike. That would've taken some explaining. I'd been used to normal superbikes. You sit up and your body catches the wind and helps slow you down, as you're on the brakes. Instead, as soon as I cross the line on the Hayabusa, I relax, let everything settle, stay in the crouched position, with the throttle all the way closed, and feed the brakes on to get rid of 100mph. This happens fairly quickly, but you're covering a lot of ground at 270mph, and the end of the runway is 0.7 miles from the cones that mark the end of my measured mile. Once the bike is down to 160–170mph it's just like riding a conventional motorbike, so I can sit up and keep squeezing on the front brakes, hardly using any back brake.

The mile that's just gone by is like nothing I've experienced anywhere else. I feel like I'm repeating myself, but it's worth it because it is so mental. A superbike is quick, but the most longitudinal g-force a modern superbike can exert on the rider is 0.6g, according to tests *Performance Bikes* have carried out, and it does that as it's accelerating between 60 and 80mph. At 120mph my Hayabusa is accelerating with such a force it's exerting 2.2g, 3.5 times as much as the Honda road legal MotoGP bike. Between 220 and 250mph my bike is accelerating as hard as Rutter on the Honda can at any speed, and I'm feeling that same 0.6g he felt hammering the Honda for all it was worth. My turbo bike will do 0–200mph in 10.8 seconds. The Hayabusa isn't acting like you might think a very powerful bike would. It isn't trying to wheelie, it isn't spinning its back wheel and snaking down the runway, it feels like it's trying to bend itself in two. I've never felt anything like it, and find it hard to put into words.

The bike is less responsive than a supersport 600, because the compression is low. With a 600cc supersport bike, like a Yamaha R6, every power stroke is having such a reaction because of the pressure that it's producing above the piston, so when the spark ignites it has a torque effect. But this bike of mine is so lazy, in comparison, because it has 6.5:1 static compression, that's really low. It makes it feel quite lazy until you give it the boost.

Internal combustion engines are either naturally aspirated or forced induction. Forced induction means turboed or supercharged. Naturally aspirated is being fed air and fuel at regular atmospheric pressure. With naturally aspirated engines you've got to make the best of what you've got. The only way to make energy, to get the biggest bang, is to squash the molecules of air and fuel as tight as you can and then light them. You have to get the inlet valve open as early as you can, as high as you can, for as long as you can get away with, to get as much charge into the combustion chamber, and then squash it as much as you can and then light it.

You don't deal with turbocharged engines like that. It's not about how tightly you can squash the air all together in the combustion chamber, because the turbo is already forcing much more in there that it has already compressed. We want to get as much in there as we can. The more air we can get in there, the more fuel we can get in there. So instead of cramming everything into a tiny tight space, you're actually leaving more room by slightly raising the head with a packer, like a thick cylinder base gasket. This is what is meant by low compression.

Cottesmore was a real find, especially as the camp's commander is on side, and it's ideal for testing, but if I could find somewhere in Britain that was a bit longer . . .

14

The World's Fastest Tractor

I GOT THE IMPRESSION JCB were dead happy with the coverage they got from 2017's World War I tank programme. The company were an integral part of the project, going above and beyond to make the whole thing happen, spending a load of time and money on something that wasn't going to earn them any sales, and I was impressed by their enthusiasm. I have done a couple of bits with them since, handing out awards to their engineers at their Staffordshire headquarters, and they'd been good enough to help with some machinery when I needed to shift muck at home. This all led to mid-2018, when JCB got in contact with North One TV about a new programme idea, saying they wanted to break the record for the world's fastest tractor, what did I reckon?

They wanted to use one of their Fastracs. JCB launched this model in 1991, and they've been good at marketing the Fastrac as the fastest road tractor. It's the Fireblade of tractors. If you know the model name of one piece of agricultural machinery, it's

probably a Fastrac. It is clever marketing, because you can spec a Fendt to do the same speed, 60km/h, just short of 40mph, so they're not faster than a modern tractor. If you listen to some folk, you'd get the idea they do 70mph, but they don't. It shows you what difference a good name makes. If they called it the JCB 4000 I bet it wouldn't be as well known.

Fastracs are popular all over the world, and they can do just about everything a regular tractor can do, but round here, Lincolnshire, they're mainly used to pull trailers and for shit spreading. The majority of that job is road work, running from the silage heap to the field, and pulling the shit spreader around the field. It's rare I see a Fastrac doing other field work in Lincolnshire, but it was the ideal thing to use for record breaking. There were a few different records that could all be considered as being legitimate. One was set by legendary Finnish world champion rally driver, Juha Kankkunen, who did a two-way average of 81mph on snow in a Valtra, a Finnish tractor. Then *Top Gear* broke the record with a Chevy V8-powered thing that looked like a tractor, but was an American car with a custom-made kind of tractor body on it. They think they've done it and they have the *Guinness World Records* confirmation that they did 87.2mph, so we had to beat that, even if it was a bit of TV bullshit.

The TV lot edited the programme to add their own bit of bullshit into the mix, but I didn't know this until I came to write this chapter. We knew from the start there had been another top speed record set in America, by Kathy Schalitz from Ohio. Her dad, Dave Archer, had built a tractor that she'd clocked 108.5mph in on a drag strip in Arkansas. The TV programme didn't mention her until much later in the programme, making out we'd only just found out about it to add a bit of drama.

Their tractor was a proper thing, a 1961 Allis-Chalmers D19, an open tractor, powered by a drag-racing V8 engine with a roll cage welded over the driver's seat. Their tractor started as a model with a top speed of 14mph.

The old boy who built it explained he was staying true to the spirit of the tractor' origins. It doesn't have any springs or suspension and he wasn't going to put any on it, because then it would've become a modified tractor. It was very original looking with a few safety elements added. Whether Kathy's speed was in the *Guinness World Records* or not, it was one that needed topping. The JCB job, I soon found out, was at the other end of the technology scale from the Americans'.

On the first day of filming I drove to JCB's impressive world headquarters, in Rocester, Staffordshire, near the Derbyshire border, somewhere I'd been a few times before. I met with Alex Skittery, who was the project leader from the design side, and Alan Tolley, JCB's Group Director for Engines, who had been involved with JCB's big record-breaking effort, the Dieselmax. If anyone was in doubt that JCB could make things go very fast they just had to look at that. Dieselmax is the world's fastest diesel vehicle, setting a record of 350mph at Bonneville in 2008. The streamliner, one of those low-profile, rocket-shaped cars with a tail fin like a jet plane, had two engines from JCB backhoe diggers, both modified to make 750 horsepower each. One powered the front wheels, one powered the back, and they were electronically synchronised. They had the right man behind the controls too: Andy Green, the RAF wing commander who drove Thrust SSC to the outright world record speed, that is yet to be beaten, of 763mph in 1997. This wasn't like some of the records we attempted for the *Speed* programmes, nowt like the pedal-powered airship that was the personal project of one inventor, and failed in the end. When JCB set their minds to something they don't come up short. I was just along for the ride.

Alex and Alan explained the limiting factors of the Fastrac for the cameras. They spoke about aerodynamics, rolling resistance and horsepower, and what needed to change to make the Fastrac do over a ton . . .

They had a designer, Jeremy Dodd, sketching on an iPad-type thing giving a gist of what the Fastrac would look like. It would end up with a front bumper, lower bonnet and lower roof, all to improve the aerodynamics – because it's a big, blunt piece of kit. They also set a figure of 1,000 horsepower and decided they wanted to lose 3 tons off the thing. The sketch Jeremy made looked trick as.

On that same day of filming I took a Fastrac 4000 for a drive around the grounds the Bamford family own, and it was an impressive bit of kit. The Bamford family still privately own JCB, it's not publicly owned with shares on the stock exchange, which is unusual for a company of its size. The B in JCB stands for Bamford, after the founder, Joseph Cyril Bamford, the current Lord Bamford's father. When I got into buying tractors and renting them out, I bought them to do specific potato-cultivating jobs, knowing there would be strong demand for tractors for that kind of work in north Lincolnshire. First, I bought a Fendt, a German tractor that I had been convinced was the Rolls-Royce of tractors, but I had bother with it and swapped to John Deere. I never seriously considered a JCB because they don't make a tractor that can do the job I need a tractor to do.

Although the Fastrac 4000, that the land speed record tractor was based on, is mainly used for road work, it is a universal thing that will pull a baler, the machinery that makes haybales, and it'll do pretty everything except pull a ridge former, because it doesn't have enough horsepower. Ridge forming is part of the profitable work my tractor does. The ridge former is a cultivating tool, it turns the soil and then shapes it for the seed potatoes to be planted. It's a big bit of kit, going on for 6 metres wide, and shifts a lot of muck, so only the most powerful tractors can pull it.

JCB make a bigger Fastrac that is more powerful, but then that won't fit down the 72-inch ridges that the company I work for demand. The 72-inch measurement is within furrows, and the inside of the tyres can't be more than that. So, the small Fastrac 4000-series could be altered to do the potato-field ridge-forming job, but it isn't powerful enough, and the Fastrac 8000-series is powerful enough, but it's too big for the very specific work I do. The company I contract for are concerned that if you're working a field and get to a headland, the edge of the field, and then you have to run back down your ridges, you'd flatten them if you didn't have the 72-inch wheel width. It's a good bit of work I do for that company, so I'm not going to rock the boat, and that's why I ended up with the 350 horsepower John Deere. So, yes, I'm into tractors.

JCB involved another influential British company to help with the record attempt. Ricardo are an engine and transmission development firm based in Shoreham, near Brighton. Their founder, Harry Ricardo, made a load of important breakthroughs in the early days of the internal combustion engine in the 1910s and 1920s, and his designs made leaps and bounds for the efficiency of diesel engines, and he even worked on the Spitfire's and Lancaster's Rolls-Royce Merlin engine during World War II. Visiting their technical centre in Shoreham was fascinating. They had a Mercedes Actros truck, a 235.1. They had it on a dyno, because they knew this 500-and-summat horsepower truck did something special to lower its emissions, and Mercedes are one of their competitors. Ricardo's engineers had wired the truck up to input false GPS data into its engine management system, the truck's brain, to trick it into thinking it was actually driving down a road. They were simulating everything that it would be doing in the real world, changing gears and going up or down hills, to evaluate its benefits. They'd done weeks and weeks of work to understand what was going on inside this truck's high-tech guts. Emissions are Ricardo's big thing, and reducing emissions is where the motor industry is going. What an honour to go down there.

Ricardo also build all the engines for McLaren supercars, including the £750,000 McLaren Senna, and they make the transmission for the Bugatti Veyron that was the world's fastest production car for a while. So, yes, they should be able to help make a Fastrac go quick.

The Fastrac engine is a straight-six, 6.6-litre diesel. It doesn't make a lot of power for an engine that big, only a claimed 235bhp and 950Nm of torque, for the 4220 model. A truck of a similar size would make 500 horsepower and 2,000Nm of torque. To explain, torque is the bedrock, horsepower is the speed between torque events. The torque is the force the piston is coming down. That's the torque event. Horsepower is calculated from the time between torque events.

We filmed a bit where I was introduced to one of Ricardo's engine builders, Shaun Haddrell. They had a Fastrac engine there that we were bolting together, oiling the liners and putting the pistons in. It was just for the camera, because they already had the engine built to go on the dyno. Shaun was using a £20,000 torque wrench. It won't torque a bolt any more accurately than a top-of-the-range Snap-On one, that sells for £450, but it costs that much because it logs what order bolts are tightened in and the history of how the tool was used. I suppose this is important if an engine fails during testing and something needs to be blamed. Was it a component, or was it the person putting the engine together? Shaun was a meticulous engine builder. I'd like to think I am, but that job is not for me, and I don't want a £20,000 torque wrench.

We moved on to watching the tuned Fastrac engine being tested on a dyno. It was like being in a NASA control room. The dyno was an engine type, not a wheel type like I have at home. The engine was out of the vehicle on a test bed, with a load of wires and sensors all over it. The Ricardo engineers spent hours looking at cylinder pressures, making adjustments, all the while checking it wasn't being overstressed. And after all that it made 500 horsepower, much less than the 1,000bhp target because they were being so reserved. Companies like Ricardo and JCB have huge reputations to protect, names they've built up over decades.

I wasn't expecting them to be like me, and be saying, 'Let's wind her on and see what we can get out of her. Let it have it!' That's not the way big corporations work, and I fully understand that, so I wasn't disappointed, or even surprised, that the first dyno runs they showed us had a power output that was only half as much as we had spoken about. I'm dealing with Ricardo and JCB, they're going to get it right. If I went in there with my mindset it would be a bomb scene and I'd be sacked by dinner time.

Just being let in Ricardo was an eye-opener, seeing the lengths they go to with the emissions and trying to find out how the competition do things differently. I didn't know they were that deeply involved in the reduction of emissions, and I'm fascinated by it, because it's using all sorts of small but clever engineering solutions to make improvements. The emissions reduction work is necessary because electric trucks are not realistic, and won't be for a long time. The size of the batteries needed to make torque are too much of a weight penalty.

While we were at Ricardo I got to see a virtual reality version of the land speed Fastrac. Not only had JCB got Ricardo on the case, they had the Williams Formula 1 team helping with the aerodynamics. JCB were investing hundreds of thousands in this, maybe even millions. Ian Turner, the Williams F1 aero expert, was at their headquarters in Oxfordshire, and I was with Ricardo and some of the JCB folk down on the south coast. JCB had used this technology with the WWI tank. You put the virtual reality headsets on and then, in the middle of the room, is a full-size land speed Fastrac, this great thing that you can see with your own eyes. You know you're in an empty room, but your brain is still telling you to step over stuff. Someone presses a button on a keyboard and we're watching how the airstream is going to flow over the vehicle. It's mind-blowing really and I'm sucking up all this new information and techniques, letting it all sink in, then, later, wondering how I can use it to my advantage with my own projects.

This being a TV programme, we had to show as well as tell. You can't just do your research into the best tyres for the job, you have to come up with an entertaining way of showing how you come to the answer, and North One are pretty good at doing that, which is how I ended up at Bruntingthorpe airfield, explaining that we couldn't just go out on the JCB's regular tractor tyres and push them to 100-plus mph.

We had a few different folks with us to help. Dave Jenkins was there with his racing truck. Dave was the driver of the truck I slipstreamed behind when I was pedalling at 112.9mph on Pendine Sands and I've kept in touch with him since then. We're both sponsored by Morris Lubricants, so I see him at some of the stuff I do for them. He's a dead knowledgeable bloke with a fair pair of hands on him. He can turn his hand to owt. He had a blast around Bruntingthorpe, this former airbase that's used for speed testing and filming. His truck showed the high-speed environments and forces specialist truck tyres could put up with. James Brighton, a professor of automotive engineering from Cranfield University, was there to explain how technology from them could be used for the Fastrac. He explained the concerns: speed rating – the tyre has to be constructed to cope with the speed it's going to be rolling at. Go too fast on a particular tyre, and it will either fling the rubber off the carcass or the tyre will blister, then blow out, possibly resulting in me, and the world's most expensive tractor, barrel rolling across the landscape. When we did the world's fastest van thing at Bonneville, Pirelli shaved most of the tread off the tyres to make them nearly bald, so there was less mass of rubber, and less centrifugal force when the thing gets up to speed. The physics of centrifugal force makes the tyre want to chuck the tread off the carcass.

To show the direction we didn't want to go in we also filmed a section with Swamp Thing, a monster truck owned by Tony Dixon. It has its own artic truck to transport it around the country, but Tony has to take the wheels off it to get it in the back of the truck. It's a right pantomime.

The monster truck's tyres were massive, and were an example of how not to choose a high-speed tractor tyre. There were a couple of scrap cars brought onto the end of the runway for Tony to drive over. He fired over the cars, jumped in the air and landed cocked off to one side with all the weight of this thing on one back wheel. I was sure he was going over, but he wasn't worried in the slightest. The tyre deformed so much that the wheel rim hit the ground and chipped a fist-sized chuck of concrete out of the runway. You wouldn't be long getting it wrong in that thing.

I never really had an opinion on monster trucks, it's more of an American thing, but they didn't have to ask me twice to have a go. Where else am I going to get chance to drive one? The whole experience is a shock. First the noise. Holy moly, it was the loudest thing I've ever been in. Too loud! It's a big American V8 engine, running on methanol to make huge, explosive power. The gearing's very low, giving it brutal acceleration, and it has four-wheel steering.

It does 56 metres to a gallon. That's 29 gallons per mile, if you were wondering. I had a go at driving over some cars. I just did what they told me. I wasn't scared because I knew it could be done. Do it like this and it'll happen, and it did. You can't see where you're going, you're so high up, and by the time the front wheels are coming into contact with the cars I was about to drive over they were in a blind spot.

The last bit of the tyre section was with this heavy-bastard aeroplane tyre. These can cope with speeds up to 300mph and can deal with however many tons of jumbo jet landing on them, but they weigh too much for what we need.

JCB didn't need us to tell them any of this, of course. They know what they're doing, and got an Indian company called BKT to make some special tyres. Between them, they specified a compound, that's the recipe of the black bit of the tyre, that had a higher content of natural rubber mixed with the synthetic rubber to give improved grip. The finished tyres were double steel belted and only grew 2mm at top speed. That is impressive.

We weren't done with brutally powerful stuff, and we found it at an unexpected place, the tractor-pulling arena at the Great Eccleston Show, near Preston. I'd been lined up to meet the Whittinghams, Kevan and his son Josh. Me, Shazza and Dot went, parked up and rode our pushbikes into this country fair, and, as normal, I hadn't done any research beforehand, so while I'd heard of tractor pulling, I didn't know much about it. I didn't know it was how far you could pull a sledge. I knew nowt about all the engineering that was involved, the size of the turbos, the number of turbos, and that it was a big thing in Europe.

Kevan showed me around his beast of a tractor, Snoopy 4. It's powered by two Rolls-Royce Griffon aircraft engines. Like the Rolls-Royce Merlin engines, they were used in Spitfires, the Griffon being used later, from MkXII onwards. Like the Merlin, the Griffon is a V12 that is twin-stage, twin-speed supercharged, but the Griffon's displacement is 36.7-litre, 10 litres bigger than the Merlin. The Whittinghams' tractors, Snoopy 4 and Snoopy 2, had a pair of these massive engines each, and I was going to race them.

A big difference between them was the fuel that they ran on. Josh's Snoopy 2 ran on regular petrol, while Kevan's Snoopy 4 ran on alcohol. That meant Kevan's tractor made 8,000 horsepower, compared to a paltry 7,000 horsepower from his son's.

You struggle to measure that much horsepower, so it's a bit of guesswork. You can measure it with a strain gauge, a solid bar of steel with a sensor on it – the sensor tells you how much the engine is twisting the bar as the amount is invisible to the naked eye, but they can calibrate it and equate the twist to horsepower. It's how they measure the power output of Top Fuel drag-racing cars, and they can make as much as 11,500 horsepower.

Whether it's an educated guess or not, it was a fuck-load of horsepower. It's the equivalent of eight F1 cars. Eight F1 cars with one steering wheel, and my hands on it. These things are mental and they're racing at a country fair in Preston, with people having their Scotch eggs and cheese sarnie picnics along the side of the strip. I loved it. There's so much that can go wrong, due to the amount of boost that's running through these engines, but it seems that health and safety haven't quite caught up with them yet.

Unlike drag racing, which is all about the time it takes to cover the course, tractor pulling is about distance. The course is 100 metres long and it's how far the tractor can pull the sledge. The sledge looks like a low-loader trailer, on wheels, and has a wedge that digs in the dirt. As soon as the tractor starts moving, a weight on the sledge slides forward and causes the wedge to dig in. The further it's pulled the more the wedge digs in. If more than one tractor covers the 100-metre distance more weight is added to the sledge for the next round.

The Whittinghams spent a few minutes giving me the basics, then I'm in, strapped into the driver's seat. I had to get into race mode, forget all the TV shit, I'm listening to you boys. I knew when it got to that stage I had a very pragmatic approach, I just do as I'm told. They're trusting me with these machines, so they have the faith I can do it. You can't spend time fannying into it, you've just got to go.

I had my feet on two clutch pedals, pressing as hard as I could on them. They're pushing back, and as the revs rise, it gets to the point you can't keep the pedals pressed any longer, so you get off the pedals and on the power. The clutch pressure is from a centrifugal force, the more you rev it, the more clutch pressure there is. These tractors have a hand throttle, like my John Deere, not a foot throttle like a car.

As the revs rise the earth is moving and I've never felt anything like it. Raw power. But it all goes to plan. When you're flat out, don't back off the throttle, because that'll break summat. On the first run, in Josh's slightly less powerful tractor, I had to steer it with the brakes because it was veering off slightly. You apply one brake to steer it one way, or the other brake to steer it the other direction. The thing is making so much horsepower it's going to overcome the brakes, but they just give it a bit of a suggestion to keep going straight and not plough into the crowd.

Kevan was happy with how I coped, so I was trusted to have a go in Snoopy 4, and this was the run that was shown in the programme. I was sat on the line, the thing idling, just trying not to stall it or do anything stupid. Then I get the signal to wind the throttle on, while still holding the clutch down, until the revs are getting to a certain level and the centrifugal bob weights are creating the force to push the pedals up. Then it's go! Noise, flames, angriness. And don't back off.

The engines have massive air intakes on the front to feed the superchargers, and 8,000 horsepower is consuming roughly 800,000 litres per minute. From what I've read on the internet, a normal shape hot-air balloon contains 2–3 million litres of air. So Snoopy 4, if it were running at full blast, would suck, squeeze, bang and blow a hot-air balloon's worth of air in less than three minutes. The amount of methanol that two 37-litre supercharged V12 engines are sucking through takes some believing, too, something like 14 gallons in a few seconds. It must have cost hundreds to do that run.

Even with this massive weight digging in, Snoopy 4 was still motoring along. The barrier at the end of the strip was coming up fast. Right at the end of the run, something felt a bit strange, so I let off the throttle. The tractor wouldn't move when they tried, so they had to crane it off the track. It wasn't anything I'd done wrong, but when you have that much torque, shit happens, and it had sheered the differential pinion, part of the transmission that shares the power between the back wheels. Obviously that component has its hands full, dealing with that power, that torque and that weight.

The Whittinghams were great people, all the tractor-pulling lot were, and I loved it. I felt lucky getting a chance to watch it, never mind getting to drive one of them.

Back at the JCB factory they were concentrating on reducing the Fastrac's weight; they wanted to lose 3 ton, the equivalent of a couple of modern Minis. I visited to do a bit of work with Phil Price. I knew Phil from the World War I tank job, he does a lot of the prototype stuff, and he was building a fabricated front axle, replacing the heavy-duty cast one the standard Fastrac has. He says he was pleased with my welding, but half the trick of that job is having your tackle set up, and he did that, all I had to do was pull the trigger.

JCB weren't messing, they'd committed to the project, it was their idea, so they weren't trying to fit it in among other stuff, and, a few weeks later, in June 2019, we met at Elvington in Yorkshire to try to break the record. It's where I first rode my turbo Hayabusa.

This was the first time I saw the finished Fastrac in the flesh and it was an absolute work of art. It's the quality of an F1 car, and there was the equivalent of an F1 team there fettling it. Loads of JCB mechanics, and all the fellas who'd worked on the project, plus three Ricardo blokes setting the engine boundaries throughout the day.

I hadn't been there long when I was handed my bright JCB yellow fireproof racing suit. No one would miss me on a dark night. I wasn't going to ask, 'Any chance I can keep that?'

The strength of any Fastrac is how easy they are to drive and this one, even with a big turbo and loads more power, wasn't much different. It was explained, and it was no surprise to me, that Ricardo wanted to build up the power and speed. It wasn't going to be shit or bust, they had to keep hold of the lead. I climbed into the cab and took it for a few laps of the apron, getting used to the feel of the thing. Alex, the project leader from JCB, was on the radio telling me he thought I had to slip the clutch more, I didn't have to be as gentle with it as I was being. The gearing is much higher than a regular tractor, to reach the top speed, but it has so much torque that you just put your foot down and it goes. Then I realised I had to murder the clutch to raise the revs to get the engine to start making boost. The clutch is oil cooled, so it can take it.

After a quick look at the engine data, I was told to take it down the runway. I was pressing my foot to the floor, but they were only allowing me to have the power that they feel comfortable with. They're restricting the power output with ECU maps, the programme within the engine control unit that controls ignition timing and fuelling, and limiting the turbo boost to protect the engine as they're monitoring it. The most important thing was for this engine to be 100 per cent reliable. Having the world's most expensive Fastrac shit itself all over a North Yorkshire airfield was not in the script.

It was dead manageable to drive and I kept doing runs until the rain came, so we had to wait for the track to dry before we went for the record. By the end of the day, if I remember rightly, the power had been increased to 800bhp, still short of the 1,000 horsepower target.

The track surface was a bit damp, but nothing to worry about with those tyres. I set off, giving the clutch some abuse, and just aimed it up the runway, with the JCB bods following in a Ford Focus RS. It was a decent run, so they said head back to do the return, the specified two-way record run. I just turned around at the end, like you would in a regular car, and drove back, no stress, no drama, especially compared to some of the records. And, I think, that suited JCB and Ricardo. They wanted it to be very business-like.

Two miles later I pulled over, and everyone is all smiles. Prav Patel, the adjudicator from *Guinness World Records*, who I've met a few times before, hands over the certificate: two-way average of 103.642mph.

On the TV show, that I haven't seen but I have been told, this is where a bit of bullshit was stirred in, because I was shown back in my workshop, where it's made to look that I've just found out about Kathy and her record, the one we knew about all along. We did a bit of FaceTime or a Zoom call or whatever and just had a chat about her, the old Allis-Chalmers tractor and the record. She told us the story of travelling to Arkansas. She knew what she was doing, good to talk to, a regular farmer's daughter driving a proper tractor with a dragster engine. It turns out she's from a family of tractor pullers, competing in the kind of events I drove the Snoopys at.

The programme was edited to look like we learned about the record there and then, meaning we had to get the gang back together and go break her top speed of 108.5mph, even though that was the plan all along, break all the records, official or unofficial.

Right at the beginning, when I first heard about this project, I was told Lord Bamford said he wanted this Fastrac to break 200mph, and that it was meant to happen in America. There was talk of doing it at the Kennedy Space Center, and the whole idea of the project was to help JCB raise their profile in America and sell more Fastracs. Even though the majority of the tackle the American military use in the desert is JCB, the company want to make more of a dent in the civilian market. The plan changed along the way, and we ended up at Elvington, where we returned to increase the record in October 2019.

The land speed Fastrac had been developed further. The second version has a bigger turbo and an electric supercharger to fill in the turbo lag. It had more aero, an undertray – to smooth the air flow under the vehicle; a rear diffuser – a type of spoiler on the bottom of the back of the tractor; a smaller cab and a massive charge cooler. They were pushing 5 or 6 bar of boost through that engine at this point, so compressing that much air, making it six times more dense than atmosphere, creates loads of heat. That rise in temperature is the waste product you don't want, and the downside of that increased temperature is a lack of efficiency. This charge cooler, that they filled with bags and bags of ice, could reduce the temperature by 240°C, a massive drop in temperature from the turbo to the inlet, which is what you want. The turbo pulls air in from the atmosphere, compresses it, then pipes it into a chamber in the charge cooler. The charge cooler is just a heat exchanger, like a car's radiator, but it's taking heat out of the compressed air coming from the turbo, transferring it into the icy water in the charge cooler system.

There was a bit of hanging around, and I had my Hayabusa with me because I knew the conditions were going to be ideal. I'd been told I could have a run on it, but on the day no one was keen on letting me ride it, and I understand, but I was ready to go on the bike. They had Tom from the TV lot have a word with me because he's so nice that they knew I couldn't have an argument with him about it. It was a shame, because it was one of those rare handful of hours per year that were perfect, and I was ready to go fast.

We were there all day, building up, more boost every time, just like the previous time. There was a button on the gear lever that allowed me to talk on the radio to them if there were any numbers on the dash that I didn't like the look of. I'd set off in second gear and got up to fifth, top gear. With the smaller turbo it wouldn't pull top gear, but this time it would. The gearing was the same, and I was revving it hard, slipping the clutch to get the revs a bit closer to the boost when I fully let off the clutch.

I wasn't nervous in the slightest. I felt protected because I was in this tractor, and only two or three weeks before I'd done 276mph on my bike on that same airfield, so I wasn't out of my comfort zone driving a tractor faster than anyone had tried. That thing's not getting blown off course.

As we got towards the end of the day I start braking as late as I dare to allow me to keep accelerating for the longest possible time. JCB had fitted a parachute on it by now, but I couldn't imagine that was going to make much of a difference when stopping the thing.

By late afternoon, one of the Ricardo men speaks to the JCB bods and decides this will be the last run, they don't want to increase the power any further.

I went for it and we were travelling at a fair old speed for a tractor. Alex Skittery, the project leader, was following in a Ford Focus RS, and it gets to the point he couldn't keep up.

We do a two-way average of 135mph, and a peak speed of 153.77mph. Yer man from *Guinness World Records*, Prav, is there again, blazer on, handing out another certificate, and everyone's happy.

I'm happy for them, but I know that anyone could get out of their manual car or van, be given five minutes instruction in the tractor and know how to drive it. It has a conventional, three-pedal set-up. The only thing I did differently was letting the thing settle for a second between getting off the throttle and getting hard on the brakes. So there are no big movements, no big spikes of torque or braking, just a bit of mechanical sympathy. But it goes to show how the quality of engineering and design mean that a 1,000 horsepower tractor, shifting at 150mph, is no harder to drive than a fast Audi or BMW. They didn't need me for this record. Their test driver could've done it. Everything up to the last few mph of the 153mph run had been done the day before I turned up by their test driver. He is a sound lad, and he's probably a bit pissed off that I came in and got the glory. To be clear, I'm not dismissing anything JCB did, the opposite, the Fastrac was so good you could stick anyone in it.

As far as I was concerned the record was never in doubt. If a company of JCB's might can't break the record, what are we doing? I can imagine Kathy Allis-Chalmers's is more aerodynamically efficient than the Fastrac, because it's a smaller thing. And they put it on the drag strip, so they had loads of grip, but they didn't have professors consulting on the tyres or virtual reality CFD simulations – that's computational fluid dynamics to see how gasses or liquids flow over and around the tractor. I'd have been embarrassed if we hadn't beaten it. I can appreciate both approaches, but my default way is probably closer to what Kathy and her dad did, because I'm a man who works in a shed. It's an honour for me to be involved with JCB. They're a great company, big employer, big exporter, and I learned plenty.

15

Don't Worry, Mr Biaggi, We've Got This Bloke from Grimsby Now

IT'S INTERESTING WHAT DOORS the Triumph streamline job in 2015 opened for me. I'd got that opportunity because they knew I was half-handy on a bike, and I wasn't easily scared, the TT and road-racing job proved that, and it didn't hurt that the TV lot would film it. Triumph always said that wasn't the reason they chose me, but I'm not daft enough to think it wasn't a big part of it.

That experience led to my own 300mph job, and spending time at airfields like Elvington. While I was there, I got talking to a man called Alex Macfadzean. He used to race sidecars at the Isle of Man TT and in grands prix. He's an engineer and a mad-keen land speed record (LSR) enthusiast. Alex is building 52 Express, a streamliner, like the Triumph, a fully enclosed two-wheeler, but instead of using traditional motorcycle engines, like Triumph, Ack Attack and the Bub Streamliner, it's powered by a Rolls-Royce

Gem gas turbine engine from a Westland Lynx military helicopter. It drives the back wheel via a Kevlar belt. It's called 52 Express because former World Superbike champion and MotoGP rider James Toseland was lined up to be behind the handlebars of it, and 52 was his race number. I'm not sure what happened with Toseland, but now Alex wants me to ride it.

It's been a long-term project, and a proper labour of love, not a business. The space frame is built, I've sat in it at Alex's workshop, but there's still a lot to do. The target for the 52 Express is 400mph. Alex has experience with turbine-powered LSR vehicles. He helped land speed legend Don Vesco and worked on the Turbinator, a helicopter turbine-powered four-wheel streamliner, that did a two-way average speed of 458mph at Bonneville. I'm not sure when it'll be ready to turn a wheel, but it should be interesting.

Another opportunity the Triumph job led to started with a call from a man called Gildo Pallanca Pastor. He owns Venturi, the French electric vehicle company. Venturi have been around since the twentieth century, making supercars that looked a bit like 1990s Ferraris. When they went bankrupt in 2000, Gildo bought the name and whatever was left, then focused on developing electric vehicles. They made handfuls of electric supercars, but they seem to want to push the boundaries of what electric vehicles can do, rather than become a manufacturer, and they have made more headlines with their electric-powered challenges. One was driving from Shanghai to Paris in a Citroën Berlingo van converted to electric power. Another was a 3,600-mile road trip through Africa, again in a Venturi electric-powered Berlingo. I came across them at Bonneville when Venturi were attempting to break the electric land speed record in the VBB-3 streamline four-wheeler, built in conjunction with Ohio State University, and funded by Venturi. Again, it doesn't look anything like a car, it's more like a half-scale Japanese Bullet train or a fighter jet with its wings pulled off. Gildo was there in a six-wheel Mercedes G Wagon that was, I was told, bulletproof. I didn't get to speak to him, he was just the person who'd drive past in this daft six-wheeler with blacked out windows.

I knew about the Venturi streamliner because I'd been reading about it for years in *Race Engine Technology* magazine. Venturi had set a few different records, and were originally running a streamliner powered by a hydrogen fuel cell, then went to electric. When I saw it at Bonneville, I think it had 1–1.5 megawatts, something like 2,000 horsepower. Then I read somewhere they got 2.2 megawatts from it, roughly 3,000 horsepower. It raised the outright speed record for an electric vehicle to 341mph. Fast, no doubt, but way off what Vesco did with the Turbinator, powered by a 1980s helicopter turbine.

Anyway, Gildo had also bought a bankrupt French motorcycle company, Voxan, and set about promoting them as a record-breaking electric bike company. One of his people contacted Andy Spellman asking if I would be interested in riding the Voxan electric land speed bike they were developing. MotoGP star, and former arch-enemy of Valentino Rossi, Max Biaggi was going to ride it, but we got the gist he didn't seem that committed to it, so they'd got rid of him and wanted me to ride it instead. Spellman mentioned the TV job and all that, and they weren't interested. It seemed like they wanted me for me, not the TV.

Come to Monaco, they said, have a word with the engineers, see what the bike is all about, and you can be part of the process. A flying visit was set up, in and out in one job.

Me and Spellman flew to Nice, in the south of France, got picked up, and were driven to the headquarters in this beautiful building in Monaco. We were taken up to this big, open-plan office, with fancy art and bits of racing car on the wall, and the place had a sea view. Everyone knows how much rents are in Monaco and this place was bloody impressive.

It turns out Gildo's family, the Pallanca Pastors, are the second most important family in Monaco, after the royal family. His mother was head of the family property business. Reports say they own 15 per cent of all the property in Monaco, and their companies are worth as much as €20 billion, earning enough to give Gildo and his older half-sister, Sylvia, €500,000 pocket money per month, according to newspapers.

But, and this is the biggest of all buts in the book, his mother, Hélène, was murdered in 2014. She'd been to visit Gildo in hospital after he'd had a stroke, and when she left the hospital his mother and her chauffeur were shot dead. It came out that Sylvia's other half, a bloke called Wojciech Janowski, had paid his fitness instructor to kill the billionaire. Half-a-million euros a month wasn't enough for him. Sylvia was questioned, but the police decided she knew nothing about it. It's like something out of a film.

So, that's why they can have such an expensive headquarters. It felt like a money-no-object operation, much different to most of the motorcycle stuff I've been involved with.

We met all the people involved in the record attempt, and saw all these amazing CAD drawings and CFD and FEA. That's finite element analysis, another complicated computer programme that helps show the different forces, and their effects, on the machine. FEA is used to confirm the components are strong enough; in this case it would be the frame, steering and suspension. You want them to be just strong and stiff enough to do the job you've given them, not over-engineered, adding unnecessary weight to the bike. The bike would have a really trick hub-centre-steering system for the front wheel, not regular forks.

We went down in a lift to see the Voxan in progress, and for me to have a sit on the frame. There wasn't much in the workshop, but there was enough to show they weren't messers. They had this electric vehicle, on caterpillar tracks, that they plan to drive to the South Pole for another of their missions. Venturi also run a Formula E team, the F1 of electric vehicles, with drivers including Felipe Massa, an 11-time F1 race winner, driving for them. Venturi use Mercedes powertrains, and me and Spellman put two and two together and decided that Mercedes might be supplying the power for the Voxan record bike. I might have that wrong, so don't sue me if I have, it was just our guesswork on the plane home. I didn't meet Gildo in person, he was in New York where he lives, but I did speak to him because he was on a telly call with us while we were at the headquarters.

I was keen. They were keen, explaining that they'd want me for 60 days of the next 12 months, and that made me wonder what we'd be doing for all those days a year? They had a plan: testing here, testing there, days in the wind tunnel. Sixty days? I'm trying to get on with my own shit here. With the TV, the farming job and doing my own stuff, tuning a few engines for friends, I think I've got the balance about spot on now, but I was still up for it.

Spellman put the deal together, quoting a vast amount of money, and they went for it. I was happy because I thought I'd learn stuff that might help me with my cause, the 300mph Hayabusa, and the project was interesting on its own with clever folks on the job. Spellman told me later that Gildo wanted me to attend a fancy function in Monaco to meet Prince Albert. Can you imagine that?

Gildo flew to England in a private jet and met up with Spellman again. We agreed terms, and things happened quickly. Within days they said I was needed in Germany the next week, spending time on the work-in-progress bike doing research into aerodynamics. This was only a week or so after the meeting in Monaco. Stuff was shifting.

The most advanced wind tunnel in the automotive world is the TGR, Toyota Gazoo Racing, wind tunnel in Cologne. Even F1 teams, who own their own wind tunnels, rent time in the TGR tunnel. And the Voxan project were in there. That says something, doesn't it?

They offered to fly me over, but I told them not to worry, I like driving. My mate Bill used his freight account to get me on the boat out of Killingholme. I always use this when I can, because the freight boat is cleaner, has loads better food, the folk on it are quieter, and it's only a 15-minute drive from home to the dock. You can't book on that ferry as a normal person, you have to be a freight operator, so I was the only van on with all these trucks. I'd much rather drive out than rely on someone picking me up from the airport and dropping me off. It's a lot of time sat in the van and I was already thinking, This won't be 60 days, we'll rattle through this. It turned out I was half-right. I wouldn't be working on the project for anything like 60 days . . .

The bike had a version of its aerodynamic fairing, but no engine in it, because we're just checking the aerodynamic drag. The fairing was a model, not the carbon-fibre final version, but a rapid prototyped thing that would help answer their questions. It answered one almost immediately. As soon as I climbed onto the bike I realised I wasn't the best fit. The Voxan is what's described as a sit-on bike, which is how land speed racers talk about them to differentiate them from streamliners. I suppose you could say the bike looked like a comic book version of a regular motorbike, something Batman might ride. Totally impractical for anything but going fast in a straight line.

The bodywork was designed to allow the rider to tuck their foot and leg in the gap between the end of the front fairing and the start of the enclosed rear section. It was tight and I couldn't get my legs into the gaps in the bodywork. They've designed it for Max Biaggi and I'm a few inches taller, broader and, it's obvious now, I have longer legs.

We spent a day in the wind tunnel, with a jet of air blowing over me, smoke added to the air so it could be photographed and analysed, and the figures they were seeing were not what the CFD analysis said they should be getting. It's all pointing at me being too big for it. I talk to the engineers about trimming the fairing back to let me squeeze my legs in, not there and then, but for the first test. They haven't made the fairing yet, this is still the prototype. It only needs small adjustments, it seems like to me, at least.

It was probably a couple of weeks later Spellman called me to say they didn't want me, they had Biaggi back on it. Maybe they just used me as the flux to get their original rider to commit to it again: 'Don't worry, Mr Biaggi, we've got this bloke from Grimsby now.' Will we ever know if that was the plan all along? Probably not. Am I bothered? Not really.

The next thing I heard about the project was when they did 254mph at an airfield at Châteauroux airport, France. When I saw it I thought, Holy moly! How have they done that so early on? I was impressed. The headline speed of 254mph, that Venturi/Voxan quoted in their press release and on their website, really caught my attention, but I have to admit I was sceptical about what they were claiming. I'm not saying they are talking shit, because the FIM, the Swiss-based Fédération Internationale de Motocyclisme, have reported it too, and they're the ones who confirm the records, but I'm looking at the facts I've seen reported and something doesn't add up.

Their website lists nine records, both newly established and existing ones they broke. They are for a mixture of distances: quarter-mile, kilometre and mile.

They set standing start and flying start records. Flying start is using space to accelerate up to speed before the bike crosses the start line, with the exit speed set as the bike exits the set distance.

So, this 254mph is a flying start, quarter-mile, on a 2.17-mile runway. You'd use a mile or so to get up speed, enter the quarter-mile, then have just short of a mile to stop. If it's easy to stop in the distance you've allowed, you'd keep moving the measured quarter-mile back to give yourself more run-up.

To set a few different records, the team ran the Voxan unfaired and partially faired, but didn't set any records with the full fairing, perhaps because of the wind. Because they didn't fit the fairing, I would have fit on it after all.

To be an official world record, the speed is an average of two runs in opposite directions, completed within two hours of each other, so if there's a hell of a tailwind one way, running into the wind evens out the advantage.

But the 254mph speed stuck out to me because it's close to what I do on the Hayabusa. The best I've done in a mile is 276mph at Cottesmore. As we'll get on to in a bit, I went faster at Machrihanish, but I was running a course that was slightly longer that one mile. I'm doing that from a standing start, while the Voxan did 254 from a flying start, but I know what's involved.

The runway at Machrihanish is about the same length as the French one they used, so 254 is more than possible, but the Voxans don't seem to be accelerating anything like as fast as my Hayabusa is. I've got it all on to get up to 254mph, their reported speed, and get on the brakes to stop before the end. Perhaps they have the electric motor programmed to brake like hell, because the Voxans don't even have front brakes, they were designed to break records on salt flats.

They set a record for one mile, from a standing start, exactly what I'm trying to do with my Hayabusa. Biaggi and the Voxan set a record for their class of 138.81mph, a two-way average, remember. They also set a standing start kilometre record, which is stated as

119.2mph. A kilometre is 0.62 miles. So, in an extra 0.38 miles they've only added 19.5mph. No one would think that was rapid acceleration.

From that you'd say, with no other information available, that once the Voxan's speed is above 120mph, the rate of acceleration has dropped right down. So how do they find another 115mph on a runway they report is 2.17 miles long? How are they getting up to 254mph and stopping before they skid off the end of the runway?

I'm doing 230mph in half a mile, from standing starts, then struggling to add another 40 or 50mph on the top speed in the second half-mile.

Their two-way averages for the kilometre records are loads slower than my half-miles (and a half-mile is shorter than a kilometre, so they had longer to accelerate). The two-way average might have really ruined it for them. They only had to break the standing records and they did that easily. Perhaps they were running 250mph in one direction and they only did 15mph on the return run. That would explain it, wouldn't it?

They were great people and I wish them all the best. I would have loved to have been a part of the project.

16

It Got a Bit *Top Gun*

WHEN I TURNED DOWN the chance to learn to fly a Spitfire, for the TV job, it sounds like 1 wasted a once-in-a-lifetime opportunity, but that alone isn't enough to make me want to do something. At the time I thought I'd done too much filming, that we were flogging a dead horse, and that alone made me say, Thanks, but no thanks. The one or two friends who found out about the decision couldn't believe I'd passed up the opportunity to not only learn to fly, but to be paid to do it, and in what is one of the most famous aircraft of all time, but if my heart's not in it, then I'm not interested. I went back to the truck yard instead.

Things change, and the TV lot know that too, so years later they came with a similar idea to see if I was interested this time. This one would concentrate on the Battle of Britain, specifically the Hurricane fighter plane and its role in the war. They explained it wouldn't be just a case of being trained to fly it, they'd want me to get to the point where I was able to dogfight in it. It felt a bit familiar, not just because of the Spitfire idea they'd put to me, but

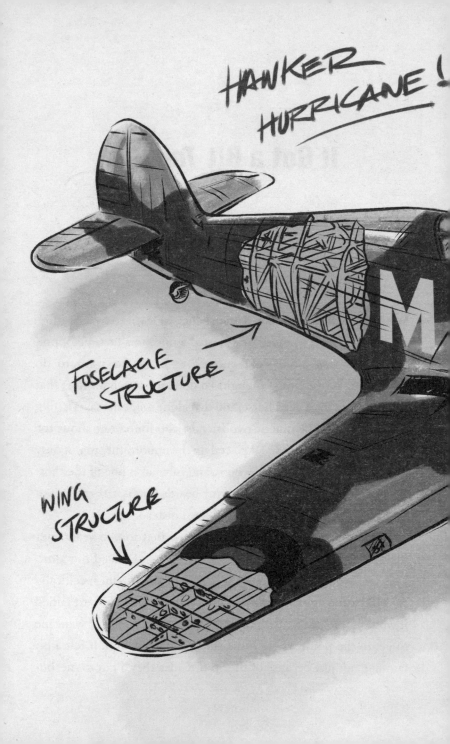

because it was planes and World War II. A bit of me wanted to say, Have we not done this idea to death? I wonder about some British people's obsession with the war. Is it because it was the last time we were great? It was vital that Britain made a stand when it did, but some people still want it to define us now, 80 years later. I'm not like that. There was a lot of pain felt, and lives lost, but how many other countries in the world are doing as many primetime shows about war as we do?

The main thing that had changed, and why I said yes, was the effect COVID-19 and the lockdown was having on everything. All of 2020's plans, programmes and trips had been cancelled, because they all involved foreign travel, and I wanted to stick to my part of the bargain of doing my agreed number of filming days a year. We were supposed to be going to Cuba, and doing another thing in America, and this was the only idea they had that gave us a chance of making the kind of programme we wanted to make while lockdown was on. At that point no one had an idea what was going to happen, how long it would last, and I doubt many people thought it would drag on for over a year, so I was up for making the best of a bad job. And, whatever I think, I get told people still watch and like the programmes.

Another thing that revived my interest in doing another World War II-related programme was meeting Squadron Leader George 'Johnny' Johnson, the last surviving member of the Dambusters raid, and a fellow Lincolnshire man. The meeting was arranged by the TV lot, and I'm not sure if they had a programme in mind for it at that time, but you don't turn down the chance. He was 98 when we met – it was before lockdown, because we met at the old people's home where he lives. Some of the stories he had were great, and all his marbles were there. He's still alive as I write this, a few months away from his 100th birthday.

That was it, I was on board. I'd learn a bit more; whether it stuck in my brain or not was another matter. I'd get to fly a few different old planes, and I'd use my words to explain what it's all like. And hopefully that's what I did. What sane person wouldn't want to do that?

Like I said, the core of the programme was the Battle of Britain. We know these famous moments: D-Day, Dunkirk, the Battle of Britain, but I'm not sure everyone knows where they fell in the 1939–45 war. My knowledge was cloudy before we started all this. Germany invaded Poland on 1 September 1939, and two days later Britain and France declared war on them. The Germans quickly spread through the Netherlands, Belgium and France. The evacuation of Dunkirk happened at the end of May 1940, when the British forces that were in Europe were forced back over the Channel. This was only a few weeks after Churchill had become prime minister.

In July 1940, the Germans were tightening the screws. After marching through Europe, they were within sight of England. They were targeting supplies coming in by sea, sinking shipping convoys, then stepped up the offensive with waves of air raids, aimed at destroying the runways, airfields and aircraft on the ground, trying to force Britain, and its allies, to negotiate a truce. They changed their tactics to bombing factories and then cities. Historians write that the Battle of Britain lasted nearly four months, from 10 July until 31 October 1940. During that 112 days, the Luftwaffe lost 1,897 aircraft and 2,662 aircrew; the RAF lost 1,023 aircraft and 537 aircrew. That's an average of 26 planes and nearly 29 men per day. The German losses, and the British resistance, were enough for Hitler to postpone his plans for the invasion, but the Luftwaffe raids didn't stop on 31 October, and the Blitz continued until the middle of May 1941. Hitler had planned all this, back in 1939, and everything had happened pretty much as he wanted, so he must have thought it was only a matter of time until he got his way. That was until the Battle of Britain, and that's why it is seen as a major turning point, even though the war with Germany continued for another five years, until 8 May 1945, Victory in Europe (VE) Day.

Depending who you listen to, or read, you could be convinced that the British were hanging on by the skin of our teeth, but Churchill didn't think so. We were always going to smash the Germans, there was no doubt, Churchill believed, and that came out in his notes that were released a few years ago. His confidence was due to the belief we had a better navy than them, and this had been proved in the early part of the war, and our air force was way beyond theirs. We finished the Battle of Britain with more planes that we started with, because we were building them so quickly. Churchill was dead confident. We had radar, or what we now know as radar, and we had the Observer Corps, who were a massive part of the effort.

The Observer Corps, OC, who were given the King's recognition and became the Royal Observer Corps in 1941, were mainly civilians who spotted and recognised enemy planes once they'd reached our coastline, and tracked their course, giving the information to Fighter Command to allow the RAF to intercept. I found out a bit about how well-organised the system of collecting and using information coming from the OC was, and how it was relayed to Fighter Command in their underground bunker.

We visited the Battle of Britain secret bunker, in Uxbridge, not far from Heathrow, and it was one of the most fascinating parts in the making of the whole programme. Germany knew about radar, but they didn't realise how sophisticated the system was that used radar combined with tons of minute-by-minute information coming from the airbases, about which planes and pilots were available at which airfields to see off the enemy. And we were building, and repairing, planes much more quickly than the Germans could.

The other part of the programme, that was hoping to be different to what people had seen before, was the plane we were going to concentrate on, the Hurricane, not the Spitfire, which normally gets the glory.

The Hurricane was a great plane. The Spitfire was a bit more nimble and a bit faster, but the Hurricane was so much easier to build. The Hurricane still had a steel, aluminium and wood chassis with lacquered linen material stretched over it. The only body panels that were metal were between the cockpit and the engine, where the Spitfire was a monocoque, with metal body panels and wings. Simply put, a monocoque construction is where the body is the structure, instead of a frame or chassis giving the plane rigidity and the body panels on top offering next to no strength. The Spitfire was more advanced, but it also took 50 per cent longer to build than a Hurricane. In the Battle of Britain, there were

19 squadrons of Spitfires, but 32 squadrons of Hurricanes, a squadron being made up of between 12 and 16 planes. And, Hurricanes shot down more enemy aircraft than all the other planes and land-to-air defences combined during the Battle of Britain. That's the background; now it was time to see if they could make a pilot out of me.

For my first day of flying I was introduced to Anna Walker, who was going to be my main instructor for the programme. Anna was born, and grew up, in Brazil, the only girl with three brothers. Her dad ran an earth-moving company, so she was surrounded by machinery and engineering. When she was six, her dad learned to fly and took her and her brothers up in the plane with him, one at a time, and she was bitten by the bug. She got into gliding, then flying, followed by racing karts. She was a bit wild, by the sound of it, so was sent to a convent boarding school in England to try to calm her down. It didn't work. She returned to Brazil, got into rallying and racing cars, then joined the family engineering business, gaining a load of welding qualifications, and helped the company expand into making oil rigs for Saudi Arabia, before eventually moving to England where she got back into flying and became an aerobatic display pilot in her spare time. She used to work for a shipping company in Hamburg, and she'd fly to work, from England, in an old biplane. Anna has flown 200 different types of plane, and gets to pilot a two-seat Spitfire all the time.

So yes, we had the right person to show me the ropes, and when we met at Damyns Hall Aerodrome, inside the M25 near the Dartford Crossing, we got straight into it. Anna had originally learned to fly in Brazil, where she didn't do loads of tests, and she only needed to the pass the exams and get her certificates to prove she could fly when she came to England. So, she was a bit old school, and there wasn't a lot of on-the-ground instruction before we were taking off.

The thing Anna decided it was best for me to start out in was a de Havilland Tiger Moth, a plane that was introduced in 1932, and was the aircraft lots of World War II pilots would have trained in. It's a biplane, powered by a four-cylinder engine, two spark plugs per cylinder. There's not a lot of technology keeping you in the air, and what there is of it is 90 years old.

I was in the front seat, Anna behind. And the one-man ground crew was there to help. The words and phrases are all from the period, so when Anna says 'Contact', it means switch the thing on, make an electrical contact, ready for the propellor to be rotated to start the engine. It's up to the pilot to tell the ground crew they're ready to move, by saying 'Chocks away', instructing them to pull on the rope tied to the wooden blocks in front of the Tiger Moth's wheels, when the plane is ready to head out on the runway. The runway we were heading for was nothing fancy, just a grass strip.

The Tiger Moth takes off at 40mph. It can do this because it's a biplane, it's got a lot of wing area, so you don't need a lot of air going over the wings to create lift. This one has an open cockpit, so there's no canopy to slide over us, we were out in the wind and the noise.

I had been in a two-seater Spitfire, about five years previously, and was allowed to fly it for a few minutes, nothing too technical, only enough to get a feel of how it went and how it handled. This was going to be a lot more involved.

Once we were at altitude, Anna told me to get ready to take control. I get hold of the joystick and do what she tells me. I pull it to the left and it goes left, point the joystick down and it goes down. Right away it feels very predictable, and it's not difficult to get the hang of. But at this point I don't realise how unresponsive this plane is compared to something like the Hurricane. She's being encouraging, saying she's pretty surprised that I'm picking it up as quickly as I am, but I think she's just blowing smoke up my arse for TV. To be honest, the plane does what I expect it to.

One thing Anna picked up on is that I was flying the plane in the same way I'd drive a van, looking forward and seeing what's ahead and side to side, when obviously, I'm supposed to be working in 3D, which takes some getting used to. Then she pointed out a plane above me and it hit home that I wasn't up there on my own, there can be other things all around you. You have to have your wits about you.

After a bit of a fly around Anna says it's time to land, and she takes control. We went over what we'd done, what she'd told me, and what we're going to move onto. Anna is far more gung-ho than the kind of instructor I reckon a paying punter might get for their first or second flying lesson and she said she was willing to trust me to take off on our next flight, later the same day.

It was my turn to say 'Contact', and 'Chocks away', and head out onto the airstrip.

The Tiger Moth, and all the other planes I flew for the programme, are nicknamed taildraggers because of how they roll on the ground: two wheels in line with the wings, and one small wheel, or a skid, under the tail. That's one downside of a taildragger; when all three wheels are on the floor, you're looking up, with your view ahead obscured by the engine cowl. When you're taxiing up a runway, you zigzag from side to side so you can get your eye in and see the runway is clear, before you accelerate to take-off. I was doing what I was told, throttling on till we hit take-off speed, then pulling the joystick back, but, just as the wheels leave the runway, the plane quickly tips to the right, the end of the wing close enough to the ground to make the TV lot jump out of their skins, even though it didn't seem that bad from where I was sat, and it wasn't even mentioned by Anna, we just got on with the lesson.

Earlier in the day, Anna explained the principle of the wing stall and, now we're in the air, she gets me to practise them. A wing stall happens when you're going so slowly that there isn't enough air passing over the wings to keep it in the sky, so it starts dropping. It's especially important for this programme because it happens when you're doing a tight turn, like you would in a dogfight. It's not like stalling a car or a motorbike, because it's not the engine that's stalling (but if it did, that would definitely make the thing fall out of the sky). As the plane drops in a wing stall, it accelerates and produces enough lift for the plane to act normally again, and to allow the pilot to pull out of the stall. Just before it's about to stall you usually get wing shudder as a warning. As long as you know about wing shudder, you can be ready for it, and if you're good enough, you can hold it on that shudder, so the plane is turning as tightly as possible without stalling. Some planes, including the Messerschmitt Bf 109, the Nazis' most advanced fighter plane, have small wings to increase top speed, but small wings don't create the same lift, so it's difficult to fly slowly. The Messerschmitt had slats on the wings that extended to help it turn more quickly, without stalling. They didn't always work though.

I'd already experienced Anna stalling the Tiger Moth when she was explaining what to do, so I knew what to expect. It's simple physics. If you have enough altitude, you're going to be all right, because it will fall, and as long as you don't have a load of rudder on it, it won't go into a spin. There's no drama. It feels like going over the top of a rollercoaster, because the Tiger Moth can't pull a lot of g's, not like a Spitfire could. We were at about 2,000 feet, around the same height I jumped out of the Dakota for the D-Day landing programme, so there was enough height for the plane to right itself and pull out of the dive.

Talking of stalling, Anna used to do aerobatics in Tiger Moths, practising flying them upside down. She was pushing the boundaries because these old planes don't really have enough fuel pressure to feed the carbs when they're upside down, so the engine can starve and stop running. There isn't a starter motor on a Tiger Moth, you have to get out and spin the propellor. When Anna and her fellow Tiger Moth aerobatic pilot would be practising routines one or the other would regularly conk out in mid-air, and have to make an unscheduled 'dead stick' landing, like a glider. Whoever still had the running plane would have to land too, jump out, spin their mate's propellor and the pair of them would take off, hopefully before anyone noticed. Like I said, she's some lass. I found all this out later. I also learned the friend she'd do the Tiger Moth acrobatics with was killed when his biplane hit another light aircraft in mid-air. So it's properly important to have your wits about you.

The world's only two-seat Hawker Hurricane, waiting for me to fly it, with the help of Anna Walker.

Wondering if I should have brought sunglasses with Mark and Jos, the dogfight instructors.

Practising jumping the
Triumph in my garden.

Proving I could clear the height
of *The Great Escape* jump.

Statue of Wojtek the Army Bear in Żagań, Poland, near the site of Stalag Luft 3.

My ankles have had some hammer over the last few years.
They could do with a service.

Digging for our *Great Escape* jump started after eleventh-hour crisis negotiations with Klaus the farmer.

Job done. Me with Andy Godbold, jump builder, Paul Bickers, who built the jump ramp, and the actor from *The Great Escape*, John Layton.

Just trying different seating positions.
In the shed and always got a job on.

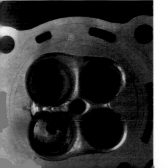

The pictures say a load of words but this one doesn't need any.

My obsession, the Hayabusa. This was taken not long before the book went to print, but the bike's probably changed another five times already.

Anna was really trusting me, and I was doing a lot of the flying while we're up there for our two one-hour sessions. At the end of the second hour Anna say she thinks I've got enough feel to land this. If an expert has faith in me, that's normally enough for me. I'm not going to start doubting myself. I just concentrate on what I have to do. She doesn't want to die so she's hardly going to trust me if there's a good chance I'm going to bury us, and the antique plane, propeller first in the ground. Still, the facts are, I've been sat in this thing for about two hours, and Anna was flying for some of that time, and now I'm going to try to land this antique. Let's have it.

I got lined up with the airfield and started to descend. I have to account for a bit of crosswind, using the rudder plenty. The plane has to be travelling slow enough that as soon as we hit the ground, we don't take off again, and quick enough that it isn't going to stall. We were just above the stall speed, with a really low engine speed, of 600 or 700rpm, less than a van at tickover. Those engines are so lazy and unstressed because you don't want them working hard and breaking down.

I was steering the rudder with foot pedals while one hand was on the joystick controlling the flaps on the wings. The skid moved with the rudder, and that helped steer it on the ground. And that was it. I landed it. Anna sounded impressed. Day one in my journey to become a part-time Hurricane pilot was over.

Before any more flying we did some filming to pad out the story. One section was with a bit of a local legend, a yakker my dad knows called Ben Jacob, of Nettleton Lodge Shooting Ground, near Caistor. He had been lined up to teach me how to blast clay pigeons out of the sky with a shotgun. World War II pilots practised that way too. The relevance is getting used to shooting ahead of the target so the ammunition and target intersect in the air; you're not shooting where the plane is, but where it's going to be. As usual, it took me a little while, but I stuck at it and then I was hitting them regularly, with a running commentary from Ben giving each of the clay pigeons the name of a German war plane as he launched them into the sky. Next, he let me shoot his more powerful rifle, me using the telescopic site. He warned me that it had a kick and not to get my eye too close to the sight, but I was still too close, the rifle recoiled and the metal sight hit me right over the eye. What an idiot. Ben saw that coming, and he had warned me twice. He called the cut it made a hunter's moon, because it leaves a crescent-shaped cut. The TV don't mind leaving something like that in, as it shows I'm just a dickhead having a go, and I'm not embarrassed either. Ben tried to tell me, but I'm too thick to listen.

Another bit of filming we did in my neck of the woods was driving around in an MG TC open-top sportscar. I knew these cars, but I was still surprised that it was small enough to turn up in the back of a regular Mercedes Sprinter-type long-wheelbase van. This was to show the RAF were very good at encouraging their pilots to enjoy their time off, so they didn't get burnt out. The ones who had the money weren't saving it for tomorrow, they might not see tomorrow, so splashing out on an impressive sportscar was a much better idea. We didn't know it at the time, but the Germans didn't give their pilots time off, plus we were bombing their airbases, so they were on edge all the time, and it can't have helped them.

The next day of flying I had with Anna was at Duxford, in a plane called a North American Aviation T-6 Texan, better known outside the USA as a Harvard, and that's what it was called all the time I was with it. Even though it was introduced in 1935, just a few years after the Tiger Moth, the Harvard has loads of differences to the biplane Anna had instructed me in. It goes to show the rate of development of aircraft design in the years even before the war. The Harvard has a 600 horsepower Pratt & Whitney radial engine, so it has loads more horsepower and is capable of over 200mph. It's a monoplane with a canopy, and has retractable landing. It has loads more instruments, more controls, but really it felt like a scaled-up version of a Tiger Moth. It felt as predictable.

Anna knew we were very tight for time, with only two short days of instruction scheduled to turn me, a total novice, into someone who could be trusted in a dogfight, and expected to fly close to another pilot, so she was pushing on. We took off for our first hour in the Harvard. I'd been in the air, getting used to the plane, and learning how it felt to stall, when Anna asked me to do a 'wingover', an essential dogfighting move that is also used in aerobatic displays. It's a tight flat turn that allows the pilot to keep their eyes on the enemy that is chasing them. Early in the war, pilots were advised that 400 yards was close enough to fire at the enemy, but that was lowered to 250 yards. That's 370 metres down to 230 metres, proper 'see the whites of their eyes' stuff. In a dogfight any speed you can gain is useful, so pilots would mix wingover with climbs and dives like a skateboarder riding in a bowl builds up speed, the pilot getting energy into the plane to increase its speed, then relying on sharp turns to lose the enemy.

For a wingover, you pick a point on the ground and you have to fly up and round, and loop back to the same point, and I couldn't get the hang of it. For the first time, I was starting to get frustrated. We landed and I tried to explain that it wasn't happening, and when I feel something isn't happening, it's best to move on and come back to it later. I even do it when I'm working on trucks or motorbikes. If there's a part that just won't come loose, or you can't work out how to get it off, go do summat else, come back to it with a fresh perspective, and normally you solve it. I'd only been in the Harvard for an hour, but I felt like I'd had enough for the day, or at least I wanted to try something else. Anna wasn't having that, and really we didn't have time to mess around, so she gave me a couple more tips and we took off again.

This time around I got it. When you do a wingover, you look at the end of your wing and pick a point on the ground that it lines up with, and the wing pivots around that point so it seems stationary, while you're balancing enough rudder and throttle to make sure you don't stall. I wasn't going to be in tears because I didn't do it first time, and once I got there I was now feeling, with a bit more time, I could have the flying job mastered. Nothing was worrying me. I just needed to build up to it, but in nearly everything to do with TV, you never have quite enough time.

If I remember right, by the end of the day we pulled 4g at 230mph, so even though the Harvard looked like an old school thing it was still a good stepping stone.

I'd had hardly any time, four hours in total, in two different planes. Normally, in peace time, trainee pilots have to do 40 hours before they're qualified for a private pilot's licence. The average age of pilots in the Battle of Britain was 20, and they were given two weeks' training before they were expected to be ready to fight.

The next day of flying would be a lesson more targeted to the dogfight. I drove to Goodwood in West Sussex, home of the Festival of Speed, the horse-racing track, and also the aerodrome, called RAF Westhampnett when it was operated by the Royal Air Force. The day of filming was 15 September 2020, Battle of Britain Day. This date was chosen to commemorate the months'-long period of fighting because it was when Allied aircraft fought against two of the largest attacks and downed 60 German aircraft for a loss of 26 of their own.

The pilots I was with were both former RAF fast jet pilots, Mark Greenfield and Steve 'Jos' Johnson. I knew Mark before, because when I was training for the Wall of Death record attempt I was sent up in a stunt plane with him to see how many g's I could handle before I blacked out. Jos is a former Harrier pilot and Red Arrow.

A couple of aerobatic/military training planes were lined up. I'd be in a Yorkshire-made Slingsby T67 Firefly, a plane designed in the 1970s, with Mark. Jos would be in a similar looking German-built Extra. Like the Hurricane and the Messerschmitt, the Firefly and the Extra both had their own pros and cons. Just like the World War II fighters, the British plane, the Firefly, could turn quicker but the German Extra had a faster top speed. Neither were massively fast, both capable of 200-plus mph speeds, similar to the Harvard, but these planes were so much more responsive, and the rate the Firefly could turn was a different league to the Harvard or Tiger Moth. When I put a bit of action into the joystick I could feel the reaction immediately, in a way I didn't with the other two, so it was a case of recalibrating the mind, and being more gentle and precise with the controls.

We took off, with Mark at the controls, to do some examples of dogfighting. We flew down to the south coast, flying over Hayling Island, on another beautiful day. I was given the controls and had the chance to do manoeuvres that were making the wings judder. In this plane, it had warning 'bingers' sounding to tell the pilot the plane is at risk of stalling. It had been a while since my lesson with Anna in the Harvard, and I was having to remind myself to think in the third dimension again, and more so, because Jos was up there with us. I'd never had to deal with that in my 39 years, so I was making sure I was looking left and right, up and down.

Mark used the phrase to describe what I had when I was doing these practice dogfights: task saturation. I was trying to keep on the tail of the other plane, and not let him get on mine; I'm making sure I don't stall or crash into anything else that's up there, or lose so much altitude as to plough into a tree, and looping to gain enough speed to escape or hunt. And checking for the other planes. There's a lot going on and nothing else you can take in, that's the saturation.

But we were over the sea, lovely blue water, I could see Goodwood racecourse, where we've flown from, and I'm being encouraged to wing stall, falling out of the sky, saving it and doing it all again. To be up there, doing this kind of flying with a couple of experts, made me think, You lucky bastard. I couldn't turn this down. And I know I had before, but circumstances change and the time was right. There are some things that I will stick to my guns on, but I'm glad they came back to me with this.

There was a point where Mark says it got a bit *Top Gun*, when I was in control of the plane and Jos was upside down, over the top of us, the canopies of the two planes lined up so we could look right at each other. Sometimes the sun was right in our eyes, and I was shielding my eyes with my hand, and it's then you realise the best fighter pilots tried to attack with the sun behind them because their enemy would have little chance of seeing them, before it was too late.

When it was over and my feet were back on terra firma, a wave hit me and I felt a mixture of drunk and seasick. This is the minor downside for inexperienced pilots or passengers in these kinds of planes. Those extreme g-forces take it out of you if you're not used to it.

I felt second-hand, because it's hard on your body and brain. We pulled 5g and it had given me a thick head, like a hangover. The last time I felt like that was when I flew in a stunt glider, in the run-up to a failed human-powered flight record, and the pilot I was with pulled some g's in that. I remember driving home in my Astra van feeling really out of sorts.

We have been made to think that the RAF are all Flash Harrys, but after my few hours of experience, I'd decided the kind of flying I'd been doing is not that hard. I reckon, if you've got a certain amount of mechanical feel, you can pick it up pretty quickly. I don't know what percentage of World War II pilots went to private school, but I don't think there were many. At the time we were filming I was working on the farm, planting potatoes or baling, so I was often fixing something that had broken down, and that meant I had my mechanical head on, and that's what you need.

Flying a light aircraft is not rocket science. It's not much different to being a farm labourer. Once you work it out, you're all right. Once you learn why it stalls you can stop it happening, cause it on purpose, or hold the plane right on the edge of it. I didn't take into account the decision-making at speed and under pressure that got me through 13 years of road racing, but that probably helped too.

While we were at Goodwood, talking on camera, Mark reminded us that every statistic of a pilot that was killed was an empty chair at an airfield's breakfast table the next morning. Unless you've been in a war you'd never know how you'd deal with it, and all I can compare it to is road racing. At some points it felt like an almost weekly occurrence, monthly without a doubt, that someone was killed racing. And it didn't change my view of racing one bit, because I didn't ever think it was going to be me. Even when my best mate in racing, Martin Finnegan, got croaked in 2008, it didn't make me think I should stop. I was racing somewhere else that weekend, and thought, Oh no, we don't want that. I didn't think, for a minute, that I wouldn't race. And that wasn't war, and I'm not trying to say anything is like war, when the balance of the world is at stake, it was just racing motorbikes, but being affected by death nearly every other meeting didn't make me want to stop. The servicemen didn't have the luxury of choice that I did. No one would care if I packed in, and no one forced me to keep doing something that could kill me. World War II wasn't like that. If you were fit enough, and the right age, you were going to war.

The last day of filming was the dogfight itself, at Biggin Hill, London, one of the main airfields for the Battle of Britain. It was under the Luftwaffe's flight path to London, so it was always in action or at risk of being targeted. Churchill regularly passed it and was said to have had more of a soft spot for this particular base. Pilots from the airfield shot down 340 planes, for a loss of 54, during the Battle of Britain.

I was back with Anna, this time in the only surviving two-seat Hurricane, a plane worth £3 million. The other plane, the enemy, was a Spanish Messerschmitt, called a Buchón (the Spanish for male dove, I'm told). They date from after the war, and have the Rolls-Royce Merlin engine in them, like the Spitfire and the Lancaster and even the Mustangs eventually did, not the Daimler-Benz 603 that the German Messerschmitt Bf 109s did. The Spanish ended up with these planes because General Franco, Spain's dictator, had dealings with Hitler before World War II, during Spain's Civil War in the 1930s. Bombers from Nazi Germany and Italy were involved in the infamous destruction of Guernica in 1937. People have described the Luftwaffe's bombing raids during the Spanish Civil War as practice runs for World War II. Deals between fascist Spain and Nazi Germany were done, and Spain ended up with the plans for the Messerschmitt. It's hard to believe, but Franco, someone who was an ally of Hitler's before the war, was still in charge of Spain into the mid-1970s.

You can tell the Spanish version of the Messerschmitt, even if it's painted identical to a German one, straight away because a proper Messerschmitt has the exhaust headers right at the bottom of the engine cowl, and the Spanish one, with the Merlin engine, has the exhausts exiting right at the top of the engine cowl. There are only two surviving German Bf 109s, and neither of them fly because, I think, of doubts about the reliability of the engine. The

Buchón we filmed with had featured in loads of films, including, most recently, *Dunkirk*. John Romain was the pilot of the Messerschmitt, the Buchón, for our filming. He's a regular stunt pilot for films and runs the Aircraft Restoration Company at Duxford, where they work on all kinds of rare old planes. The last time he flew the Messerschmitt was for the filming of *Dunkirk*. I've had dealings with him before, but there was a bit of a frosty atmosphere on the day because Biggin Hill also restore Spitfires and the like, and they're in massive competition with John's company, they don't get on one bit. John wouldn't even enter the hanger. He dealt with Anna, who was the Switzerland of this situation, so it was no skin off my nose and didn't affect anything we had planned.

The bad news was the weather was shit all day, and it was looking like we were going to have to come back the next day at, I'm guessing, huge expense to North One, but just when it was looking desperate the weather cleared and it was all go.

We taxied out to the runway with the canopy open, and I got a faceful of unburnt fuel, enough to make my eyes water.

We took off, Anna doing that, of course, and flew over the sticks, outside the M25 over Kent, where actual dogfights took place in the Battle of Britain. Anna flew out there, let me have the controls for a couple of minutes to feel the Hurricane for the very first time, then she said, 'Are you ready?'

I was expecting to get the feel for the Hurricane pretty quickly, but I struggled a bit, and Anna was barking instructions at me. The plane is three or four times more powerful than the previous ones

I'd flown, and that was for less than four hours in total. The Hurricane was as quick-turning as the Firefly, that I'd flown from Goodwood, but with that massive engine up the front. So it was responsive, it would change direction quickly, but once it started turning it wanted to keep going, so I had to counteract it, and I wasn't ready for that, which is why Anna kept shouting, 'Left! Left! Left!' to get me to correct it. It wasn't very difficult to fly, it was just different. I only needed the tiniest movements to manoeuvre it. You're counteracting stuff all the time, and I think Anna was getting annoyed with me, but it was a big ask for me to pick it up that quickly.

When she thought I was as ready as I was ever going to be, John came in with his Messerschmitt. This is what it's all built up to. It's not hard for me to imagine what it must have been like to be a pilot in the war. You're looking for a speck that could be coming at you from any direction at 350mph. It's not like when you're on the ground and the noise is a clue to where to look. There's a lot of sky and not a lot of plane. You can't hear anything but your own engine.

Now there were two historic planes worth, I don't know, but £4 million might not buy the pair of them, concentrating on their pretend dogfight, and one of them was being piloted by a truck mechanic who has been in control of any plane for, at the very most, three-and-a-half hours, and in charge of this Hurricane for three-and-a-half minutes. Into all that you chuck the cameraman's helicopter. It would be a recipe for disaster if it weren't for Anna, John and the pilot of the helicopter, Will Banks, who is an absolute master.

I was doing the moves I'd been taught, and then comes the chance to get on the Messerschmitt's tail, and at that point he couldn't shake me. It doesn't matter how good a pilot is in front, it's difficult to lose the plane following you. That's how it is, and I don't think I'm any kind of pilot. So if it was life and death, I would have come out on top that time. If you were in the Messerschmitt you just have to hope that they weren't a good aim with those three-second bursts of gunfire. Anna was instructing me, and it made it good for the TV that John, playing the part of the German, allowed himself to get in a position where I could get him in my sights. Normally he'd have smoked me.

Once we've got the footage it's time to head back. Biggin Hill is within the M25, between Bromley and Sevenoaks, Kent, and when we flew back, with the sun setting, I could see the Shard in the distance, and it looked trick.

I was happy, and so seemed everyone else. Then I did what I always do, said thanks and goodbyes to everyone, got in my van and drove home. I don't need to go to the pub and say what a great job we've all done, or turn up to what TV and film people call the wrap party at the end of filming, because I've got stuff to do. It was brilliant, but what's next?

We've told some great stories about World War II. From the experiences of my mum's dad, to my dad's dad, D-Day, the machinery involved, *The Great Escape*, and now the Battle of Britain. I've learned shitloads and I hope people who watch the programmes have too, and that some of it is passing down to younger generations, because it is important stuff.

While I had the chance to fly a Hurricane, chasing a Messer-schmitt over Kent, if I had to choose one thing that stood out about the experience, it would be a person, Anna. I can't imagine a better teacher, and a brave woman too, giving me enough rope to hang myself how many times? Fantastic.

17

Now Boys, Don't Ask Me Anything Complicated

TO HELP PROMOTE THE BATTLE of Britain programmes I was asked if I'd be a guest on a podcast all about World War II called *We Have Ways of Making You Talk*. They wanted to have a yarn about the filming and what I knew about the history of the Battle of Britain. The podcast is hosted by war historian and author James Holland, and the comedian Al Murray, who is probably best known for his character the Pub Landlord. Recording a podcast like this means I don't have to go to London to do any PR interviews, and it's over and done in an hour, so I wasn't complaining. The North One TV director, James Woodroffe, had been picking James Holland's brain and checking details with him about this programme and others we'd made, and he'd set up a Zoom type of thing on his laptop when we were filming summat else. The interview took place a few days before the Battle of Britain programmes were first shown on Channel 4, in April 2021. The podcast hosts had been sent a link to watch the programmes before they were shown on TV, so they could see what we'd been up to.

They were at their homes, on their own computers, and me and James were at MIRA, the Motor Industry Research Association centre, in Warwickshire, where we were filming. These Zoom and Skype calls give people the chance to show how intellectual they are by sitting in front of a bookshelf. Doing that you are saying it all by saying fuck-all, and both these boys did it. Al Murray had some cool shit, drums and stuff as well as his books, while James Holland just had books, but I could tell they'd both really thought about it.

Before the podcast started I said to them, 'Now boys, don't ask me anything complicated because I'm thick as fuck.' They started laughing, and obviously they might think I'm trying to have them on, or make them laugh, but I'm not. Also, the first thing I do is swear, to set the scene. Then everyone knows this is the way it's going to be, we know where we are. I'm naturally sweary, so when I'm on camera I'm having to work out what to say without swearing, and it's a struggle. I could be far more efficient with my language by using swearwords, and, instead, I end up using a longer, more complicated sentence when really, I want to say, Fuck off, it's a load of shite.

I know that James the director thinks I'm thick, because he's sat next to me. They don't trust me, and I don't care. I get to do some amazing stuff, so does it matter if they think I'm stupid? I don't think that they know that I know that they think I'm thick. I think they think I'm joking. But obviously I know they think that, but it doesn't change the facts. I know what I know, and I'm clever enough to know that I don't know everything. I will never try to bullshit my way around anything.

I'll admit there are lots of ways I'm definitely not thick, like when I'm diagnosing problems. I'll go back to the beginning, the basics, and work through it in a pragmatic way. I learned that word, pragmatic, from Jonny Twelvetrees, the team manager when I was riding for Honda Racing at the 2017 Isle of Man TT. I'm not saying that season of racing was a disaster, because no one got killed, but it wasn't great. I'd crashed the bike, or it had chucked me off, and McGuinness was injured from being flung off it at the North West 200, suffering a compound fracture of his leg, cracked vertebrae and three broken ribs, if I remember right, so he wasn't even racing at the TT. We sat in what you could call a crisis meeting. It was time for me to have my say, and I started with, 'I'm as hard as fuck, I'm the hardest man I know, no one needs to kid anyone, we know this bike isn't right, because of where we are, but I'm willing to go out, have a ride and take any shit that's thrown at me.'

I was trying to explain we could get through this without falling out. I'd done the Tour Divide the year before and I was still strong in the head from that. I let the Honda bods know that they could tell the media whatever they wanted and blame me if they liked, as long as we, the team, know the truth, that being, the bike has a lot of problems. If you start a statement with 'I'm as hard as fuck', you're buggered really, but I was trying to set the scene, that the bike and the team weren't failing because I was afraid of anything. Then Jonny Twelvetrees agreed we had to be pragmatic about things. The word didn't mean anything to me before then, but I use it a lot now, and there wasn't a better description of how we had to be to get through that TT. We did get through it, and no one died. So, most of the time, I'm pragmatic.

As soon as the Zoom connection was made, James has put on his phone voice. I might have tried to use some big words years ago, but I soon learned not to. Being myself means I'm never a fish out of water. I've already told them I don't know what I'm doing so they're not expecting a genius. I've learned plenty filming all those programmes, but I've forgotten a lot because I've no real reason to retain the information. The stuff I'm learning about electric cars is useful for the future, and I'm remembering most of that, and some other stuff sticks in there, but just because I've been told it once doesn't make me an expert on it.

James explains to them that North One make the programmes with me, because I look through a normal man's eyes, a polite way of saying, 'Can we succeed in making this dickhead into a Battle of Britain pilot?'

When it's my turn to talk I come out with some stuff about the Hurricane being the unsung hero, all we ever hear about is the Spitfire, but the Hurricane got more kills during the Battle of Britain, and then I give a simple description of the programme and what was involved.

James Holland and Al Murray are intelligent, they've been doing this war-related podcast for ages – I was on episode 305 – they really know their stuff, of course, and they're well into it.

We got talking about the Messerschmitt Bf 109, the fighter plane that the Hurricanes and Spitfires were up against. I learned that once the Messerschmitt was off the ground it was probably a better plane, at the time of the Battle of Britain, than what the

British had, but it sounds like the Germans weren't using it right. They were making this advanced fighter accompany the heavy bombers, and fly at their speed. When the enemy showed up on our radar they were lumbering over the Channel at the speed of a bomber, so the RAF squadrons had that bit more time to scramble and get in the air. In some ways it makes sense, because the Germans weren't sending the fighters to pick off the odd Hurricane or Spitfire, they wanted the bombers to get through and do some proper damage, but it did mean their fighters lost a lot of their advantage.

Also, from what I understand, the Messerschmitt was only superior to what we had for a while. The development was cat and mouse throughout. The Allies would make an advance, and have the better fighter, then the Germans would improve their machinery. Some of the changes were hurried along by nicking ideas from each other's crashed planes.

That then got me onto the subject of the Daimler-Benz inverted V12 engines, like the 601 and 603X, the type that were used in Messerschmitts. This is an amazing engine from my point of view. At the time, it was so technologically advanced, a really amazing piece of engineering, but it was unreliable. When I say it was inverted V12, it was mounted upside down, compared to a car, with the cylinder heads at the bottom and the crank at the top, and all the problems that need solving when it comes to having the sump at the top of the engine. But it had direct fuel injection, a roller bearing crank, and a constantly variable supercharger operating through a hydroscopic coupling, and all this in the 1930s. The later version had desmodromic valves. It blows my mind. I told them

I thought they were far more advanced than the Rolls-Royce, and I got talking about some of the technical details of this inverted V12 engine. The Rolls-Royce Merlin was an amazing engine, but it wasn't pushing the boundaries. I suppose you could say it was being pragmatic.

I told them I loved the German way of engineering. I got on about the Messerschmitt and what an evil plane it was. One in three of those was lost in a take-off or landing incident. I think the TV programme made it out that the reason for that was that the German pilots weren't as good as the British, but Anna Walker's partner, PK, Pete Kynsey, told me what he thought was the real reason. PK is one of, if not the, most experienced civilian pilots of warbirds, and he says the Messerschmitt was so difficult to take off and land because the distance, the width, between the wheels was so narrow. The pivot point, where the wheels folded out of, was straight under the fuselage, and that why the landing gear came out at such a wonky angle. The Spitfire's wheels folded in and out of the wings. I was told that the Germans didn't use that design because they wanted to be able to dismantle the Messerschmitt, stick it on a train, and transport it easily to the airfields it was going to fly from. The German command thought, First things first, this is a tool to do a job, and we have to transport it where it's needed, and while it might be hard to take off and land, you boys are going to have to deal with that. This is how it's going to be. Part of me loves the German attitude.

Also listening into the recording of the podcast was someone from Channel 4. That just shows, to me at least, they think I'm thick, because he was listening in to make sure I didn't say anything that could put the TV channel in a bad light.

After the recording finished he said, 'They're not going to include that bit about Hitler, are they?' I'd only said I was pro German engineering, but he was panicking. Now he definitely thinks I'm as thick as fuck.

18

I've Never Taken Drugs, but It Might Feel Like This

AFTER SPENDING A FAIR AMOUNT of time at airfields for the Battle of Britain job, I was back to using them for what they were really designed for. The runway at Cottesmore is great for running the Hayabusa, and I'm lucky to be able to go there and ride, but the one problem is the length of the runway, it's only 1.7 miles, so it's not safe to run more than a mile there, it's borderline even running that because it's tight for stopping at the end, especially if I start getting closer to 300mph. Elvington is slightly longer, so a mile is safe, but I found out about a disused former airfield in Scotland through another mate, Alan Shand.

I've known Alan for years. He must be in his early 60s, he was a scrutineer at the Isle of Man TT, and races a sidecar. I'm going off on a tangent here, but hopefully it's worth it. Alan lives right up in the far north of Scotland, top side of Aberdeen. Back in October 2018, he came down in his camper van with his sidecar to race at

241

my local track, Cadwell Park in Lincolnshire. He travelled down on his own, and met a mate who passengers for him at the track.

That weekend I got a phone call from Alan's phone, but it wasn't him, it was a doctor from Cadwell's medical centre. The medic said, 'Your mate's not very well and we're going to airlift him to Hull.' Being airlifted anywhere is bad, but if you're being airlifted to Hull Royal Infirmary from Cadwell, you know it's really bad. Normally you'd be taken to Louth, Boston, Grimsby or Lincoln. If you're going to Hull, you're fucked.

Me and Shazza went to Hull Royal Infirmary that afternoon to see him. He'd broken his pelvis, smashed his ribs and his lung had collapsed, but he was sort of all right. He was conscious, he could sort of talk, so we made a few phone calls and rang his missus, Jen, who ended up staying with us. Jen doesn't drive, so Shazza was taking her to Hull every day, and I'd go see Alan every day after work. At one point he was getting worse and worse, and it was getting to the stage that I was thinking he wouldn't see tomorrow, but, luckily, he improved. He was in hospital for a month and, 18 months later, as I write this, Alan is 100 per cent. What was the point of that? If you crash and they tell you they're airlifting you to Hull, it's time to start panicking.

Anyway, I asked Alan, do you know any runways? He did – Machrihanish on the far side of Scotland, a 15-hour round trip from Grimsby. It's a former airbase that's now owned by the local community. He put me in touch with a bloke called Robbie, who helped me set up a visit. Me and my dad drove up there, stayed the night before and we were on the runway at 4.30 in the morning waiting for the sun to come up.

Machrihanish has a longer runway than Cottesmore, so I could run 1.12 miles and still have room to brake. The ultimate aim is to go 300mph in a mile, but I'm nowhere near doing that yet, so having that extra 0.12 mile helps while I'm still building up.

The hassle of organising and the long trip was worth it, because the conditions were as good as I can remember, and I did 282mph, the fastest I've ever been.

When I've done a fast run I know it. Two-fifty isn't fast any more. When I go more than 270 I know I've done a fast run, and I don't sleep much that night. Normally I'm out like a light, because I can hardly keep my eyes open later than half-nine. After a fast run on the Hayabusa I'm fine loading the van, driving home and unloading, but when I get into bed, I'm not calmly wondering, What if I tried this, or that? It's FUCKIN' HELL! I've never taken drugs, but it might feel like this, because I'm wired and so much is going through my head. I feel like I've survived something.

I explained that the land speed job at Bonneville felt risky, but this mile riding feels like the most dangerous thing I've ever done. It might not seem like that to people who have seen the TT or Irish road racing up close, but being brutally honest, if anything I've ever done is likely to kill me, it's probably this.

I don't shy away from the dangers. I've thought hard about them. Everyone knows what the dangers of the Isle of Man are, the sudden stops. We've seen MotoGP and Superbike racers crash at the same speeds that have killed TT racers, and the short circuit riders walk away, get back to the pits and try to get out in the next session. On the runways, there's nothing to hit, but if you're coming off at 270mph, you're going to slide a long way and I'd think that blood loss would be an issue. Leather is only going to last so long, skin won't last and then there'll just be the nuts and bolts left out of my back. I was concerned enough about it to ask Dainese to make me some thicker leathers. Normally they're making leathers as thin and as light as possible, while still offering the protection, but I explained my worries and they made me a special set that are twice as thick and weigh loads more in comparison to my Dainese road-racing leathers.

The danger comes from the way the wind acts on the bike. These are outside influences I can't do anything about. When I was at Machrihanish I thought the conditions were fair enough for another run, but once I started going I was leaning so much, in a straight line, that I caught my toe on the ground. I was putting in that much lean and that was on a day that was as still as still. I might have had my toes stuck out a bit to counteract the wind, but I had my foot on the footpeg and the bike, though it had modified suspension, isn't lowered much compared to standard, so if I'm catching my foot on the ground that is some amount of lean, and that's forced me to make some more changes to the bike.

People who have been trying to do the same thing as me, go fast on sit-on motorcycles, not streamliners, have been killed. The fastest man over a measured mile on a motorcycle, Bill Warner, lost his life in 2013 attempting a mile run. Reports say he was clocked at 287mph before he crashed. Ralph Hudson, another land speed racer, who had clocked a two-way average of 297.97mph on a longer course, died at Bonneville in August 2020 when he crashed at a speed of 252mph. In reports I read, both crashes were blamed on wind conditions.

When I got the chance to take my Hayabusa to a wind tunnel for an afternoon's session I wanted to see what I could find out. When I got the results back I learned the bike, with me on it, has a 0.42 coefficient of drag, when it is fitted with the big land speed fairing and seat unit, but the figure is 0.7 when the bike is naked. That roughly translated to needing 400 horsepower to do 300mph with the fairing, and over 600 horsepower without it, but that's only roughly because I want to do the speed in the measured mile, so I might need more.

With the bike fully faired there are only a handful of hours per year I can exploit that coefficient of drag, because it becomes too dangerous to ride in any kind of wind. I just have to park it. If the bike doesn't have that big area of land speed racer fairing, and the wind can blow around and through it, I should be able to safely ride it when there is more wind, meaning there are more days I can consider. Or that's my thinking. I came out of the wind tunnel having made the decision to go with a semi-naked look, so only have the top half of the fairing, and go back to the original Suzuki seat unit.

I went to Cottesmore on a weekday morning, conditions were good, I had cut up the front fairing and put a rough Hayabusa seat unit back on it. I had a load of wastegate trouble, I had a bearing go on the end of the driveshaft, and a misfire I couldn't cure, but I did 250-odd easy, and that was the last ride before the winter of 2020–21. At that point I was still using a lot of the £5,000 bike I'd bought a couple of years before. The wheels, brakes, forks, frame, swingarm, crankcases, crank, cylinder heads, throttle bodies, fairing bracket, bottom yoke, steering damper, shock linkage … It's definitely not the bike I got off Jack, but the backbone of it was still his work.

Piloting the Bonneville streamliner is nothing like riding a motorbike, it's very unconventional. The Hayabusa follows all the rules of a normal motorbike, just with brutal, brutal horsepower. I've never had to deal with anything like that before. I went 273mph in the Triumph Streamliner, and I've been 282 on the Hayabusa. You look at the pair of them and you'd never think my Suzuki was quicker.

The majority of stuff I've done has been half-baked. I can see now that when I've raced mountain bikes or motorbikes, I've never been fully dedicated to that one thing, I've let work or something else compromise it. I don't regret any decisions I made, but looking back I'm honest enough with myself to admit that. I also know I've spent a good part of my life racing and I don't really want to be part of a race. This 300mph record is the one thing, outside of truck-fitting, that I'm not half-arsing. I'm going for it. I made Cottesmore happen. I made Machrihanish happen. I'm taking the bike to wind tunnels and talking to anyone I think can give me a different perspective. I want to do 300mph in a mile. And I'd like to be the first person to do it.

19

I've Got the
Breaking Strength
of a Kit Kat

WHEN IT COMES to the truck job, during 2020 and the lockdown, it became the dog wagging the tail. It turned from the truck yard telling me what time to be in and which days they needed me and which days I could have off, to me telling them which days I could go in.

There have been a couple of times I've used tractors as the flux to make what I want to happen actually happen. A few years ago, I'd been at Moody's for eight years and wanted to get out of it and have a change. One of Moody's drivers, who had worked for him for years, had been banned from driving for working too hard. That's how we used to describe someone with a tachograph offence. That meant there was an extra pair of hands in the yard, and the driver could do a lot of the maintenance stuff that was keeping me busy.

At the same time that I'd decided I'd just about had enough of doing the same old stuff at Moody's and felt I needed to tax the grey matter again, young Ben Neave, the brother of the racing twins Tim and Tom, was driving my tractor on the potato-lifting job. Ben had to go to college, so I now had an excuse I had to have time off to drive the tractor for six weeks, so I did that, and never went back to Moody's. I knew I wasn't going back the day I left, but instead of just manning up and handing my notice in, I had to make an excuse. I felt if I told Mick Moody I was leaving I was allowing myself to be asked, 'Leaving to do what?' I didn't want to say 'Nothing' and sound like a lazy sod. 'Leaving but you haven't got a job to go to?' That's the little mad man in my head saying that, it's no one else.

That first week of work on the tractors, me actually driving not just renting out my tractor, wound up with the end of the potato harvest, like it always does, at the end of October, early November. AKP, the big potato-producing firm in north Lincolnshire, that I had been contracting for, wanted me to do some maintenance on their machinery, so I did that for a while. Then I was told that a local haulage firm needed help because two of their fitters were off sick, so could I go and give them a hand for a while?

It wasn't like Moody's, which was mainly sales work, getting new and used trucks ready to sell, this place was back into the frying pan, servicing working fleet trucks. I was straight into it, 80 hours a week, in at five on a Saturday morning, home at two. I thought it was great when I started because the trailers they use are different technology to what I was used to. It's all blowing work, so I was learning. The products they specialise in transporting are powders: powdered lime, ash, cement. They take ash from power stations and transport it to cement works. They take lime from quarries to water treatment works and to steelworks.

The product is dumped into the trailer through the hatches in the top, out of a hopper, but when it comes to emptying the trailer, the powdered product is blown out. The trailers have on-board systems that push a massive amount of air through the trailer, 1,500cfm, cubic feet per minute. There is a semi-permeable membrane at the bottom of the trailer that the air blows through in such a volume that it almost liquefies the powder, meaning it runs out. If you saw it, you'd say it was dirty water because of the way it flows, but it's dry. To pump that volume of air you have a blower unit, a screw compressor, about the size of the motorbike engine, that works off the truck gearbox. This was all new to me, so I was enjoying the job, because I was learning lots and fixing different bits of machinery.

I loved it for a year or two, then I learned it all and it got to the point that it wasn't taxing me any more, so I decided I was getting out of it, because I had so much on at home in the shed, and I could have twice as much. Everything I was doing at home was compromised. And I still stuck it out for three years, because it was a good crack, and great money for a fitter. After a while I started thinking, What are you doing? and at the beginning of 2020 I told Shazza I was definitely going to leave. She said, 'You won't. You always say that.'

I came to use the tractor as flux again to get out of a job I'd had enough of. Maybe it was a hobby when I first bought the tractor, but it isn't now. The tractor goes from one massive farm to another, doing different stuff. Sometimes I'm in it, sometimes I put a driver in it. I wanted fingers in pies, because I was looking at the big picture, thinking of the future. I'm not greedy, but I always think the TV job is going to end, if not tomorrow, then sooner or later, and the tractors earn good money for me.

Just when I was looking to get out of the truck job, in spring 2020, when the UK was going into lockdown, I had a tractor lined up for some work, and I had a driver in it, so he'd be earning, and I would too, but he let me down at the eleventh hour. I couldn't drive it, because I was supposed to be going to Cuba for a filming job. I was shitting myself because I had no one for the tractor and I couldn't change the filming dates. This was all middle of March, and the corona situation was looking dodgy, so I didn't think we would be going, but the TV lot were still full steam ahead. Everything else was getting cancelled, but they were telling me, right up to the week before, we were still going, definitely, pack your bags, see you at the airport. We hadn't quite gone into lockdown, but I just couldn't see us going.

In the end, what I reckoned, though it was never confirmed, was that the TV lot couldn't cancel the trip because they wouldn't get their insurance back. The airline had to cancel it, or the government had to say no one's travelling, then the insurance would pay out.

So it all helped me out. I couldn't go to Cuba, but I could get on the tractor, so it meant I was leaving the trucks to get on the tractor job. The tractor was the flux.

If you're wondering what all this is about, the talk of 80-hour weeks, and still working even though I end up being too tired to do my own stuff, when, behind it all, the TV job pays enough to keep me comfortable and pay for everything I need or want, it's because I need to be doing a normal job. I don't need the money. The most rock and roll thing I've got is my electric bill and I'm trying to lower that. The consumption for this house is massive, and I'm trying to become self-sustaining, but that's a long-term plan. I think it's because all I've known is work. My dad worked to build his business up. My mum worked hard for years, my brother and sisters are the same. It's what we do. It's what I do.

Tractors are different to trucks. It's a lot less physical, most of the time. Get in the tractor, listen to a podcast, get away from those trucks. I'm not using my head in the tractor, but I'm learning plenty from the podcasts I listen to. It reminds me of the days when I was labouring at the factories, the docks, building and maintenance, in the time between leaving my dad's and working for Moody. I was working my hole out on that job, but I wouldn't think about work from leaving on Friday to going back in on Monday.

The tractors can be boring, moving along at 5km/h while you're ridge forming, but if you have something to listen to it's all right. I can even have my feet up, reading a magazine, and the tractor beeps at me when we get to the headland, the edge of the field. It's easy as long as everything is going smoothly, but you have to be on it when things go wrong, like if the destoner gets bunged up, or a belt breaks, that can be a big job. The biggest trouble is I'm thinking about food all the time because I'm not concentrating on anything. I've eaten my pack-up by nine in the morning.

The hours can be daft on the tractor because, if the weather's good, you're working. Six in the morning to eight or nine at night, seven days a week until the job's done, but you're only at it for eight weeks at the most. In that time you're beyond busy, but you can have a life. Trucks aren't quite as busy, but they're non-stop 52 weeks of the year where farming is seasonal.

The year is split into different sections. First, there's something like eight weeks of ridge forming, destoning and planting the potatoes. The destoner takes the stones out of the ridge and puts them in the bottom of the ridge, then the planter comes through. A lot of the potatoes that AKP grow are for McDonald's, so they need to be a uniform size and shape to go into a certain machine for chipping, so the land needs to be well-prepared to make sure you don't have any wonky potatoes. If there are any stones in that ridge or muck that's too firm, that hasn't been broken up by the tiller, the potato grows around it and then it's no good for McDonald's.

After preparing the fields for tayties and planting them, there wouldn't be much for me or the tractor to do until we get into baling and harvesting. It sometimes starts slowly, a couple of days a week in late July, until the weather gets better in August and then it's baling seven days a week. When you're baling you're driving faster than when you're ridge forming and destoning. You can't start too early either. You have to wait for the dew to dry off, because you don't want too much moisture in the bale. We have a probe to stick in the bale, and if there's too much moisture in the first bale of the day you sit and wait a while. I was on the baling for two months, me and one other tractor, and we did 20,000 bales between two of us in that time.

Then there's a bit of overlap – just as we're finishing the bales, the potato lifting starts. The ones we planted in April are now ready to pick. AKP have summat like 800 acres worth. A lot of potatoes. With the tractors, you tend to be moving all day, unless you're on the potato-lifting job, when you have folks in the back of the potato harvester, sorting the good tayties from the bad, on the riddling belt. They need their breaks.

The draw of the trucks is always there. The owner of the haulage firm, and one of his fitters, Lingy, are always on the phone asking if I'll come in, and I can never say no. I've got the breaking strength of a Kit Kat. So, I'm back on the trucks. I'll do Friday afternoon and Saturday, which are the busy times in this job because the drivers don't need the trucks then. On a Saturday I'll start at five, and finish one or two o'clock. I come home and do some work in the shed or fix stuff around the house, if it needs it, sit with Dot, reading or while she watches telly, then I try to watch a film with Sharon, but I can't stay awake and I'm in bed for nine.

Beyond trucks and tractors I have to keep reminding myself what side my bread is buttered. Channel 4 have signed me up to another three-year contract, and Spellman says I'm the only presenter on their books they offered more than a year to in 2020, so I can't really say I'm on the tractors for six weeks when they want to do summat. But wait another five minutes, and I'll probably contradict myself again.

20

I'm Right on His Arse, Thinking I Can Have Him

I'D KNOWN FOR A FEW YEARS I wasn't enjoying road racing for teams, but I still wanted to race when it suited me. A lot of my favourite tracks run classes for classic bikes during the same meetings where I'd compete on superbikes, so I decided I'd build something I could turn up and race every now and then. I ended up with a Rob North with a BSA triple engine, that I wrote about in *We Need to Weaken the Mixture*. Rob North is a British engineer who designed racing frames for Triumphs in 1971. His design was successful straight away, and they're still the thing to have, in classic races, 50 years later. North is still alive, at the time of writing, living in America, I think, and over the years various companies have had the rights to build and sell his design of chassis. It's a lightweight, tubular steel frame, nothing like Triumph ever made, and they're fitted with a big aluminium petrol tank, again, nothing like a 1960s or 1970s Triumph road bike, the era the engines are from. The tubes of the frame curve around the side of the engine, and the petrol tank follows the lines of the frame. It was ahead of its time. The bike I have now is very similar to the first bike I ever rode on track, because my dad had a Rob North he let me ride, and still owns the same one now.

I ended up with mine from a connection I made when I was doing the Wall of Death programme (that's covered in *When You Dead, You Dead*). I decided I wanted to build my own bike to attempt the record and chose to build my version of a Rob North BSA triple, a 750cc three-cylinder engine. I bought a frame that had just been made for my mate Gary Hewitt, and a load of bits from Les Whiston of Rob North Triples, who is the current rights holder of Rob North frames. After the Wall of Death bike was built, and Les had found out I was right into this kind of bike, he offered me a road-racing special frame and some parts to do what I wanted with. I actually ended up with a full bike, a prototype he'd used to test parts with. Les explained he hadn't had it running right yet because he'd fitted so many prototype parts to it.

So this Rob North that I've had in my shed for years now is not my bike, but I treat it like mine. It's trick and unique, because the frame is a bit narrower at the back than an original Rob North. Les had fitted a throttle position sensor for it to communicate with the ignition, so it was really pushing what anyone had done with an old triple. One of the biggest leaps he was making was with a design of gearbox, trying to use modern gearbox technology in the old gearbox casing. I wrote about all the headaches we had with the gearbox, and how many we broke, but it's close to spot on now, because Les really persevered with his idea, and I admired that.

Until we got the gearbox right there wasn't a lot of point in trying to tune the engine, even though it wasn't powerful. My dad's was tuned by P&M, Peckett and McNab, who are well respected tuners of these and other engines of this sort of age. When my dad was racing, he chose P&M to tune his Kawasaki, which was a modern bike at the time, and his Rob North triple has a full P&M engine tune, which is what triple people say is the best going, and it makes 74–75bhp at the back wheel on my dyno. People might quote bigger power numbers than that, but I just refer to what I see on my dyno, so I'm comparing apples with apples. Mine wasn't making much more than 40 when I got it. I fitted a different ignition and increased the horsepower to 50. Then I started messing with the carburettor's jetting and the ignition timing, and got 60bhp. At that point I didn't want to strip the engine, and it was running lovely, didn't smoke, didn't rattle, but I was banging my head against a brick wall when I tried to improve it. I tried all types of fuel, all types of jetting and ignition timing, but I couldn't improve on 60 horsepower.

Then I started messing about with valve timing, something no one really did with these engines any more. P&M had worked out what they liked, proved it worked and was reliable, and that's what people stuck to. I must have been inspired by how much Les Whiston had experimented, because I started going radical with the valve openings. When I did my engine made more power, but still not as much as my dad's. I was going in the right direction, but mine was now making maximum power at 10,250rpm, where Dad's made its peak power at 8,500rpm, which is a big difference. I had increased the overlap – the time when both the inlet and exhaust valves are open, which alters the natural scavenging of the engine, how the maximum amount of fuel and air is drawn into the combustion chamber, and that's a bit of a black art. There are waves and vibrations that can help or knacker you when you're trying to get rid of the burnt exhaust gas, and suck in the fresh fuel and air mixture, and it was fascinating me. Once I changed the valve timing to my new way of thinking, the engine started responding to conventional tuning techniques again. Octane level, the carbs' air/fuel ratio and ignition advance all started to make a difference to how it made power. Still, at the very best, it made 70 horsepower, less than my dad's. Next, I increased the compression ratio; this, in basic terms, is the amount of pressure the piston creates as it squashes the air and fuel charge in the combustion chamber. I had done a static compression test and the engine was only something like 9.5:1, where a modern road bike, like a Suzuki GSX-R1000, would be 13:1. The problem is, the old combustion chamber design doesn't lend itself to high compression. The piston has deep valve pockets, depressions in the top of the piston that clear the valves when everything is spinning. If you're running high compression, there's more stress, more heat, and the heat concentrates in the corners this design of piston and cylinder head has, and that causes detonation, also known as knock. If the engine is knocking you have a bomb scene before you know it.

My goal was more compression, so I machined the cylinder head, skimming 0.15mm off it. That lost me 1cc of cylinder volume, but increased the compression ratio to 10.1:1 and increased the maximum power to 71.6bhp. It had never made that. By that point I'd done as much as I could with the pistons I had, so I got hold of some blank pistons that I could machine to my own specification. I'm not stopping until I make more power than the P&M ones do. I'll persevere with my way of going.

I enjoy working on the bike as much as, if not more than, I do racing it, but I do still want to race it. In case you're new to motorcycle racing, I'll explain a couple of terms before I start using them. There are few types of racing a bike like the Rob North triple can compete in. The most common is short circuit racing. This takes place on purpose-built tracks like Donington, Brands Hatch, Silverstone. Then there's real road racing, where regular public roads are closed to allow bikes to race on them. The Isle of Man TT is the most famous real road race, but it's different again, because riders leave the line one at a time, at ten-second intervals. Every other real road race has a mass start, with bikes and riders in lines on a grid, all leaving at the same time (or, if there are a lot of entries, in two different groups, a few seconds apart). Real road circuits can be anything from a couple of miles long up to the 7.3 miles of the Ulster Grand Prix in Northern Ireland, and beyond to the 37.73 miles of the Isle of Man TT.

Then there's endurance racing that takes place on short circuits, normally over a period of between 4 and 24 hours, two or more riders competing in shifts. I've done plenty of short circuits races over the years, and I really enjoy the teamwork and challenge of endurance racing, but real road racing is what I like the best, and also where I had the most success.

I'd raced the Rob North a few times on short circuits and the odd real road race, and in 2019 I signed up with the Classic Racing Motorcycle Club, CRMC, to compete in a two-day meeting at

Cadwell, the short circuit closest to my house. I pushed my luck to get a late entry, and like they have always been with me, the CRMC were great. It pissed it down the first day of the races, but I worked it out that I could listen to the commentary using an app on my phone while I was parked up on my own, right in the back corner of the pits. Because I could hear the commentary I knew when my race was coming up, so I could sit in the back of the van reading my magazines until the last minute, get the bike out and ride to the holding area. I didn't get my first race till dinner time, that's about one o'clock, because there was loads of crashing in the rain. Then my bike started playing up because I got water in the electrics. Looking at the time, and how many races there were still to run between my first and second race, I decided there was no way I would be getting another race that day, so I went home, and drove back Sunday morning.

When it was time to go, I rode down to the holding area, where the marshals line you up before you roll out to the grid. There was some confusion with who should be in this position and you should be in that place, and I just said, 'Don't worry lads, I'll start from the back.' I set off three rows from the back row, and I wasn't bothered, because I was only there to test a new ignition on my bike before I raced it in Ireland.

The bike behaved this time, but when I got back to the pits I wondered, Why am I doing this? I'm not enjoying it. I put the bike in the van and came home, not bothering waiting for my next race. I had some Irish road dates in my diary to look forward to.

I'd already raced the Rob North on one of my favourite real road circuits, Tandragee in Northern Ireland, and I'd entered

Skerries, a race on the outskirts of a small town on the coast, north of Dublin, somewhere I hadn't raced since 2004. I got the overnight crossing from Cairnryan to Belfast, the cheap boat, then drove down to near Newry, met my mate Alan, went for a fry-up, and got to Skerries in time for scrutineering.

Because I hadn't raced there for 15 years I was allowed out in the newcomers' five-lap practice, as well as the practice for my classic race, because I genuinely couldn't remember the track. There's a load to remember. It's narrow, fast and bumpy, with big jumps down the back straight that I wouldn't fancy doing on a superbike now.

I did the newcomers' practice, getting my eye in, following a few boys, most of them on modern bikes, a few classics. I loved being on this circuit. I've always enjoyed racing in Ireland, north and south, more than anywhere else. Now, more than ever, I'm not out to prove anything to anyone. It is just about having fun on the bike, but I got a bit of a shock three laps into classic practice. I felt I was doing all right when a Norton twin came past me, Bruummmmm! It turned out to be a rider called Richard Ford, who sucked the stickers off me, he went past that fast. I thought, I'm going to have my work cut out with him. I wasn't bothered because I was back into it and enjoying it. I qualified second row, and was happy enough, but still lacking a bit of track knowledge. And that was it for the day, no racing till Sunday morning. Loads of people want to say hello, even if I'm in the middle of summat, so I get mithered at these Irish road races, but it's worth it to ride a track like Skerries. That's the difference between this and somewhere like Cadwell. I don't get anything like the same enjoyment from short circuits.

The next day, before the race, I saw the fast bloke on the Norton, Richard Ford, getting ready to sneak out in the practice before the racing. It was an official session they put on for riders who'd either broken down and not had a proper practice, or had changed something and needed to try it out for safety reasons. I thought to myself, I need to get out in that practice. I made out I needed to test a change to my back brake, and at times like that it helps that people probably know who I am, know that I'm not too much of a dickhead, and they're happy to let me out. My race wasn't until two in the afternoon or summat, so I'd have had to wait all day for that one race. I knew any practice lap I could do was going to help me in the race. I didn't try to tuck in behind the Norton, because he was miles faster, but I learned a bit more of the circuit and gained some more confidence in the track and the bike.

My race came around and I rolled out to the start line with the mindset that I'm not bothered if I win, lose or draw, because I'm in love with it all again. I don't go mad from the start, but within a few laps I'm fourth. I pass a couple more boys and I'm up to second. I can see matey-boy on the fast Norton up ahead. I catch him up, and, through a tight section of bends, I'm right on his arse, thinking I can have him. I sit there for another couple of laps, before putting a hard pass on him that he wasn't expecting at one of the first gear road ends, a T-junction in the normal life of the road. By now I'd followed him closely for a couple of laps, so I'd seen where he was fast and I realised, if I tucked in for the next tight, rough section I could probably build up enough of a gap that he couldn't pass me on the straights where he was much faster. I pressed on, did a lap, back to where I'd overtaken him, and he hadn't come back past me, so I kept doing what I was doing, being neater and neater, riding my own race, not looking over my shoulder once. He might have been stalking me, checking my lines and weak spots, but looking over my shoulder wasn't going to change that.

The triple engine is 50 years old, but I bet I was doing 150mph in some places. You need more mechanical sympathy with a classic, but you're still licking on. I'm hitting the jumps at speed, and it was landing rock steady, letting me think, The job's a peach.

Then I got into the backmarkers, and that slowed me up, because I wasn't willing to make do or die moves to pass them, showing them a bit of respect, and I did just enough to win the race, with the Norton right on my back wheel. I can honestly say I wouldn't have minded finishing second, but it was good to win, and I broke the lap record for the class by summat like two seconds.

At that moment I thought, This is the best thing in the world. It's nicer to race the classic, I've got time to think about it, and I'm riding the bike, it's not riding me, and I'm hanging onto it. With 60bhp, which is about what it had then, you're not feeding in the power, searching for grip, like you are on a 200-horsepower superbike. On a classic, the throttle's either on or off. I used to live for racing superbikes on the roads, now I can't think of anything worse. People change, don't we? It was the near-death thing that got me hooked, knowing that if you got it wrong you were done, and that's what I loved. I was young and didn't care if I killed myself. Then the older I got, I don't want to kill myself road racing because I have more interesting things to do. I evolved, and the classic is a good compromise. I'm still riding it as fast as I can, so

I'm enjoying it. I get to build the bike, too, and I couldn't when I was racing for Honda or TAS.

That was it for 2019, and even though we all know what happened in 2020, I still managed to fit one race in on the Rob North BSA. The new organisers of the races at Oliver's Mount, Scarborough, squeezed in a race, with spectators, in the middle of 2020.

Oliver's Mount was my first real road race, and I've done a lot of winning there. While it is thought of as a road race, not a short circuit, it's not like the Irish tracks, the layout is in between a track like Cadwell and an Irish road race. For as long as I've been racing it has been organised by the same person, Peter Hillaby of Auto 66, but this race was the start of a new era, with new people. The famous old racer, Mick Grant, is part of the organisation now, so I told him I wanted to race, but I didn't want any fuss. I just wanted to park out of the way and come ride my bike. 'No bother,' he told me. Two weeks before the Scarborough meeting, there was a track day at Cadwell that I went to because the Suzuki lot were there, testing the classic GSX-R they'd made some changes with. Mick Grant turned up to get me to sign an entry form. Oh heck, I thought, I didn't like that. I felt like he was going out of his way to guarantee I was going to be there. Oliver's Mount would often advertise which racers were entered to try to attract a crowd, and I'm not saying I would attract anything but flies, but in the past they put my name on the advert. It was part of it, because I, and other racers, would be offered start money to turn up, and that's part of the deal, but now I'm racing the classic, I just want to turn up quietly and do my own thing.

I'd been told they were only allowed 2,500 spectators, because of coronavirus, but it looked like they had all that and a bit more, it was a decent crowd. I don't know how they got around it because professional sports weren't allowed crowds at the time.

Mick Grant was good to his word, there was no mention of me in the advertising, so me and my dad drove up on the Friday to qualify for the races on Saturday or Sunday. The race meeting was held in the middle of harvest, when I was flat-out on the tractors. So if I wasn't working, I thought I'd do one day at Oliver's Mount and go to Elvington, on my Hayabusa, the other to do a few runs at their top-speed weekend.

Scarborough turned out to be interesting. Interesting in the sense I didn't enjoy it one bit. I didn't enjoy the riding and I don't know why. I qualified on the front row on the BSA triple and front or second row on the 1980s Suzuki GSX-R750, in what they call the post-classic class.

It was nice to get out for the ride, even though we had to wait till two in the afternoon for the mist to clear. I wasn't pushing, but I got straight into it. The last time I rode there was on the TAS BMW S1000RR superbike in 2015, five years previously. It's strange, but the braking points are similar for the cutting-edge superbike and the classic BSA. The BSA isn't travelling as fast as the BMW, but the British bike's brakes aren't as good, and the BSA is heavier, so the difference is not as drastic as you'd think.

The BSA's bottom gear has always been an issue because of the prototype gearbox, and getting into first gear was a problem, but I eventually sorted it, I think. At a road race, somewhere like Skerries in Ireland, you can get away with it because you're only going into first gear once, maybe twice per lap, but at Scarborough you're in first gear five times every lap because of the hairpins and chicanes. When it won't go into first, I have to pull the clutch in and really rev it to try to get it, while all my teeth are on edge as the gears are crunching, trying to engage.

Dad was mad keen about the event, but I was driving home after the first day of racing wondering if the weather was going to be good enough to go to Elvington or even go farming. I was already looking for an excuse not to go back, but it was too windy for the Hayabusa and there was no tractor work on, so I went back to Scarborough.

I started on the back row of the post-classic race, on the Suzuki, even though I'd qualified near the front. I hadn't raced in a group for so long I didn't want to be sat at the front. I didn't feel comfortable riding with people. Nothing had happened, except the passing of time. If, when I was racing more often, I saw another rider I knew put themselves on the back of the grid in a race like this I'd think, His head's gone, and it would be fair for anyone to think that of me.

I used to love getting stuck in, thinking, I'm going to shove this under you. I liked a bit of that. Now all I want to do is the Hayabusa thing. I sound wet, saying I've no interest in racing, but that's how it is. I don't care how it sounds. I'd told Mick Grant I'd do the meeting, and he never told anyone, so I kept my part of the deal.

So I had a wobble round, getting into it, picking a few riders off. I think my best finish on the triple was third, starting from the back. All this is very unlike me, because if we're doing it, we're bloody doing it. No one said anything, and I don't know if it's because no one felt they dare ask me, but even I was thinking my head's gone. I've lost my love of it and I was disappointed that I wasn't more bothered.

All I was clinging onto was how I felt while I was racing at places like Tandragee and Skerries, because I don't want to fall out of love with the roads. I want to enjoy them when I go. I blame the Hayabusa for changing everything. Nothing comes up to the knees of that. I'll do another road race, somewhere I really like, and if I'm still not feeling it, it might take a lot to convince me to do another.

21

Simulation Is Like Masturbation

THE PODCASTS I'VE BEEN listening to all day in tractors include history, science, engineering, I'll try most things. I was listening to one from *Autosport*, when the guest was Andy Cowell. He was one of the top bods at Mercedes-AMG High Performance Powertrains for 16 years, and was the managing director there from 2014 until he left in 2020. He was a big part of the development of Mercedes's F1 V6 hybrid engines that powered Lewis Hamilton's car, and that Mercedes won six consecutive drivers' and constructors' titles with.

The podcast presenter asked Cowell what his favourite engine was. I think *Autosport*, who are a car racing magazine and motorsport news website, were expecting him to say the DFV or the FQ or one of the Cosworths, because he worked there for years, but he said, 'The Rolls-Royce Merlin,' and added that he planned to own one, one day.

He got talking about Sir Stanley Hooker, who was a big part of the development of the supercharged Merlin engine; was the brains behind the engineering when Rolls-Royce aero engines went from piston to turbine; then led the design of the jet engines used in the Hawker Siddeley Harrier, the Jump Jet, along with a load of other stuff. Hooker has been called Britain's greatest ever engineer.

Hearing Cowell say he wanted one of these engines made my ears prick up, because I have one. I bought it because I'm into engines and there's no better piston-powered engine than a Rolls-Royce Merlin. Four of them powered the Lancaster bomber, they were in Spitfires and Hurricanes, and the American World War II fighter, the Mustang. They're a 27-litre V12. Twenty-seven litres is more than 20 times the cylinder capacity, the cc, of your average hatchback. It makes 1,600 horsepower. That's enough to push a Spitfire through the air at 350mph.

Once I decided I wanted one it took me four years to find mine. It came out of a 1942 Lancaster bomber, and I bought it as a runner, mounted on a custom-built trailer. It had its own 10-gallon petrol tank and a dashboard and controls designed so it could be started and run. It had a propeller fitted too. It gave me goosebumps every time I started it.

When I bought the Merlin it was limited to 1,800rpm, but I knew these engines made maximum power at 2,800. I have told this story in the first book, *My Autobiography*, but in case you forgot, it was a quiet afternoon at Moody's, when I was working there as a truck fitter. The Merlin was being stored there and I thought, as I didn't have much else to do for a while, that I'd start it up to blow the cobwebs off it. It was in the big, high-roof shed where I worked on the trucks, and it sounded great, but the fact it wouldn't rev out was niggling me. I cut the engine and took the gubbins off that were restricting the throttle opening, so I could rev it to 2,800rpm. When I started it up again I gave it a bit more throttle and it sounded even better. I can't have been thinking straight, because I gave it a few more revs, then a few more, then it started moving. Before I could do anything about it, the propeller had demolished the parts store's wall, chopped a wooden staircase to matchsticks and cut my pushbike in half. I can't think of many times I've been more scared than when that engine started moving.

After listening to the podcast I asked a man who knew a man, who knew a man, to tell Andy Cowell that I might sell my Merlin. The message got through, because I got a text message saying he'd heard I had one, was it still for sale?

I have a bit of a relationship with the Grampian Transport Museum in Aberdeenshire, and they put some of my stuff on display up there. At the time I started talking to Andy Cowell the museum had my Merlin and I was happy for them to keep it until they planned to close in October 2020. A few months passed, and it was coming up to the time the museum was closing, when Cowell texted me again asking if it was still for sale, so he was serious and we did a deal.

I had the Merlin delivered to a local truck yard where I'd been working, because it was brought on an artic and I thought it might get stuck down the lane I live on. It was brought on the same truck as a rare E-Type Jaguar that was being returned to Beaulieu, I think, and a Ford GT40 that was going somewhere else. It had been sat for four years, so I wanted to recommission it before I sold it. I took all the spark plugs out, and wound it over.

When Cowell came to see it I told him I didn't want to offend him, but could I ask a few questions? I'd heard he'd had 1,000 people working underneath him, just on F1 engines. A thousand people! There was a thing about the Mercedes engine that had fascinated me for a while. I thought if it was top secret he wasn't going to tell me, so there was no harm in asking. I wondered if the Mercedes engine's spark plugs spark on every firing occasion. He said, 'Yes, 100 per cent,' but he knew what I was getting at.

'They think this . . .', 'They think that . . .', 'They know a lot . .' 'They' think the Porsche 919 Le Mans racer doesn't have spark plugs, but uses controlled detonation, a system called HCCI – homogenised controlled combustion ignition. No one is confirming this happens, but 'they' are saying it might. Car racing series have been lowering the amount of fuel a car can carry without reducing the distance of races, so the engineers have to design more fuel-efficient engines if they want to make the same power. To have an engine running as efficiently as the Porsche 919 does, it must be running beyond lean, it must have a stoichiometric value of more than 1 to get the fuel consumption they are returning. If a car is running rich, its exhaust is full of unburnt fuel. That's wasteful. If it's lean, it's burning all the fuel it's being delivered, but running lean also means running hot, hot enough to easily cause serious damage.

Cowell said Mercedes were so successful when the new era of Formula 1 began in 2014 because they were the masters of knock. Knock is detonation; that is the charge – the air and fuel in the combustion chamber – igniting before the spark plug ignites it. It's also called pinking, and I've mentioned it before in the book because it's something I have to deal with on both the Hayabusa and the classic Rob North BSA. Heat is your enemy, but you need heat for your efficiency. A lot of it comes down to combustion chamber shape. You want it hot, but you want the heat evenly distributed through the combustion chamber. If you have hot spots, that is what causes the detonation. It's science and engineering and it's fascinating to me. What Andy Cowell confirmed is Mercedes were still using conventional four-stroke technology. Even the Porsche is, but, I read, there are certain phases, certain engine strategies, when they can run controlled detonation.

We talked a bit more and one thing he said made me laugh. We were discussing testing and simulations; that is, running the engine in lab conditions when track testing is not available, when he said, 'Simulation is like masturbation, it's not real.' It's another way of saying, we're not racing dynos, the track and race conditions are different.

He was saying when he was at Mercedes they were buying motorbike engines to take them to bits to have a look inside. It blew me away that they were getting ideas for F1 engines from superbike engines, because they're dinosaurs in comparison. Cowell explained they wanted to see how bikes could have their cylinder bores so close together and how they did the rev. He was impressed at how compact superbike engines are.

I didn't try to make anything on the sale of the Merlin, because it was an honour for me to sell it to someone like Andy Cowell, and I got to meet him. He's definitely a good man to have in my phone.

I had my fun out of it and got my money back. It was the ultimate in stationary engines, and I still have the memories of starting it in my back garden and at Moody's. I'm a bit of a hoarder, but I realised I don't need half the stuff I've ended up with. It's more clutter. I still have stuff all over the place, but I've been getting rid of it too. I've scratched the Merlin itch, it's someone else's turn now.

22

Brand New to
Disintegrated in 2 Miles

THE HIGHS OF DOING 282mph on the Hayabusa at Machrihanish, or running the bike semi-naked and realising it's an improvement over the big fairing, can soon get forgotten, because this bike can break my heart.

At the back end of 2020 and into 2021 I was dead set about having my rear brake on the handlebar, but because of the aero penalty of having wide handlebars I don't have the option of running two normal levers on one side of the handlebars. With a regular modern motorbike the right-hand handlebar has the throttle and front brake, left hand has the clutch lever, right foot is rear brake, left foot changes gears.

I want to be able to operate my rear brake with my left hand, because I want a lot of control and feel for it. The idea is, if anything happens to the bike that would normally make me want to close the throttle, to calm it down, I want to use the rear brake instead. The bike's so powerful that the rear brake is just adjusting it slightly.

Like I wrote earlier in the book, I want to be able to keep the throttle steady, and use the rear brake almost as a throttle to calm down whatever is happening, without actually closing the throttle. The turbo is so big and the engine makes so much power that, say the bike's getting wild and I have to close the throttle 10 per cent, then let the thing settle, and then I want to go again, I want to go again *now*, but, because of the size of the turbo, the bike hesitates for a fraction of a second while it gathers its thoughts. If I do close the throttle, even the smallest amount, then the run is ruined, or at least not as good as it could be, because the momentum is lost, the boost is lost. I'm working with such fine margins to improve on my best run that those fractions of a second matter. I'm riding this thing. It's not like a rocket that you launch and just have to steer, there is a lot going on that needs reacting to and adjusting with the brake, throttle, body position. Anything that can give me more control is going to help.

So I thought, I could use the rear brake pedal as a clutch, because I hardly have to use the clutch for this kind of riding. I tried it on my dyno, the rolling road I have in one of my sheds, but I couldn't get it to work as well as I hoped and I didn't persevere with it. I was going to convert the clutch from being operated by hydraulics to a cable, and I rang Jack Frost to see if he had ever done it. He gave me a suggestion, but then called me back the next day to ask, 'Why don't you use a slider clutch, like the drag racers do?' I looked into that, then ordered one, and waited two months for it. It's almost an automatic clutch, and it takes a bit to set up all the spring weights. The makers, MTC, couldn't give me any advice because they had no experience of anyone using these kind of clutches in land speed race bikes, but they suggested settings.

The first time I went out to test the new clutch was at the first top-speed event of 2021 at Elvington, in Yorkshire. I was happy to turn up to someone else's event, instead of going down the road of private hiring an airfield just for myself, because there were too many things to test and sort out. The bike has changed so much from when Jack handed it over in 2020 that I knew I'd have a lot of niggles to sort out, before I can concentrate on improving my top speed and think about private hiring.

I got a feel for the clutch and thought it was all right, but the bike was misfiring. That turned out to be a coil problem. A coil is the electrical component that fires the electrical charge to the spark plug. I'd done four or five runs, trying to get used to this coil, but the bike wasn't really ripping, only doing 200, 210mph.

One of my mates from the top-speed runs – Samosa Joe, I call him that because he gives me samosas every time I see him – had a scrap Hayabusa in the back of his van, and he let me borrow the stock coils off that to try to cure the problem. I use heavy-duty coils for a more intense spark, but these road coils would work fine, and it would help me confirm if they were causing the misfire.

I fitted the coils and new spark plugs, set off, and the bike felt mint. I did 220mph in half a mile, then, just as I went to change gear, it died, like I'd just turned the ignition off. No rattles, no bangs, no smoke, so I thought I'd blown a fuse. I rolled back to the pits. Looked at all the fuses, they were all right. Then I plugged the laptop into the bike's dash to look at the data. I could see the point on the graph that the bike had shut off, and just as it did it lost the signal from the cam sensor. I thought that was strange. I pressed the starter button once and the engine sounded different to normal. Not bad, just different. So I loaded it up and headed home to strip it. It turned out the cam chain had broken, allowing the valves to drop and hit the piston, bending six of the valves. Bastard.

I had been running with a standard cam chain because, really, even an engine like this one, that's putting out four times as much power, the cam chain isn't dealing with more stress than a road bike. Anyway, I ended up putting a heavy-duty cam-chain kit in it when I rebuilt it.

The cam-chain failure meant I never really got an assessment of the clutch. Still, it felt mint, but it hadn't been under a lot of stress.

While the engine was apart I had to machine the head for bigger valves, because the only ones I could get in the material I wanted, Inconel, were bigger than standard. I'd bought a serious bit of kit, a valve seat cutter, when I sold the Merlin engine, and that had arrived in time to do it. Then I built the engine back up, and went back to Elvington on the Sunday of a bank holiday weekend. Me, Shazza and Dot went. It was the first time the Straightliners had run the 2km course at Elvington, a longer run than they normally measure out.

I did a couple of runs. Got up to 230 or summat. Did another run, got up to 237mph and the clutch blew to bits. I'm covering more distance than a drag racer, so the clutch is under stress for longer. And drag racers are not running the gearing I'm pulling, so the clutch on my land speed bike is working a lot harder, due to my bike being geared to run at a theoretical 311mph. Drag-racing

Hayabusas hit 230-odd at the end of the quarter-mile. It's violent acceleration, but it's not sustained.

The original idea had been to get some Sunday dinner on the way home, but I wanted to get the bike fixed to be able to run the next day, so I rang up Pete from B&B Suzuki in Lincoln, who'd ordered me a spare clutch and I hadn't been to pick it up. But now I needed it. He did me a big favour by going to the shop on bank holiday Sunday to get the clutch because now I really needed it. By the time we started looking for somewhere to eat everything was closed so we ended up outside a McDonald's, having our Sunday dinner in the front of the van.

Lingy, who I work with at the truck yard, had gone to Elvington to help me, and he came to my shed on Sunday night to help get the engine stripped, cleaned out and rebuilt so I could go back on Monday for another go.

Everything was full of metal filings from the disintegrated clutch plates. The alloy had melted, so the temperature must have reached 2,200°C in eight seconds. That's a lot of energy. I should've taken the engine out of the bike, but I wanted to run on Monday, and in the end we finished rebuilding at 10 or 11, Sunday night. I'd be back in Yorkshire the next day.

When I got back to Elvington I was told I set the record on the 2km course, at 237mph, because it was the first time they'd ever run the course and all the other fast riders had trouble too. Someone will break it next time they run a 2km course there.

I got ready, went out and did a decent run of 250-summat straight away, but thought I might have felt the clutch slip, so I looked at the data in the pits. I took the casing off, everything was all right, so I made an adjustment to put more spring pressure on the clutch, to push the plates together more to reduce the chance of clutch slip, then lined up for another run. This time the clutch disintegrated again. Brand new to disintegrated in less than 2 miles. That was it, I'd had enough of my new slider clutch. That experiment could be marked as a failure, so now I've gone back to the MTC manual lock-up clutch I was using before.

On the plus side, even with everything going wrong with the clutch and all the new things I was trying, including different bodywork, this Hayabusa had never felt easier to control, so it confirmed to me that I was on the right track with the thumb brake lever to operate the back brake. My left thumb presses the lever, rather than using my fingers to pull in a regular lever. Brake set-ups like this came into use when 500cc Grand Prix champion, Mick Doohan, mangled his right leg so badly in an accident that he couldn't operate the brake pedal properly, and this was the solution he worked out with his mechanics. Then other riders started using them, even though they weren't injured, because they liked the feel and also the ability to leave their toes right on the footpeg, not move to reach the brake pedal. Short circuit riders and road racers had begun to climb all over their increasingly powerful bikes to get them to turn, and tyres were offering mad amounts of lean, so just moving your thumb a little bit, rather than your foot, ankle, and perhaps whole body position, was a big benefit for those riders who could adapt.

Like everything on a machine this extreme, solving one problem usually has a knock-on effect. Now I'm using the back brake more it's finding weaknesses with the rear disc. It's designed to hold back 80ft.lb of torque, and my bike's making 400ft.lb. and that's causing discs to keep cracking. One idea was to fit a carbon fibre disc, like they use on the front of MotoGP bikes and Formula 1 cars, but that material of brake only works at high temperatures, and a brake expert told me I wouldn't get enough heat into the disc, how I plan to use it, to make it work properly. Obviously, it would at the end of the run, when I slow down from 270mph or more, but not when I'm dabbing it to settle it down as I accelerate. The next idea is a steel front disc from a Moto2 bike, the 765cc Triumph-powered triples that are the support class to MotoGP. The Moto2 front disc is a bigger diameter than my current rear disc, and thicker, so it's more suited for extreme braking.

Even though the failures are a kick in the teeth, I look at the bike on the workbench and don't consider stopping for a second. I love it. The trying, the failing, it's everything. I don't have mad expectations. The hope for 2021 is I can go as fast as I did in 2020. If I do, it'll be amazing with my new set-up. I was speaking to the ten-time European Top Fuel drag-race champion, Ian King. His bike makes over 1,000 horsepower, cost over £100,000 to build, does 0–60mph in 0.7 seconds, and covers a quarter-mile, from a standing start, in under 6 seconds. Top Fuel drag bikes, like his, are mind-bending. Ian suggested adding weight to the bike to make it more stable, not trying to lose it like I had been doing. It hadn't occurred to me, but it made sense as soon as he said it. I had two boxes, made from sheet aluminium, welded to the bottom of the swingarm, either side of the rear wheel, and filled each one with 16kg of lead shot, 32kg in total. That's five stone, if that's easier to visualise. I'm experimenting all the time.

There's no doubt 0–300mph within a mile can be done, it's just if it kills me before I get there. If someone beat me to it, I'd still try to do it, but I'd like to be first. I do wonder if I deserve it, because the American Shane Stubbs and Jack Frost have been in the sport for so much longer than me. Bill Warner did 311mph unofficially, the month before he died in 2013, on a 1.5-mile run. It was all unofficial, but if he said he did it I believe him. Even he hadn't done 300mph in a mile, but it's the kind of challenge that I need.

23

Reset the System

LOOK AT ALL THE STUFF that's come off the back of saying yes to the TV job in the first place, when I was really in two minds. I've been doing it for more than ten years now, starting in 2010 with the narrowboat job. For a lot of that time I wasn't comfortable with any of it. I could do all the talking to camera and all that, but I was a truck fitter who'd fooled someone into giving me a chance, and I'd sometimes dig my heels in and force the TV lot to cancel stuff they'd been working on for weeks because I had two trucks to MoT, and I wouldn't back down. I felt I was doing it because I couldn't let myself be a TV wanker. I didn't think the people I worked with were wankers, even though I have called them that in my books. It was just my way of staying true to myself. I feel I have nothing to prove to anyone any more, and, while I've always said I don't care what people think of me, now I think it's probably more true than it's ever been.

The TV lot haven't got wise to me, or perhaps they have and they still want me to do it. It shocks me that Channel 4 still want me. I haven't got the biggest vocabulary. When I listen to podcasts I wish I could word stuff like that, but I'm not trying to be something I'm not. I'm just blunt with the job. I'm never going to be silver-tongued, so there's no point trying to be something I'm not. I'd pay to do most of the stuff the TV lot line up for me. I just like doing stuff. And I've never left a filming job thinking, Those blokes think I'm a wanker. Even when I was doing stuff with Formula 1 bosses.

People's mental health is talked about all the time, especially since lockdown. Brian the inner chimp makes appearances all the time, but I know how to deal with it. I gave my inner chimp a name, and I don't know if that helped me deal with the way I reacted in certain situations, but now I know what to do. I know I have to get out on my bike, fix trucks, keep things real. I don't want Brian to the front, because he turns me into an arsehole.

I wrote about being diagnosed with Asperger's syndrome, a type of autism, in the first book, *My Autobiography*, and I only think about it when someone brings it up, but I got in a bit of bother and had to have some kind of expert assessment. I met this bloke, and we had a cup of tea and talked while I was waiting for him to start the assessment. Next thing, he says he's done, and asks can I take him back to the train station? I was honest, and told him I think 'my' Asperger's thing is a load of shit. When he put his report in, he reckoned I was worse than he thought I was going to be. For a week I wondered if there might be something in it, but now I reckon it's a load of bollocks. What I do think is that we're all different. There's labels on everything and I don't know if it's always helpful.

When it comes to dealing with stuff, I've learned I can do some simple things to reset the system. Biking, spannering, and when the Hayabusa disintegrated two clutches in the same weekend I came home, took everything out of my van and washed it inside and out. I normally only wash my van when I service it, every 10,000 miles, whether it needs it or not. That afternoon giving it a proper wash was enough to sort me out and get thinking, Right, what next?

I don't spend much time in the 'real world'. I've got my shed at home, or I'm in the tractor on my own, or I'm at the truck yard. The only other times I'm out are if I'm riding the Hayabusa or filming. I do go out, every day to walk the dogs or fetch something, but I'm not around people.

I don't like being the centre of attention, so I say something stupid to get myself out of it. If I get talking to people and someone is trying to be the big man, I just say, 'I don't understand that, you'll have to explain.' And that seems to diffuse them. It's a good tool in the box.

Like I explained earlier in the book, after packing in the trucks, I was asked if I could go back and now I'm doing a couple of days a week, most weeks. So, on Fridays, I work on my own stuff at home till midday, cycle to the truck yard, have pie and peas, then work till seven, and cycle home. The next morning I'm up at half-three, take the dogs out, bike to work, work from five till two in the afternoon, and bike home. I'm on double time, and usually it's me and my mate, Lingy. He's had his pacemaker fitted so he's all set. Jack, the boss's son, sometimes works, and my nephew, Louis, comes and helps. He cycles there too, and he's there for five on a Saturday morning, like me. He's keen as mustard.

After ten years doing TV stuff, I don't have to worry about money. I wouldn't do the trucks for free, it's a job with job satisfaction, not a hobby, but it's part of my life. I love working on them, but I like the mix of trucks and driving tractors. Just enough of one thing, not too much. I've never had a plan, and if I did it was work hard, fix trucks. I just do what I want to do. If that's a couple of days a week on the trucks and tuning bike engines the rest of the time, then that's it. If it's going to Cuba to film for two weeks, I'll do that. If it's 14-hour shifts harvesting with the tractor, then that's it.

The TV is great, and I enjoy it, but it doesn't give me a lot of job satisfaction. Like with the Battle of Britain, I made a pig's ear of it, so I don't get any satisfaction. Enjoyment is one thing, but job satisfaction is a completely different thing. I can't think of many occasions when I have felt any kind of job satisfaction from filming jobs. I'd say Pikes Peak; Nürburgring van; breaking the speed record for a bicycle on the beach, and they're all things I had to put a lot of effort in. Yes, the TV experience is great, I get to meet all sorts of interesting folk, and I'm definitely not knocking any of it for a second, I'm just trying to explain the difference between TV work and truck work.

The TV lot have looked after me the best, even when I get all my priorities wrong about other work, and I know I'm a dickhead. Perhaps I don't deserve to be happy, so I have to put myself through some misery, but it's good to have choices even if I do sometimes make the wrong ones.

I'll be 40 by the time this book comes out, the back end of 2021, and I'm going on a bike ride. I've half worked it out. I'm going to leave in November: cycle to Dover, cross to Calais, through Belgium, then into Germany and follow the Danube, through Germany, Austria, Slovakia, Hungary, Croatia, Serbia, Romania, to the Black Sea, maybe to Istanbul. I think I can get through Georgia, Azerbaijan, Kazakhstan, and maybe even into Mongolia. There's no plan, just take it as it comes, and see how far I can get in six weeks, then fly back.

That'll be a good reset.

24

Jack of All Trades, Master of Nowt

A BIG TV PROJECT started while I was writing this book, and will still be going on after I've finished it. It's called *Guy's Garage*, even though I said that's a word I'd never use. I reckon it's going to be one of those programmes where I get a bit of enjoyment and job satisfaction. It is filmed in my shed at home in Lincolnshire. I chose this house because there was a shed bigger than the house, so there's enough room for what we're getting up to.

The idea for the series is to buy an old vehicle and prepare it for a specific race or competition. Like the Hurricane programme, it is similar to an idea that we had talked about before. At first, and this is a few years ago, I wasn't that bothered about the idea because it sounded like a few other things that had been done, but once we found actual races we could get involved in it gave me a proper target. I'd be competing against people who were really into that particular type of racing in something we'd built, so it wasn't a TV bullshit challenge.

Ewan, North One's director for these programmes, had an idea of having one of my mates be in the series. In the past ten years, I've only made one series, the very first one, *The Boat That Guy Built*, with a co-presenter or a sidekick or whatever you want to call them, and that was my mate Mave, Mark 'Mavis' Davis. All the others have had experts or specialists we've used in that particular programme, involved them, and relied on them, for that one challenge.

After that very first series some of the North One bods came to visit me in Caistor, and I told them they should use Mave instead of me for whatever they were doing next. He could talk in front of the camera, he could get in character, he had the skill that I'm never going to have. He was brilliant. I wasn't trying to double bluff them, because I honestly believed he was the better man for the job. So, while I wasn't that bothered about making another programme, I told them that if they did, I would only do it on my own. It felt too much of a mismatch for me to be with someone who knew what they were doing. It didn't feel real. It felt like Mave was being a TV presenter, and that's not how I go about the job.

When it came to the *Guy's Garage* planning, North One spoke about who could work on the programmes with me, and I suggested Cammy, Cameron Whitworth. I met him through the racing, he has been, and still is, a mechanic for some of the top British teams, and he works as a cable splicer's mate, too, installing high-voltage national grid cables. I thought he'd be the best person for the job because he knows the same as me about what we'd be doing, which is fuck-all, but he'll have a go. He'll never put on a phone voice or try to use big words, and if he doesn't know what he's doing, he'll say. He won't try to bullshit his way out of it. He is also meticulous and methodical, but with a pragmatic approach to things. Meticulous is useful when you're preparing race vehicles, but sometimes you have to cut a few corners to get things finished in time for filming. I was sure we'd be all right. It also helped that the TV lot knew him, because Cammy was involved in the Pikes Peak programme, and I liked the experience of filming that, racing the Martek Turbo out in Colorado, sorting problems, trusting him, and doing a bit of road-tripping too.

These new programmes appeal to my 'Jack of all trades, master of nowt' mindset, and we're working on four vehicles at once. We have a Volvo 240, a Land Rover, a Trabant and a Piaggio Ape. I'm doing the Ape, Cammy's concentrating on the Volvo, and I've subbed out some of the work to experts, otherwise it wouldn't have got done in time. Dave from Tornado Motorsport, who builds racing Defenders, is doing the Land Rover, and my mate Tim Dray is getting the Trabant ready.

It would suit the TV lot for it to look like I did it all, and that's how a lot of these type of programmes are done, someone does the grafting and the presenter takes the credit, but that's definitely not me. I said, 'Look boys, what are we, eleven years into doing TV stuff? We're not starting to be bullshitters now.' Dave was bringing the Land Rover here and they wanted me to bolt stuff to it that he'd already sorted out, and I wasn't into it. I've put a head gasket on it, and different turbo, which was actual stuff that needed doing, but I'm not making out I've built it. My life's a contradiction, but I don't want to tell porkies. If we're handing work over to people, I can't put my name to it, it isn't going to work. I want to do it all, and if I had to choose I'd always rather be the person to build it than be the presenter driving it, but I do usually bite off more than I can chew, and that causes problems. I'll just get on, and do a few late nights. It usually works out in the end.

So, the Ape, the little Italian three-wheel delivery truck, is the one I'm most involved with. It looks like the tuk-tuks you see in India and other places. I call it the Ape, pronounced like a gorilla ape, but the name comes from Italian for bee. It's made by the same company, Piaggio, who are famous for building Vespa scooters. Vespa is Italian for wasp, and you can imagine why; the little scooter can buzz through gaps in traffic in busy cities. Ape, pronounced ah-pay if you were Italian, still buzzes, but it's bigger than a wasp and doesn't move as quickly, or the standard Apes don't. This one will.

There is a race series for the three-wheelers in Italy, and within it is a Proto class where virtually anything goes, so I have a Kawasaki ZX-10R racing engine to go in mine. My brother, Stu, packed in racing a few years ago because he kept crashing and spannering himself. He hurt himself, got fit, came back, and then broke his pelvis, so, rightly probably, he called it a day and sold up. There wasn't much to sell, except the front sprocket and a few other bits and bobs, because he'd mangled the bike that much. He did have a spare engine left, and at the back of my mind was always a thought I'd do something with it. The Ape was the opportunity. Lots of people use 1998 Honda CBR600 engines in their racing Apes, but this Kawasaki engine will have loads more power than those Hondas, and the throttle goes both ways, so why wouldn't I use that engine? When it comes to power, it's better looking at it than for it. My brother had the well-respected engine man Frank Wrathall tune it, and it's supposed to make 200bhp. The original 50cc Ape, that we got as a runner for £1,500, makes 2.5bhp. That isn't a mistake, it produces less than three brake horsepower and 2.4ft.lb (3.3Nm) of torque. I've probably got a Snap-On drill with more power than that.

But it's not as simple as bolting a 1,000cc racing engine to it. This style of racing is off-road, almost rallying or motocross, so the suspension needs sorting.

First thing I thought was, we need to get an Autograss car and cannibalise that. I've dyno'd a few Autograss cars and there's a load of engineering that goes into them. I had a load of ideas, and all the Piaggio Apes that are raced in Italy are trick, but they all look mismatched because there's nothing available off the shelf for the Proto Ape class. Everything is custom made as a one-off.

I hadn't been thinking about the Autograss route for long before I was put off the idea by someone saying the engine position and the weight would be all wrong, because the Ape needs some weight over the front for steering, and the Autograss racers do all their steering with the rear. That made me doubt the Autograss route because, in my experience, when one of the Autograss racers brings their cars to mine for dyno testing, and I'm pushing them around the yard, they don't steer, they just want to go straight on, whatever you're doing with the steering wheel. The steering wheel only suggests where you want to go. The drivers make them go around the oval by powersliding them. And, what I've seen of this Ape racing, it looks the same; they're driving these mad, little three-wheelers like rally cars, but no one's got any grip.

I spoke to Jack Frost because he's always putting daft engines in daft things, and he pointed me to speedcars. They're a type of rallycross buggy, often fitted with a Suzuki GSX-R600 motorcycle engine. They have a kind of dual-wishbone suspension that would be perfect for the job. This kind of racing is not big in England, but it's popular in Ireland and Spain. Jack had me convinced. As far as I know, this type of racing buggy is called a speedcar, but Speed Car is a Spanish company, who are one of the chassis manufacturers. There's another called Semca, from Eastern Europe.

Jack got me the details of the Irish importer, and I asked for a price for the rear wishbones, the suspension, driveshafts, wheels, brakes, CV joints, all that, and I'd make the chassis to mate up with it. A full chassis is £18,000, but it sounded like £5,000 would get me everything I needed, so I put the order in and waited. When I chased, the importer said he couldn't get any sense out of the company because the woman he dealt with had left, and no one in the factory could speak English, so it dragged on.

When I'd originally said I was going down the Autograss route, Tom at North One TV got straight on the phone to a racer and arranged for me to have a drive in one, before I had thought to tell him I'd gone off the idea of them. I tested it in Wales and, man, it was quick.

I got talking to the owner, Graham Bennett, who told me nothing is faster on a grass oval than an Autograss car, not a World Rally Car, nothing. The Apes race on dirt, but with left- and right-handers. It was enough to change my mind back. Another reason I did is because Graham reckons Autograss racing is British motorsport's best kept secret. If I use ideas from this sport I've got a chance of doing something different to all the established Ape racers, and part of that is by putting more weight on the back wheels to give more traction than the other Apes have. I'm less worried about the steering being ineffective, because in the Ape, I'm sat on top of the front wheel and that will help change the weight distribution and help it steer. The Italians have been mint, giving us the rules and loads of suggestions about how they modify their Apes, but I've not really taken any of their advice. We've done our own thing. I'm going into the unknown, but I like that, and we've got absolutely nothing to lose. I'd much rather go to Italy, having tried something different, and fail. But we could go and smoke them.

I learned from Graham that Autograss race engineers have found the sweet spot of the angle between the pivots of the two suspension units of their oddball wishbone set-up. It's taken them years of trial and error to get to this point, but now they have I can use that knowledge for my Ape. And there is a grey area in the rulebook that I'm going to exploit, where it says, try to get the engine as close as possible to the back of the cab. The rules don't dictate where it has to be. Well, we've tried and we've put it as close as we could get it.

I asked if I could buy all the suspension stuff from Graham's company, BB Motorsport, and he said we could do that, but I really needed to go to him with the Ape to work out how the suspension would work with the roll cage. Then I rang him back and said, 'I'm mucking about here. I've got a Volvo 240 to get running in two weeks, the Hayabusa's shit a cam chain, I have one Yamaha R1 and two R6 engines to do, I know I want to modify the Ape, but I have to be realistic. Can you mount the engine and make the back chassis for it?'

If you're wondering why I've got bike engines to tune, when all this TV stuff is going on, you aren't the only one. The truth is I can't turn down the engine-building work because that's the big picture. If I dropped everything else and just did the TV job I wouldn't be true to myself, and it wouldn't last. I contradict myself all the time, because I want to do everything but it gets to the point I can't. I could buy all the parts, but BB Motorsport would do it in half the time, probably for less money and do a better job. There'll still be a lifetime of work to do when I get it back. It's no different to what I've done in the past, when I subbed bits of the Nürburgring Transit out to people, but I still built it, it was still my van. BB might be completing a bigger bit of the puzzle, but I want it to be as good as possible, then go over to Italy and spank them.

Even though they race Apes, no one has ever done anything like this, as far as I can tell. It has a live axle, no differential, so there's equal drive to left and right. Just like the Autograss cars I've dyno'd. You can't turn the Ape when you're pushing it around with the engine off. It'll only turn under power. What I'm clinging on to, what Graham Bennett at BB Motorsport said, is that it's based on the fastest thing on grass. Why do what everyone else is doing?

BB Motorsport did a great job, then the Ape came back to mine for me and Cammy to make the roll cage to protect the cab, tying it all into the steering tube at the front and the chassis at the back. Then I got on with a few more details.

I weighed-in a load of scrap from my yard, and bought lengths of tube and a pipe bender so we can have a go at making our own roll cage for the Ape's interior so it won't crumple if it lands upside down.

When we needed a roll cage put in the Transit, ready for us to take it to the Silver State Classic, we had Safety Devices put it in, and we made it clear they'd done it. They're specialists, they made a great job of it, no problem, mint. But for *Guy's Garage* programmes, they want people to believe that we're doing stuff here even if we aren't. I don't want to be taking credit for anyone else's work, and I won't. So if there's something I think I can do, I'm going to have a go.

Apes have handlebars, not a steering wheel, and a motorcycle twistgrip throttle. You change gear by twisting the left-hand grip, just like a regular manual Vespa. But I think I'm going to fit a thumb throttle because this thing is likely to be bouncing all over the place, and I can have a better grip on the bars. I've got a Translogic auto-blip gear-change system, with two buttons on the handlebars to shift up and down.

If it's anything like 200 horsepower, it's probably going to wheelie, even with all my weight in the cab, over the front wheel. The Italians fit massive tyres, but they're still spinning up. Grasstrackers use narrow wheels with remould tyres. I want the limiting factor to be the tyre spinning.

While the Ape is taking shape, me and Cammy were building the Volvo too. The TV lot ended up buying one that, really, was in too good condition for what we were going to do to it, and it was an automatic, not a manual, so it was no good for racing. We thought we could get a gearbox and convert it, so we started stripping it, ready to fit a roll cage, but it was going to be a load of hassle, so we bought another, a manual estate, paying loads more than we should have, just so we could carry on with the programme. By this time the automatic was stripped to shell and pushed out into the yard.

We're preparing the Volvo to compete in a Swedish Folkrace. Folk racing is like banger rallycross, with one important rule, called a claiming rule, that a competitor can buy a lottery ticket to try to win the chance to buy another driver's car. If they win the lottery, they can buy the car for about £700. The idea is to make sure people don't spend too much on their cars, for fear someone can just buy it and the owner can't say no.

We made the roll cage in the estate, and the TV lot booked a track day, the Volvo's first proper test, at Blyton airfield. The old Volvo was quicker than I thought it would be, but it was terrible in the corners. As soon as I got tramping the body would roll, the inside rear wheel would lift up, and the thing would start freewheeling because the diff, the differential, was doing its job. The diff allows a rear-wheel car to turn better than cars with live axles, because the diff allows the back wheels to spin at different speeds. Imagine a car is driving in a tight circle, the inside wheel is covering less distance than the outside wheel, so the outside wheel has to spin faster than the inside wheel.

We were looking for a cheap solution for the rear-end freewheeling, and decided that we'd weld the diff up. It's hillbilly engineering, but that's what I do full-stop. Anything Tim Dray does will be bordering on F1 spec, but I don't profess to be anything special. I get the job done. Most of the time. Solving stuff is good for the programme. If it all went right first time it could be boring. And it definitely wasn't all going right. Six laps into the test and the engine shit itself.

Back at my shed, Cammy started stripping the engine, and straight away we could see it was full of black gunge. It had been run on old, non-detergent oil before I changed the oil ready for the track day. When the cam cover was lifted off, we could see the head was full of carbon, so as soon as I'd hammered it for a couple of laps some of the gunge in the engine has dislodged, blocked the oil pick-up pipe, starved the engine of lubrication, and caused the bottom end to go. It is a 1988 car, I'm the second owner, and it's never been radged about, so it had the equivalent of blocked arteries and couldn't cope with the exercise I was making it do. Something else going wrong added a bit of drama, so the TV lot will have loved it.

Straight away, I got thinking about what we'd do with the blown motor, and told Cammy we should put in a Ford V6 engine and gearbox. The rules say you can do whatever you want, as long as it isn't turbocharged, but Cammy didn't want to go down that route because there'd be a lot of mucking about making it fit, so he'd rather stick to the Volvo 240 engine. There were a couple of scrap cars we could have bought, but did we want to take that chance? Then we found a reconditioned bottom end in Bristol for £400. We had nowt on the next day, so I said Cammy could borrow my van, pick up the engine, and we'd have it. Then the TV lot said he could go in their hire car, so that was happening, then they couldn't get him on the insurance, so it didn't happen. And while we didn't need the bottom end the next day, it's better having it, so I thought he should've just gone in my van, like I'd suggested. Anyway, the TV lot picked it up a few days later, so it happened and no harm was done, but it could've been simpler.

A few weeks into the filming I'd realised it doesn't matter who I ended up with, I'd have differences of opinion, and I'd end up being annoyed by anyone I was doing this with, because I'm a bit of a loner by choice. I like being in my shed by myself. Cammy's work is mint, but he sometimes fannies about. If there's a decision to be made, he gets on to the TV lot for them to ask the organisers if the battery can be here, and I'm thinking, Jesus Christ man! Just get on with it. I don't think he wants to make the decision but, like I explained, he's meticulous, and he's good at remembering to film with the little camera they left us. Where I'd never bother.

Right, the Trabant . . . It's the old East German car that became famous after the fall of the Berlin Wall, in November 1989, and the collapse of the Eastern Bloc, when loads of folk, looking for a better life, drove out of former East Germany in them. The Trabant 601, the model everyone thinks of, was built from 1963 to 1990, with 2.8 million of them rolling out of the factory in that time. It has a two-stroke engine that dates from the 1930s, and a type of GRP, glass reinforced plastic, body like a Reliant Robin. And they race them, on short circuits, in Germany.

Our Trabant was going to be modified by someone the TV lot lined up, but he stopped answering the phone so they had to get it back, and now my mate Tim Dray, who helped with the Nürburgring Transit van, is on the case. As I write this he's working through building the roll cage, altering all the suspension system, making his own steering. That man is universal, he can do anything. So I'm not worried about that.

We're going to race the Trabant at Hockenheim, Germany, at a classic race event. It's got to have the original two-stroke engine, that made 25 horsepower originally, but you can tune it. The TV lot have arranged to buy an engine from a bloke in Belgium, and that one is meant to make 50 horsepower. It hadn't arrived before I finished the book, so we'll have to wait and see if it does.

We spent a filming day at Thruxton racetrack, me driving an Austin A30 on track, getting used to driving slow, shit, old cars before I race the Trabant. Of course, it's too much to ask someone to film in Thruxton, near Andover, Hampshire, for a day, then drive 160 miles to Pembrey, south Wales, to film the following day. We only use impossible for special occasions, but I think that would be next to impossible. So, after we were done at Thruxton, I drove home to Lincolnshire to get stuff done at home the next day, then drove five hours to south Wales the day after that. I didn't have the option of a travel day, I had too much on. I had a cylinder head to finish, my van to service, Shazza needed some shit moving. I had to do a bit of this book. It would have been good to do two days back-to-back. I keep repeating, they're the nicest people, but sometimes the schedule . . . holy moly.

The last project to talk about is the Land Rover that is being prepared, by Tornado Motorsport, to go Comp Safari racing. You don't have to go on safari, because Lincolnshire Land Rover Club do it. It's a mixture of high-speed, low-speed and technical stuff, off-road racing around a lap normally 3 to 6 miles in length. There's not much more I can write about this because I haven't had my hands on the car much yet.

Guy's Garage will be four hour-long programmes, and it's a load of effort for four hours of television. Take the adverts out, and it's more like three hours. We plan to road trip out in the van to the different events, but the dates can't be set because of all the travel restrictions, continuing in 2021. We can film the whole of the Land Rover show in the UK, but the other three cars are being built to take part in European races. I'm not confident we'll be able to travel, but I have to keep ploughing on with the projects and get them the best we can.

I am enjoying the process, it makes a change from some of the other stuff we've been doing. It's time in the shed, building daft stuff and having a race at the end. I've had enough of looking at the stopwatch for all these years, so let's go have a crack, win lose or draw. Go do these daft races in the van, it'll be mint.

25

Willing to Die

I HAVEN'T MISSED serious road racing for a second since I packed it in. The opposite. I still reckon I stuck at it far too long. The reason I walked away, when I still had top teams offering me rides, was dead simple: I wasn't arsed about dying for it. Back in 2003, 2004, I would have died for road racing, but that attitude, that passion for it, gradually wore off, but I was still trying to make it happen, to get that feeling. Those early years, when it was all new, especially when it was me and my mate Trellis living in the truck, were the best and I did love it. I knew I loved it, because I knew I was willing to die for it, and vice versa. That feeling I had for the sport only lasted so long, maybe five years at the most, then after that I was flogging a dead horse, but there were still a few parts of the racing experience I enjoyed and I kept going back. I liked working with the teams for most of it, because the mechanics were on my wavelength, and I learned from the cleverest of them. I was happy to be part of a team.

Sat here, four years after walking away from Honda after the TT balls-up, I do wonder if I ever enjoyed the riding, the competitive riding, and I don't think I did. I got the job satisfaction from improving the bike and making it as good as I could. There wasn't one moment that changed my attitude. I'd been missing that feeling, that commitment to racing those tracks, for quite a while, without realising that was the main problem I had with racing.

The spark went out of it, but now I'm doing this 300mph job I've got it back. When I get my helmet on for a run and tell myself, Right, let's have it!, I'm back feeling like I did in the early days of road racing and I am, without exaggerating, willing to die attempting the 300mph record.

That might sound stupid or overdramatic to some people, especially people who don't ride motorbikes, but I think it's the opposite. It's realistic and honest. Motorcycles are dangerous. Trying to go that fast is dangerous. I try to make it as safe as possible, and if the conditions are right, I don't push my luck. But you can't make it 100 per cent safe, and if it was, I probably wouldn't be that interested. By admitting that I am willing to die for it, I'm acknowledging that I might.

Riders trying to do 300mph on sit-on motorbikes have died in recent years. No one really knows what caused the crash that killed Bill Warner in 2013. He had done 311mph in 1.5 mile, then died at a strip in Maine, New England. He'd done 296mph that day, riding a turbo Suzuki Hayabusa fitted with a great big land speed racing fairing and seat unit. He was interviewed before his final, fateful, run, saying, 'Hopefully we can keep it on the ground,' and telling the interviewer how scary it was if the bike wasn't exactly planted on the ground. He was doing 287mph when, eyewitnesses said, his bike suddenly veered to the right and off the runway. He'd come back from the big crash the year before, so he knew the risk and, I reckon, he'd decided he was willing to die for it. He was 44.

Folks lose their lives commuting to work on bicycles. They might not have ever thought they were willing to die for that sweaty ride to the factory or the desk in the corner of the office, but that is a possibility if you're cycling in a big city on busy roads. Just because I've admitted that I know the risks of competing on motorcycles, either on the roads or in land speed events, doesn't mean I want to die. Motorcycling has never been some daft suicide mission for me, but I've been around a lot of tragedy at races and lost some good friends. It's just I'm more willing to describe the risks than most people.

My life hasn't been champagne and blowjobs all the way through, but I wouldn't change any of the decisions I've made or the direction of my life. I've done stuff I regretted, but not many things. I've spannered myself a few times, too, but everything came right in the end.

Things that went tits-up did so for a reason. It took me a long time to stop thinking about some decisions, times when I'd been an absolute arsehole. You can look back at your life and only see the good stuff, and wonder why you made stupid decisions. If I think about the choices I regret, I realise I did things for a reason. It wasn't all rosy, there was something wrong and that's why I made the decisions I did. Realising that helps.

I never have these conversations with people close to me, because I'm not asking permission and there is no discussion. This is just the way it is and how my adult life has always been, and I can't see it changing.

Index

GM indicates Guy Martin.
Page references in *italics* indicate images.

INDEX

Acknowledgements

Thanks to Andy Spellman and Gary Inman, for putting up with my shit and making the book happen, to Sharon and Dot for putting up with my shit and keeping the wheels on, to Lorna at the book company for putting off deadlines, to all the North One TV lot, for making the TV job happen. To all at Red Torpedo, Dainese, AGV, Morris Oils and Snap On tools for making my projects possible.